PERFECTION

Heston Blumenthal

Bloomsbury

First published in Great Britain in 2006

Bloomsbury Publishing Plc
50 Bedford Square
London WC1B 3DP

By arrangement with the BBC

The BBC logo is a trade mark of the British Broadcasting
Corporation and is used under license

www.bloomsbury.com

Bloomsbury Publishing, London, New Delhi, New York, Sydney

Chefs on p.149 (left to right): Wylie Dufresne, José Andrés,
Heston, Ferrán Adrià and Sam Mason, pastry chef at WD50

A CIP catalogue record for this book is available from
the British Library

ISBN 9781408849422

10 9 8 7 6 5 4 3 2 1

Designed by Caz Hildebrand, Here+There

Printed and bound in China by South China Printing Company, Dongguan Guangdong

All papers used by Bloomsbury Publishing are natural,
recyclable products made from wood grown in well-
managed forests. The manufacturing processes conform
to the environmental regulations of the country of origin

To Zanna, Jack, Jessi and Joy.
My energy, my everything.

CO

INTRODUCTION

erfection n. the state of being perfect; the process of making or becoming perfect.

erfection? Oh, here we go – another book from some puffed-up, Michelin-starred chef who thi
e can tell us how to cook. Do we need it …?'

No, you don't. And this isn't that kind of book.

Although my restaurant, the Fat Duck, does have three stars, and I'll use what
arned there to cook these dishes in a way that I hope really brings out their essential charac
m not claiming that my recipes are perfection. (Indeed, as you'll see, I think that's impossib
his book is more a kind of exploration, a journey that I hope you'll make with me. You'll m
ome extraordinary artisans: a visionary pasta-maker who sees his day job as funding for his t
alling, creating a golden pasta that tastes better than any other; master butchers who comp
ach year to produce brand-new bangers; a brother and sister determined to create the perf
hocolate, and to do so in a way that benefits the poverty-stricken farmers who harvest the bea
ou'll meet historians who cook to unlock the past, have Sunday dinner (on a Thursday) with
mous French chef in his *village gourmand*, and hunker down with a very patriotic chicken. Ma
these people have spent decades pursuing their own ideals of perfection, and the results a
lly inspiring. This book's title is, in part, an acknowledgement of that, and a tribute to them.

Before I set out on this journey, however, I had in mind two other forms of perfectio
First, perfection is the ultimate, the best something can possibly be. For many of
e perfect meal won't be some fancy restaurant food. Stuck on a desert island, our dream d
more likely to be something we grew up with and have taken to our hearts. An entry in *Scho
od & Drink Miscellany* details last-meal requests of prisoners on death row in Texas and reve
ed eggs, fried bacon, ice cream, chocolate milk, burgers and French fries to be the fro
nners. Before you ascribe this to penal-colony demographics, note that chefs exhibit simila
omespun desires. In *A Cook's Tour*, Anthony Bourdain describes a lower-stakes version of t
eath-row dilemma that he plays with other cooks. He calls it the Last Meal Game. Braised r
nd cold meat loaf are among the choices, and, as he points out, 'No one came back with "t
sting menu at Ducasse".'

So food perfection means a dish with a history, a meal that means something to us a
okes fond memories. The role of memory and nostalgia in food is seldom explored and h
ecome a fascination of mine, so I was very excited when the BBC invited me to do a series
ogrammes in which I would cook dishes that people generally consider perfection itself. Eig
ogrammes, eight dishes. The producer, researcher, directors and I went into a meeting room a

vowed we wouldn't leave until we'd thrashed out a running order.

Of course, any list like this is going to provoke dissent. 'The perfect dish? Where's steak and kidney pie, toad in the hole, bread and butter pudding? Where's prawn cocktail?' I hear you cry. Some dishes were sacrificed to the need for balance. Italian cuisine, with its roots in *la cucina di casa*, offered many contenders for our list of eight. But we weren't making an Italian cookery series, so out went risotto and lasagne and zabaglione. Other dishes fell victim to our schedule or balance sheet: for steak I managed to wangle a trip to New York, but it seemed unlikely that we'd have the time or the money to visit India. Goa wasn't a goer. So out went curry.

In the end, however, we came up with a list that seemed to have something for everyone – a range of undeniably popular meals that also offered lots of interesting challenges in the kitchen. Eight dishes that people could really get their teeth into.

Even so, there was heated discussion among us. Roast beef or roast chicken? Italian or American pizza? Bolognese with spaghetti or tagliatelle? There were fierce advocates of all points of view. It seemed that, when it came to perfection, none of us could agree completely. It was too subjective, too personal. It brought home to me how elusive an ideal perfection is, and how foolhardy and arrogant it would be for me to claim my versions of these dishes as perfection. Yet I reckoned that, by using all my technical and scientific expertise, by talking to producers and artisans and chefs and their customers, I could pin down what made these dishes work. I could isolate the elements that a cook would have to bring into harmony to make his or her own 'perfect' meal.

Which brings me to the second meaning of perfection: honing a recipe through continual experimentation. Trying out ideas and then revising and retrying them until you've got something special, unique. The BBC series gave me the opportunity to try my hand at all sorts of things I'd never encountered before, and I was as excited about this as I was about the chance to explore memory and nostalgia in food, because that's how I started in the restaurant business.

Although I've had help and advice from many people, I'm a self-taught chef. My passion for cooking began when my parents – uncharacteristically – took me to a Michelin three-star restaurant when I was sixteen. I was knocked out by the theatre of it all, and knew at once that I wanted to be part of it.

For the next ten years – like a car enthusiast dedicatedly stripping down and reassembling a vintage TR7 or Morris Minor – I took apart and examined every aspect of classic French cuisine, trying to perfect the kind of experience I had had in France. As the results of my cooking got better and my confidence grew, I began to explore how I might actually improve these dishes – producing meat in which the robust, earthy, browned surface gave way to a gratifyingly soft and velvety inner texture; or a parsley mousse whose silky airiness seemed too fragile to contain any strong taste, so that when it melted in your mouth the depth of flavour came as a distinct and pleasurable surprise.

It was a journey of discovery that took me down many strange roads, and into a world of centrifuges and digital probes, vac-pacs and liquid nitrogen. If physicists and chemists could use science and technology to unlock the secrets of the universe, I reasoned, then surely I could enlist their help for something as humble as refining my techniques in the kitchen. If the freezer could revolutionise what we bought, ate and stored at home, why couldn't I, for example, use an ultrasound gun to make mayonnaise? Perhaps, by using some of the amazing advances in science and technology that had taken place over the last decade, I could produce dishes, or effects, that simply hadn't been possible for chefs in the past because of the limited technology available to them.

I had almost no scientific background, so I consulted chemists and physicists, psychologists and biologists with the aim of understanding, at the most fundamental level, what went on in cooking. In so doing, I hoped to gain enough knowledge about the real science of cookery (the atoms and molecules; the physical processes of oxidation and evaporation) to help me build something new, different and, perhaps, better. When the Fat Duck opened in 1995, it showcased the fruits (and meat and vegetables) of my labour.

As everybody knows, the road to perfection is a difficult one. At the Fat Duck the technical demands of many of the dishes mean they take days to prepare and require the attention of a huge number of people: there are more staff in my kitchen than there are customers in the restaurant. Although the dishes in this book represent a different sort of cuisine, exploring their potential proved equally challenging. Searching out the best ingredients took me to dubious back-streets in London and New York, and on several wild-goose chases in various parts of Europe (I was taken, with great solemnity and assurance, to a canning factory that turned out to be processing completely the wrong sort of tomato, and visited a dairy farm whose standards fell so far short of perfection we couldn't film there). Refining the culinary techniques for each recipe, I ended up hand-milking a cow, inflating balls of mozzarella with a gas tank, and nearly burning down my house in an effort to get the oven hot enough for a proper Neapolitan-style pizza!

It was a hectic but fascinating undertaking, and I hope the pages that follow convey something of the sheer enjoyment I experienced while doing it – the problem-solving no less than the exotic locations. The end result is a set of recipes that I'm really proud of. I wanted to make them as accessible as possible, so I've endeavoured to keep the more obscure ingredients to a minimum. The Directory at the back of this book will tell you where to obtain anything that might not be readily available in your local shops, from malt syrup and rice flour to smoked sea salt and dry ice. Similarly, I've worked out recipes that don't require the kind of high-tech equipment that costs a fortune and requires a science degree to operate – even if that's what what was used to refine a recipe in the first place. Two thermometers (one to monitor oven temperature, another to probe the temperature of food and liquid) are more or less the only investments you'll have to make before starting. Both can be bought relatively cheaply and they are, to my mind, as essential a part of the kitchen as a sharp knife or wooden spoon. The section entitled 'Equipment' will tell you wheere to obtain these and any other items you might need.

Despite my desire for accessibility, some of the recipes are long – perhaps at first glance dauntingly so. But they're designed to leave nothing to chance: by taking you step by step through the processes involved, and giving background information that shows not just how to do things but *why* you're doing them as well, I aim to provide a knowledge base that eventually makes the dishes easier. (Two other things will also simplify the cooking: with complicated recipes, it's worth reading through and visualising what's involved before you start; and weighing out and preparing ingredients beforehand cuts down the number of tasks to be done at the same time.) If a meal ends up wrong, or not how you like it, you should be able to look back over the techniques and shape and adapt accordingly. In any case, I'm sure that, like me, you'll enjoy the scientific investigation as much you'll take pleasure in eating the meals themselves.

As I've said, the menu at the Fat Duck is different from the foods you'll find here (though my pub, the Hind's Head, is set more squarely in the British tradition), but the approach in both cases is the same – combining technique, science, innovation and, yes, history, romance, folklore, sensory perception and passion to bring magic to cooking. My hope is that you'll try out these dishes and, equipped with the principles, processes and ideas in these pages, play around with them until you've got a meal that matches your best memories of it. I'd like to see you bringing that dish to the table and thinking, as you bite into the first morsel, 'Yes, that's it. That's what I had in mind all these years.' And I'd like to hear the noisy chomping, slurping and laughter round the table – as your guests or family tuck in with gusto – which shows that they think so too. Now *that* is perfection.

Heston Blumenthal, 2006

CONVERSION TABLES

The recipes in this book use the metric system: to have included imperial and American measurements would have added a bewildering number of figures to each recipe. Below are conversion tables that will help translate measurements to whichever system you prefer to use.

Conversion is not an exact science, as it tends to round up or down to the most convenient number. Therefore it's best always to consult the tables rather than doubling or tripling a known amount (notice, for example, that 200g = 6oz but 400g = 14oz; and 30ml = 1fl oz but 90ml = 3½fl oz). And for ultra-accurate conversion from Celcius to Farenheit, use a thermometer or multiply the Celcius figure by 9, divide it by 5, then add 32.

It's important also to note that the recipes in this book were cooked in a conventional oven. If you have a fan-assisted oven, you will need to decrease oven temperatures in the recipes by 20°C (68°F), and you may find that the cooking times need to be reduced slightly.

Temperature

30°C	85°F	110°C	225°F	Gas ¼
40°C	105°F	130°C	250°F	Gas ½
50°C	120°F	140°C	275°F	Gas 1
60°C	140°F	150°C	300°F	Gas 2
70°C	160°F	170°C	325°F	Gas 3
80°C	175°F	180°C	350°F	Gas 4
90°C	195°F	190°C	375°F	Gas 5
100°C	212°F	200°C	400°F	Gas 6
		220°C	425°F	Gas 7
		230°C	450°F	Gas 8

Weight

10g	½oz	100g	3oz	300g	10oz
20g	¾oz	150g	5oz	400g	14oz
25g	1oz	200g	6oz	450g	1lb
50g	2oz	250g	9oz	500g	1lb 2oz

Measurement of Volume

5ml		1 teaspoon	130ml	4$\frac{1}{2}$fl oz		
10ml		1 dessertspoon	140ml	5fl oz		$\frac{1}{4}$ pint
15ml	$\frac{1}{2}$ fl oz	1 tablespoon	155ml	5$\frac{1}{2}$fl oz	$\frac{2}{3}$ cup	
20ml			170ml	6fl oz		
25ml		5 teaspoons	185ml	6$\frac{1}{2}$fl oz		
30ml	1fl oz		200ml	7fl oz		
40ml	1$\frac{1}{2}$ fl oz		225ml	8fl oz		
50ml		$\frac{1}{5}$ cup	285ml	10fl oz	1 cup	$\frac{1}{2}$ pint
55ml	2fl oz		400ml	14fl oz		
60ml			425ml	15fl oz		$\frac{3}{4}$ pint
70ml	2$\frac{1}{2}$ fl oz		565ml	20fl oz	2 cups	1 pint
80ml			710ml	25fl oz		1$\frac{1}{4}$ pints
90ml	3$\frac{1}{2}$ fl oz		850ml	30fl oz		1$\frac{1}{2}$ pints
100ml		$\frac{2}{5}$ cup	1 litre	35fl oz		1$\frac{3}{4}$ pints
115ml	4fl oz					

Measurement of Distance

5mm	$\frac{1}{4}$in	10cm	4 in
1cm	$\frac{2}{5}$in	20cm	7$\frac{3}{4}$in
2.5cm	1in	50cm	1ft 7$\frac{1}{2}$in
5cm	2in	1m	3ft 3$\frac{1}{2}$in

Liquid and Dry Measure Equivalents

2 tablespoons	1oz	25ml	30g
1 cup	$\frac{1}{4}$ quart	250ml	225g
2 cups	1 pint	500ml	450g
4 cups	32oz	1 litre	
4 quarts	1 gallon	3.75 litres	

Ounces to grams	multiply by 28.35
Teaspoons to millilitres	multiply by 5
Tablespoons to millilitres	multiply by 15
Fluid ounces to millilitres	multiply by 30
Cups to litres	multiply by 0.24

Measurement of Dry Goods by Volume

Butter, Shortening, Cheese and other Solid Fats

1 tablespoon	$\frac{1}{8}$ stick	15g	$\frac{1}{2}$oz
2 tablespoons	$\frac{1}{4}$ stick	30g	1oz
4 tablespoons ($\frac{1}{4}$ cup)	$\frac{1}{2}$ stick	60g	2oz
8 tablespoons ($\frac{1}{2}$ cup)	1 stick	115g	4oz ($\frac{1}{4}$lb)
16 tablespoons (1 cup)	2 sticks	225g	8oz ($\frac{1}{2}$lb)
32 tablespoons (2 cups)	4 sticks	450g	16oz (1lb)

50g = $3\frac{1}{2}$ tablespoons   100g = $\frac{1}{2}$ cup minus 1 tablespoon

Flours (unsifted)

1 tablespoon	8.75g	$\frac{1}{4}$oz
$\frac{1}{4}$ cup (4 tbsp)	35g	$1\frac{1}{4}$oz
$\frac{1}{3}$ cup (5 tbsp)	45g	$1\frac{1}{2}$oz
$\frac{1}{2}$ cup	70g	$2\frac{1}{2}$oz
$\frac{2}{3}$ cup	90g	$3\frac{1}{2}$oz
$\frac{3}{4}$ cup	105g	$3\frac{1}{4}$oz
1 cup	140g	5oz
$1\frac{1}{2}$ cups	210g	$7\frac{1}{2}$oz
2 cups	280g	10oz
$3\frac{1}{2}$ cups	490g	1lb

100g = $\frac{3}{4}$ cup minus $\frac{1}{2}$ tablespoon   250g = 2 cups minus 3 tablespoons
400g = 3 cups minus 2 tablespoons   500g = $3\frac{1}{2}$ cups minus 1 tablespoon

Granulated Sugar

1 teaspoon	5g	$\frac{1}{6}$oz
1 tablespoon	15g	$\frac{1}{2}$oz
$\frac{1}{4}$ cup (4 tbsp)	60g	$1\frac{3}{4}$oz
$\frac{1}{3}$ cup (5 tbsp)	75g	$2\frac{1}{4}$oz
$\frac{1}{2}$ cup	100g	$3\frac{1}{2}$oz
$\frac{2}{3}$ cup	130g	$4\frac{1}{2}$oz
$\frac{3}{4}$ cup	150g	5oz
1 cup	200g	7oz
$1\frac{1}{2}$ cups	300g	$9\frac{1}{2}$oz
2 cups	400g	$13\frac{1}{2}$oz

250g = 1 cup plus 3 tablespoons plus 1 teaspoon 500g = $2\frac{1}{2}$ cups

Brown Sugar

$1\frac{1}{2}$ cups		450g	1lb

Confectioners' Sugar

4 cups		450g	1lb

Breadcrumbs

Dry	$^3/_4$ cup	115g	4oz
Fresh	2 cups	115g	4oz

Egg Whites

1	2 tablespoons
8	1 cup

Egg Yolks

1	1 tablespoon
16	1 cup

Fruit, Dried and Pitted

Plumped	$2^2/_3$ cups	450g	1lb
Cooked and puréed	$2^1/_3$ cups	450g	1lb

Fruit, Fresh

Raw and sliced	3 cups	450g	1lb
Cooked and chopped	$2^1/_3$ cups	450g	1lb
Puréed	$1^1/_4$ cups	450g	1lb

Nuts

Chopped	$^3/_4$ cup	115g	4oz
Ground	1 cup, loosely packed	115g	4oz

Vegetables

Carrots & other roots, sliced	3 cups	450g	1lb
Carrots & other roots, puréed	$1^1/_3$ cups	450g	1lb
Onions, sliced or chopped	3 cups	450g	1lb
Potatoes, raw/sliced/chopped	3 cups	450g	1lb
Spinach & other leafy greens	$1^1/_2$ cups	450g	1lb

ROAST CHICKEN & ROAST POTATOES

I gotta thing about chickens.

Mickey Rourke in *Angel Heart*

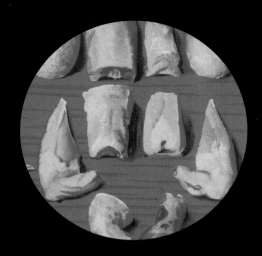

INTRODUCTION

It is hard to think of a more perfect meal than roast chicken. Not so much because of its taste or simplicity, but because it gets people round the table. It's an event, a celebration of food and a magnificent social ritual. There are the *Carry On*-style innuendoes – 'Are you a leg man or a breast man?' – the carving customs, the tussles over the dark meat, the 'oysters', the wishbone. 'Come for Sunday lunch' is an invitation that almost invariably conjures up a vision of a glisteningly juicy, golden-brown chicken, sitting in a well-worn roasting tin, surrounded by a scree of paler gold roast potatoes. It's a meal we linger over, still picking at the desecrated carcass long after the kids have left the table, as though abandoning the bird might end the feeling of well-being.

Certainly, in my household, it's a family affair. One irony of being a chef is that you get to spend almost no time cooking and eating with your family. Sunday evening is about the only chance I get to do it, and it's sacrosanct: come 7 p.m. you'll find us eating roast chicken and roast potatoes. Nostalgia demands that I still call it Sunday lunch, though my kids correct me: 'Dad, it's *dinner.*' It's an anarchic business – my daughters demanding the legs, my son the breast; all of us taking a slurp of water and gargling Pachelbel's *Canon*.

Like freshly baked bread, it's the smell that gets to me, the golden aromas snaking round the kitchen as the meat softens and colours. When I was child we'd go for picnics in Windsor Great Park. On the way we'd stop off at Andrianov's deli in Connaught Street to buy a roast chicken and a buttered baguette. That delicious smell would torment me until we reached the park, opened the bag and slipped the chicken into the baguette. Even now that smell, for me, summons up a pleasure all the sweeter for being deferred.

HISTORY

• Chicken •

Charles Darwin first identified the red jungle fowl of south-east Asia as the original ancestors of the modern chicken because they showed the ability to breed with domestic birds and produce fertile offspring. The chicken's domestication seems to have taken place early in human history, with some archaeologists – perhaps following Darwin's lead – dating it to around 3000 BC, in India. Others argue that domestication happened in Burma or the Malay peninsula. Remains discovered in China confirm that, no matter where domestication first took place, it was certainly under way by the second millennium BC, though it's not clear whether these birds were raised for food – or for fighting.

The chicken's progress westwards was gradual and meandering. It was probably introduced to Europe via Egypt: Greek writings from the fourth century BC refer to the Egyptians not only keeping chickens but incubating them as well. The Greeks also kept domestic fowl – there are texts referring to chickens as *alektryones*, which means 'awakeners', a description that anyone who has ever slept near a farmyard will agree with.

From Greece the chicken went to Rome (there are many references to chickens being served up at symposia, and several recipes appear in the classical cookbook *Apicius*; the physician Galen recommended chicken soup for regular bowel movements), but when the Romans reached Britain, they discovered that the chicken had beaten them to it, probably brought there by Celtic tribes.

Tricking with chicken

Although chickens of the past didn't suffer the cruelties of intensive farming, they had other indignities to contend with. Here's a piece of food theatre from the fifteenth-century French cookery manuscript *Vivendier*. Don't try this at home!

To make a chicken to be served roasted.

Get a chicken or any other bird you want, and pluck it cleanly in hot water. Then get yolks of 2 or 3 eggs; they should be beaten with powdered saffron or wheat flour, and distempered with fat broth or with the grease that drips under a roast into the dripping pan. By means of a feather, glaze and paint your pullet carefully with this mixture so that its colour looks like roast meat. With this done, and when it is about to be served to the table, put the chicken's head under its wing, and turn it in your hands, rotating it until it is fast asleep. Then set it down on your platter with the other roast meat. When it is about to be carved, it will wake up and make off down the table upsetting jugs, goblets and whatnot.

(Translated by Terence Scully)

For centuries chickens remained little more than farmyard scavengers. Towards the end of the 1700s, however, attitudes began to change. The selective-breeding theories of Robert Bakewell (who created longhorn cattle and shirehorses), along with Darwin's ideas about genetic transmission, alerted agriculturalists to the breeding potential of chickens. The fuse of more widespread enthusiasm awaited only a match – which came in the form of Queen Victoria. In 1843 Sir Edward Belcher presented her with Cochins from what is now Vietnam. When they were displayed at the Dublin Show three years later, they sparked off a national mania for poultry breeding and exhibition. By 1865 the Poultry Club of Great Britain was drawing up the world's first Standards of Excellence and the Victorian era had become recognised as 'the Golden Age of Rare Breed Poultry'.

That we have gone from the chicken's golden age to its opposite in less than 150 years is just one of the many shocking features of modern-day intensive poultry-farming.[*] In the scramble to produce birds with the maximum amount of white meat, everything else has been sacrificed – taste, health concerns (for both the chickens and those who consume them), ethics and, above all, humanity.

Broiler chickens (i.e. those raised for their meat) spend their scant six weeks of life crammed in an unclean shed with 10,000–40,000 other birds, each of which has a living space about the size of an A4 sheet of paper. The mortality rate is high: anything between 6 and 30 per cent. Those that survive often spend their final weeks on their knees, enfeebled by drugs and poor diet, and unable to carry the abnormal weight of their artificially fattened bodies. This is the life of 98 per cent of broiler chickens in the UK – some 735 million chickens every year.

• Potatoes •

It must be very nutritious, or it would not sustain the strength of
thousands of people whose almost sole food it constitutes.

Eliza Acton, *Modern Cookery for Private Families*

Potatoes were cultivated at least two thousand years ago in Peru, and possibly up to six thousand years earlier. Archaeological excavations suggest that their history extends even further back: in southern Chile there is evidence that wild potatoes were being gathered in 11,000 BC. They undoubtedly became a central part of Andean culture: potato designs have been found on shards of Nazca and Chimu pottery, and South American Indians measured time by how long it took to cook potatoes to various consistencies.

The transformation of the potato from knobbly, somewhat bitter tuber to universal staple began in 1537 in what is now Colombia. As with so many of the foods in this book, it was a by-product of conquest: the Spanish forces of Gonzalo Jiménez de Quesada discovered the potato while in search of the golden city of El Dorado. (It is not recorded whether Jiménez de Quesada was disappointed that, instead of the wonders of gold, he found the Golden Wonder.) Within twenty years it was cultivated in Spain and Italy.

The potato's history continued to be linked to various adventurers, though it's impossi-

* Poultry's sorry tale has taken a new twist with the worldwide advance of the H5N1 virus, commonly known as 'avian flu'. Poultry sales have collapsed as a result, even though H5N1 is not a food-borne virus. While the effects of the outbreak of the virus should not be underestimated (millions of birds have died from it in the last decade), they need to be kept in perspective. At the time of writing, the World Health Organisation has confirmed 105 deaths from the virus. In each case it is believed to have been caused by close contact with sick birds.

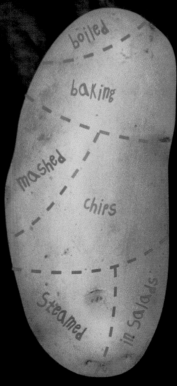

In any way...

boiled

baking

mashed

chips

steamed

in salads

...potatoes are goo...

GERMICOPA
CRÉATEUR VARIÉTAL DE POMME DE TERRE
POTATO VARIETIES CREATOR

ble now to unravel the truth of these stories. Sir Walter Raleigh, it is said, brought the potato to the British Isles around the 1580s and planted it on his estate at Youghal, in Ireland. Others claim that Francis Drake obtained some roots in Cartagena, or that the potato was part of the booty from a wrecked Armada vessel. What is certain is that, despite its dramatic arrival in Europe, and its mass acceptance in modern times, people didn't at first take to the tuber. As part of the night-shade family, it was considered poisonous or liable to cause leprosy or syphilis. Protestants refused to plant it because it wasn't mentioned in the Bible, and it was still viewed as a delicacy in England some eighty years after its introduction. Despite the Royal Society's recommendation in 1663 that it be grown as a precaution against famine (a cruelly ironic fact, given the famine caused by potato blight in Ireland 200 years later), the potato only really became available to all classes in the early eighteenth century.

The spud was always going to win through. Born of conquest and adventure, it was a suitable cultivation for troubled times. As an underground crop it was difficult for soldiers to destroy: it couldn't be razed to the ground like a field of corn. It was also easier to grow than oats or barley. With each poor cereal harvest in Britain in the eighteenth century, potatoes grew in pop-ularity until, by the end of the next century, it was the main vegetable crop in the country. (The Second World War gave the potato a further boost: the 'Dig for Victory' campaign in Britain – an initiative designed to compensate for lack of imports by means of home-growing – led to a doubling of the acreage devoted to production.) It is now the staple food of two-thirds of the world's population and, along with rice, wheat and maize, one of the most important food crops on the planet.

The early Peruvian farmers worshipped a potato goddess, depicted with a potato plant in each hand. It seems that their faith was well-placed.

THE QUEST FOR THE BEST

• Chicken Stock •

We researched what are considered to be the best chickens you can buy in the UK and came up with five: Label Anglais, Ark Chicken, Linda Dick, Ellel free-range and Waitrose organic free-range. Even before cooking, the differences between them were marked: one was a monster almost as big as a turkey; another had the attractive mellow yellow skin of a corn-fed bird. Some had a long breast shape, others a fat one. They all went in the oven for five hours at a low temperature, though at this stage the temperature wasn't the key detail: they just needed to be cooked to the same degree so that I was testing like for like, with the aim of finding the right combination of flavour, juiciness and texture.

These chickens were unlikely to taste like any of the usual fare. A properly reared bird has done a lot of running around, searching for stuff to eat. It has worked for its food and the work-out gives it muscle, which results in a denser, tougher bird with a much gamier flavour. It can come as a surprise if you're not used to it (some people prize chicken precisely because it's bland: another example of how subjective perfection is), but for me it's how chicken is supposed to taste – and I reckon it's a far better eating experience.

My expectations were borne out in the tasting. All the chickens were superior to most of what you find on supermarket shelves: they had a genuine flavour, a decent meatiness to them. One even had a touch of almond in the flavouring, which was enjoyable, if a little weird. Tasting made it clear to me that it was the combination of flavour and texture that was important: the flesh of some of the birds tasted great but was too loose. Label Anglais had neither the strongest flavour nor the densest flesh, but in combination it proved the most satisfying to eat.

So, Label Anglais was our benchmark, but this test was always going to be a game of two halves. I'd wanted to try out British chickens partly because it's important to seek out and support local producers – that's how a good food culture grows – and partly because it's always worth exploring beyond the products with an established reputation. Sometimes you stumble across something little-known but truly exceptional. None the less I'd always known that, no matter which chicken impressed the most in our taste test, there would still have to be a showdown between it and the titan of the chicken world – the legendary Bresse. Now the moment had come. I had to travel through the countryside round Lyon to find out more about a chicken widely considered to be the very best.

The Cult of the Chicken

The queen of chickens, the chicken of kings.

Jean-Anthelme Brillat-Savarin

I'd visited the area where Bresse chickens are reared, and I'd cooked and eaten them loads of times. It is undoubtedly a superb chicken. But, either things had changed since I was last here, or maybe I'd simply underestimated the *poulet*'s pull. The cult of the chicken seemed to be growing …

This came home to me as we pulled off Autoroute 39 into a service station and were confronted by a chicken sculpture four storeys high in tubular steel. It was both monumental and surreal. (Imagine exiting the M5 near Cheddar Gorge and coming face to face with a gigantic fibre-glass wedge of cheese.)

The same level of devotion continued inside. The place was decorated with photographs of Bresse chickens happily running through green fields. In the shop you could buy the chicken in many forms – on T-shirts, oven gloves, aprons, candlesticks, tea towels, or in the flesh, ready for cooking. There was even a postcard of the tubular steel chicken, as though it had already become a tourist sight to tell the folks back home about.

As it turned out, this service station really is on the tourist trail. The A39 is a major route south for Swiss, Germans and Belgians, and many deliberately plan their journey so that their lunchbreak falls in the department of Ain and they can get their fill of the fabled Bresse chicken. (It's the only stop on the motorway that sells it.) The area manager, Laurent Berthelin (his blue tie was printed with little chickens; I wondered if you could get that in the shop too), told me that they sell 15,000 chickens a year – more than any other place in France.

'It's one of those ideas that now seems such an obvious winner, but when we started selling Bresse chickens in our cafeteria a few years ago, we had no idea if it would take off or not. Even though the chicken is far cheaper here than in Britain, it's still an expensive bird, and we had to gamble on whether people would pay that bit more for a quality product. Now we're selling forty to fifty a day.'

Although L'Arche cafeteria had the same inexpensive furnishings and signage of motorway service stations everywhere, exposed beams gave it a homely, rustic look. The food on offer also marked it out as being different from most such places: there was a wide range of cheeses, a well-made *crème brûlée* and several sorts of bread. I caught sight of the baguettes as I joined the chicken queue and was instantly transported back to Andrianov's deli. I bought bread and chicken and, as the hot savoury aromas tormented me, just as they had in the past, set about recreating my childhood experience. It may not have been the best-cooked chicken I've ever had (though Andrianov's probably wasn't either), but it was a wonderful reconnection to an important memory. How often does a service station manage that?

• Coq au Chauvin •

I want there to be no peasant in my kingdom so poor that
he is unable to have a chicken in his pot every Sunday.

Henri IV of France

Part of the Bresse chicken's appeal comes from the packaging with which nature has obligingly furnished it. With its red comb, snowy white feathers and blue legs, it is decked out in the colours of the *tricolore*. What Frenchman (or, for that matter, foodie or Francophile) could resist? It certainly looks good, but I wanted to find out why it tastes so good, so I visited Christian Chotard's farm near the village of Viriat.

As I arrived I passed a line of men in green army fatigues with shotguns slung over their shoulders and bright orange caps on their heads (presumably to make sure they didn't end up in the guns' sights by accident). They were farmers hunting boar and, had they seen any, they might have made a mockery of the otherwise peaceful scene. As it was they simply stood waiting for hours at the forest's edge, patient and impassive, as dusk gradually faded them to grey. They were

a reminder that I was on different territory: country rules applied here, where the death of animals is a way of life.

However, Christian's farm, Bon Repos, was far from forbidding. There was, of course, a sculpture of a chicken in the front garden, though this one was carved from wood and quite manageable in scale. The buildings had a pleasing lopsidedness to them that suggested great age. Clusters of sweetcorn hung from the balconies and bushy wisteria twisted up the sturdy beams. The neatly tended plots of geraniums and marigolds marked this out as a well-run farm that paid attention to details. No space was wasted: in the earth around the outbuildings both curled and flat-leaf parsley were cultivated.

Like the hunters, Christian was dressed in military green. He has been rearing Bresse chickens for twenty-five years, as did his father and grandfather before him, and he often wins prizes at Les Glorieuses, the Bresse chicken farmers' equivalent of the Oscars. Standing on the stony track that runs through his property, I asked him what gave the chicken its marvellous flavour.

'The Bresse area is small – maybe one hundred kilometres by fifty – but unique,' he said. 'There's almost no chalk in the ground here so the birds' skeletons are thinner and lighter. You get more meat for your money but a more fragile bird. And there's a lot of acid in the soil which acts like a bleach, whitening the feathers and making the feet pale blue.'

He opened the door of a roomy plywood shed strewn with straw. Panicky chatter filled the air as chicks scattered at our intrusion. Too young to have acquired their patriotic colouring, they were pale yellow with a slightly unkempt look, as though they'd just woken up, but already they looked energetic.

'These birds are two weeks old,' Christian told me. 'They'll stay in here another two weeks because they're still little babies and can't stand the cold. Then they'll go outside.'

'They look pretty healthy already. What are they fed on?'

'While they're inside they get a standard chicken feed. Then comes a big change – they eat what they can find in the grass.'

We looked over to where chickens wandered around tussocky fields, alongside long-bodied, creamy-coloured Charolais cattle. The fencing was deliberately set high enough that the chickens could wander where they liked. They stayed here because they wanted to.

'An unusual landscape like this one creates a very particular ecosystem,' continued Christian. 'The soil that the birds peck in, the herbage, the insects – it's all very different from the neighbouring areas, and it's what gives the Bresse chicken its distinctive taste.'

In acknowledgement of the formative interplay of bird and environment, the Bresse chicken was awarded *appellation d'origine contrôlée* (AOC) status in 1957, and its production is now regulated as rigorously as that of any wine or cheese. 'Each bird must have plenty of space to strut around in – at least ten square metres,' Christian explained, 'and they must spend the majority of their life outdoors, to grow up healthy and get the benefits of the Bresse soil. Chicks have to be put out at five weeks old at the latest, and stay out for a minimum of nine weeks. So, except at night, when they're shut in to protect them from foxes, the chickens roam free. The only supplement to their diet is maize plus a little wheat and milk. Nothing else. Certainly no antibiotics, chemicals or hormones. Then, at the very end, the last one or maybe two weeks, we put them in wooden coops – *épinettes* – to fatten them up.'

The chicken that fulfils this regime ends up decorated like a war hero: an identity ring on the left leg bears the name and address of the rearer; the coveted AOC red diamond label adorns its body; and a tricolour metal seal with the name of the dispatcher is attached to the neck.

There are about 400 farmers rearing birds in this fashion, producing about 1,500,000 per year, most of which are sold in France (export accounts for a mere 5 per cent).

• Les Halles de Lyon •

Later, I got to see plenty of these extravagantly bedecked chickens in Lyon's foremost food market, Les Halles.

I had been here before, of course. Before I opened the Fat Duck I spent years teaching myself the principles of classic French cuisine, and I would visit France each summer to build on what I'd learned. With its famous chefs – Alain Chapel, Paul Bocuse and Georges Blanc – and its reputation as one of the gastronomic capitals of the world, Lyon had been an important stopping-off point for me during my summer travels. I had fond memories of the fantastic range of produce on offer in Les Halles, particularly at Mère Richard, which sold some of the best cheese in the country. I wondered whether it would all be as good as I remembered.

The area had another special significance for me: barely an hour from here was L'Oustau de Baumanière, the restaurant that had first opened my eyes – and tastebuds – to the wonders of cooking. Nestling at the foot of a tower of rock, amid olive groves, with the air carrying wafts of lavender and the whirr of cicadas, it offered total sensory overload. Waiters poured sauces into soufflés, carved legs of lamb at the table or crunched over the gravel wheeling chariot-sized cheese trolleys. The sommelier, a formidable figure with a handlebar moustache and leather apron, presented the wine list as though it were a stone tablet from Cecil B. DeMille's *The Ten Commandments*. As if to match this solemnity, the wineglasses were a foot high. I'd never experienced anything like it. Perhaps that's why it had such a dramatic, life-changing effect on me: as far as fine dining went, I was a blank canvas. L'Oustau sketched out my future. On that day, cooking got into my blood, and there was nothing I could do about it.

Les Halles is situated in a bland, unprepossessing part of Lyon, between a Guggenheim-style car park and the anonymous tower blocks of hotels and banks. The squat two-storey concrete building with its sliding glass doors gives no indication of the wonderland within. Even so, it seemed somehow tidier and trendier than I remembered. But as I wandered up and down the market's three long passageways, I could see that the place still had the air of an Eastern bazaar. A jumble of small premises – bakers, butchers, game merchants, charcuteries, pâtisseries – were squeezed in together, each vying for attention and setting out elaborate displays of produce to tempt you. Pyramids of Pouligny and Valençay cheese gave way to the crescent curlicues of langouste-tail halves or the iridescent green of ducks' heads. Different aromas – aniseed, cumin – waxed and waned enticingly as I walked. La Mère Richard was still there, as were some of the quirkier places that add to the market's character: Chez Georges appealed to me, with its six types of oyster and counter in the form of a boat.

This wasn't just a trip down memory lane, however. I was here to visit the Boucherie Trolliet. Maurice Trolliet is a master butcher who really knows his craft: in 1986 he won the hugely prestigious Meilleur Ouvrier de France award. His was the place to buy a Bresse chicken – and perhaps pick up some advice as well.

Maurice's shop is professional, formal and discreet. On the façade, ornate neon handwriting picks out his surname. Below it, five butchers wearing long white aprons and black tunics with *tricolore* edging trimmed meat with the speed and precision of surgeons, placing it on the counter wrapped in folds of thick waxy paper. They were all busy, and their customers knew a thing

or two about meat as well. Transactions were accompanied by passionate, informed discussion about the quality of the produce and how it should be prepared.

Maurice got down to business in brisk, no-nonsense fashion, reaching across the counter to put a dead bird in my hands. The head lolled over the end of my palm; it still had its fan of white plumage topped by a brilliant red comb. There was no doubting this had once been a bird: it was about as far from the supermarket's anonymous, pale, prepacked meat-blob as you are likely to get.

'The female chicken has a finer flesh,' Maurice advised. 'Less *ramasse*. How do you say that in English?'

'Dense?'

'Yes, compact. The males toughen up as they chase the women around. So here we sell only the female.'

The bird I was holding had tell-tale yellow spots beneath its skin – signs of fat deposits that had built up and spread through the flesh. They would give a marvellously rich texture to the meat.

I handed over fifty euros and Maurice wrapped the bird in paper and popped it in a natty Trolliet bag. It was certainly expensive, and it would be much dearer in Britain. But it's a very special product, and proper care costs money. It's an animal, not a mass-produced bit of plastic. You're paying for the time and care, the passion and humanity and history that go into the farming of a perfect chicken.

And there's no substitute for that.

By now the queue around the *boucherie* was several deep and the hubbub of voices had increased. Everyone seemed to know everyone else, as though this were a small village within the city. The customers were all sorts: old couples for whom this had become a ritual part of each day's entertainment, fastidiously dressed gourmets, families with kids larking about or sucking lollipops. The children might look a little bored but, without even realising it, they were gaining a valuable education in food: seeing the proud care and knowledge of the retailers; hearing their parents' confident negotiations for exactly what they wanted. This was how they, in their turn, would be able to come to the market and partake in passionate, informed discussion with master butchers and fishmongers and cheesemakers. This was how the great French culinary tradition stayed alive. It was encouraging to watch, and I could only hope that kids were getting equally bored in farmers' markets all over Britain.

• The Blanc Generation •

I'd followed the chicken from green field to butcher's slab. It seemed right to finish what I'd started and track it to the table. And although there are many famous and talented chefs in and around Lyon, there was really only one person to talk to about cooking the Bresse chicken: Georges Blanc.

The Blanc family enjoys a 130-year-old tradition of gastronomy and has practically become a national institution. In 1872 Jean-Louis Blanc and his wife, Virginie, created a small *auberge* catering mainly to the poultry dealers who came to Vonnas every Thursday for the market. It was their daughter-in-law, Elisa, who put the town on the map, creating food that drew in people from miles around and earning two Michelin stars in the process. By the early 1930s the name Mère Blanc was famous throughout France, and the celebrated gastronome Curnonsky had called her 'the best cook in the world'. Georges Blanc's parents, Jean and Paulette, maintained

both the quality and the tradition before handing over to him in 1968. Georges has since not only earned a third star but also embarked on a magnificently ambitious historical building project based around the *auberge*.

In Lyon it had been raining fit to bust and, for the only time during this series, the camera crew wrapped early, so we headed over to Vonnas to check in to Blanc's Résidence des Saules hotel. From the balcony of my room I had a great view of some of Georges's achievements. Before me lay the market square – a patch of sandy earth that I could imagine was a favourite with boules players – bordered by two stately ranks of plane trees and a small river. At the far end was the solid brick of the original 1872 *auberge*, now transformed into the Restaurant Georges Blanc. This was just one of fifteen buildings around the square that Georges had lovingly restored to create the spirit of a *village gourmand*: '*Vivant, gai, harmonieux et protégé, illustrant "l'art de bien vivre".*' It's a kind of living museum and homage to the past – a little insight into the way life was lived. And I'd say that the sense of context and tradition that Georges manages to evoke only serves to increase your enjoyment and appreciation of the food he cooks.

• Like Mama Used to Make •

The following morning I got another small insight into the way life was once lived – at least in the Blanc household while Georges was growing up. He had generously agreed to show me the *poulet à la crème* that his mother used to make every Sunday. And, in concession to British tastes and traditions, he'd agreed to prepare a roast chicken as well.

It had stopped raining. I walked across the square and entered the restaurant a few minutes early, so I could have a look round. As befits a great chef who is part of a long-standing tradition, Georges's establishment is covered with testimonials from satisfied customers. In the lobby black and white photos of Deneuve, Belmondo, Delon, Yves Montand and Johnny Halliday graced the walls, along with handwritten words of praise. Rowan Atkinson and Nicole Kidman were there as well. Richard Burton declared, soberly, 'Many thanks for your wonderful hospitality.' There was a photo of Bill Clinton, who, though I didn't realise it at the time, was to become a kind of leit-motif for my travels; wherever there was good food to be had, Bill had got there first, and had his picture taken for good measure. In Georges's case the Clinton connection came about when he was asked to cook for a G7 meeting in Lyon and came up with Bresse chicken with roast garlic and a foie gras sauce. The president apparently asked for seconds, which Georges claims as his finest moment.

I turned to discover I'd been caught snooping by Georges himself. He has a schoolboy-ish air, and the glint in his eye suggested he enjoyed catching me off guard. He led me through to his kitchen, a spacious warren of interconnecting white-tiled rooms, where chefs in tall pleated hats were frying ceps and snipping bay leaves into more pleasing shapes.

'For you, Heston, Sunday dinner is roast chicken and roast potatoes.' As if to illustrate this point, Georges put an onion into a chicken's cavity and placed the bird in a pot which he then slid into an oven preheated to 160°C. 'But I'm from a different culture. Of course, we too had the family meal on Sunday. It was a great ritual, and *poulet à la crème* was the main course. When I was young, every Sunday was this. Do you want to see how it was done …?'

Hmmm. Did I want a three-star chef to cook his traditional Sunday dinner for me – a dinner that was part of his heritage and had many memories for him, that had been enjoyed and perfected by four generations of legendary French chefs, and that contained possibly the world's finest chicken?

It wasn't a tough call.

Georges put butter in a copper pan and let it froth before adding the two parts of each leg plus salt and pepper. 'I don't support an excess of salt,' he declared, 'but I do like a lot of pepper.' The legs began to brown. 'It's very important to have the right colouration because ... how do you say in English, *le sucre*?'

'The sugars?'

'Yes, in this recipe the caramelised sugars give the sauce its flavour. I use no stock.'

The butter was foaming vigorously round the panful of chicken pieces. They were already a lovely shiny brown colour, like the patina on polished pale wood. Georges had kept back the neck and wingtips because they'd take less time to cook. He added them now. 'To give more *sucre*.'

Half an onion studded with a clove or two went in the pan. A head of garlic with the top lopped off. Then more onions, this time cut into smaller pieces. A little flour was spooned in, along with some chopped mushrooms.

Georges is softly spoken and gentle but his voice acquires a sharp edge of authority when he's in the kitchen. Instructions were rapped out whenever an ingredient wasn't to hand. There was a brief, tense moment when someone mislaid the white wine, but it was soon found. A glass or so was poured into the pan, sending up a marvellous smell of caramelised chicken and alcohol. By now the chicken had a darker patina. The onion and garlic were flecked with brown too. Georges turned the pieces, leaned low over the pan and wafted the aromas towards him – perhaps having his own Proustian madeleine moment.

'Has this recipe changed over time?' I wondered out loud.

'Never. Less flour maybe, so the dish is less heavy,' Georges said. But cooking the dish is a kind of revisitation of the past, and he kept remembering details he'd forgotten, little changes that he and others had made.

'There didn't used to be mushrooms or white wine. They'd cook the chicken pieces with the roux, then drain them and add cream. Cream mixed with a yolk. And a drop of lemon. Now it's different. The acidity is introduced at the beginning, with the white wine. We don't use lemon at all.'

He picked up a big glass jug of cream and poured in the lot. 'No water or stock. Just white wine and cream. Very natural. So the sauce has only the taste of the chicken and its aromas.' He slurped a couple of spoonfuls. *'Oui, c'est bon.'*

A touch more seasoning and it was left to cook for thirty-five minutes.

In the meantime, the roast chicken was ready. It sat there, a beautiful pale gold, with its blue legs sticking up out of the pot in undignified fashion. It still had the ring on its leg, as if to remind me that, even when cooked, this bird was an aristocrat.

Georges lifted it respectfully out of the pot and let the juices drain off before setting it down on the chopping board. He carved and placed the pieces artfully round the plate: leg, two slices of breast and one of the 'oysters'. He ladled over some juice and a handful of girolle mushrooms. 'For me, it's important to use a male bird. The leg is more interesting – less tender but with more meat; a more interesting texture.'

'What is it about the Bresse chicken that makes it so special?' I asked.

'The price,' Georges deadpanned. 'OK, seriously. The marbling – the fattiness – gives it taste, just as it would in red meat. In the Bresse chicken the fat is nicely spread out rather than in big deposits. And the fact that it has been running around means it has nice dense flesh. The diet, too, is good: what it gets from the ground gives it more flavour.'

'And roast chicken is such a wonderful family dish,' I said. 'It stirs up emotions and memories of sitting round a table together. Everybody has strong opinions – male or female bird, leg or breast, white meat or dark, skin on or off – often for no apparent reason, they've just developed over time and out of habit. It's great.'

'Yes,' Georges agreed, 'and the quality and taste are perfect for me. It's a simple dish. That's the beauty of it. Even the juice to go with it is simple – no stock, just a drop of vinegar at the last moment.'

Georges was right: simplicity was the key here. He backed up a conviction that had been growing in me since we first arrived in Lyon to investigate the Bresse chicken. Many farmers and butchers devoted their lives to a careful rearing and preparation of the bird, taking great pains to avoid a production-line approach, in the belief that it benefited both the chicken and the consumer. In this context, I felt, the recipe I developed should be an extension of their efforts, celebrating the basic flavours they had worked hard to produce. In other contexts I might attempt something extremely complicated, but here it seemed right to keep it simple, keep it pure. Let the chicken speak for itself.

We turned our attention back to *poulet à la crème*. Georges took a carving fork and fished out the pieces, giving each a final sloosh round in the juices before placing it in a heavy black cast-iron pot. He grabbed a ladle and a conical sieve, which he held over the pot. The thick creamy sauce was scooped into the sieve and allowed to trickle gradually over the chicken pieces.

'You know, Heston, it's very interesting for me to revisit the tradition in my cuisine, and to change little things. People come to my restaurants for the local specialities and for authenticity. It's very important for me – as I hope it will be for my sons, Alexandre and Frédéric, who are both chefs too, and for my grandson, who already shows an interest in cuisine – to preserve the classic traditions of the area. Because we have our roots here in the Bresse region, where people are still very close to the land and its products, the good cuisine that comes from it.'

It was a beautiful sentiment. French cuisine was in good hands with people like Georges around. I too hoped that an awareness of tradition would inform the cooking of his sons and grandson.

The sauce had made its way through the sieve. It was time to sample Sunday dinner in the Blanc household. *Poulet à la crème* – a real example of what Georges was talking about: good cuisine that comes from the region.

He set out two white plates and placed a leg on each. Cream was gently spooned over each piece. It ran down the meat and spread out across the plate – simple, decorative, tasty-looking and very rich. You'd need some form of potato with it or, better still, bread, to mop up every last drop.

'With this dish,' said Georges, 'it's important that the meat doesn't colour too much or it starts to harden and ends up dry.'

The first plunge of my knife told me there was no danger of that here. The flesh simply fell away as I cut. The sauce had a lovely natural aroma, almost a perfume to it, and it did indeed contain a marvellous roasted flavour, the result of Georges's careful browning of the chicken in butter. We both put far too much in our mouths at once, and the director complained that he couldn't understand what we were saying.

'So, Heston,' said Georges, once he'd swallowed, 'now you know not only how the Bresse chicken feeds, but how he cooks as well. In that spirit, to finish with, I'd like to show you what we offer in my restaurant. I call it "La Bresse en Fête", a celebration of the chicken to show that every part of it is good. This is what a third of our customers order.'

He laid before me a sequence of six beautifully presented dishes. I especially liked *Le sot l'y laisse et l'huître creuse, dans une nage mousseuse et iodée avec des soissons* – a preparation of oysters and chicken oysters – and *Le poulet et la grenouille: duo de cuisses entre Bresse et Dombes 'façon blanquette' sans crème, au vin jaune et cerfeuil* – in which chicken and frogs' legs were cooked together. I was attracted by the play on words that underpinned each dish, but they were more than just witty flourishes. Both were light, beautifully balanced and enshrined the respect for the region that Georges was so passionate about (the frogs are a speciality of neighbouring Dombes). It was marvellous cuisine – playful, informative and precisely executed.

• Spuds-I-Like 1 •

What I say is that, if a fellow really likes potatoes,
he must be a pretty decent sort of fellow.

A. A. Milne, *Not That It Matters*

I'd got some way towards sourcing the perfect chicken. Now I needed roast potatoes to go with it. For most of us, potatoes can be divided into two groups according to use. You need a dry, floury variety for mash, roast and chips, and a waxy, creamy one for salads, gratins and purée. So Maris Piper and King Edward for mash; Charlotte and Belle de Fontenay for purée. *Sorted*.

When I first became obsessed with the idea of the perfect chip, however, I'd had to go into more detail. I spent years researching complicated questions such as starch conversion and dry matter (I even persuaded my wife, Susanna, to sneak round the local supermarket with a bucket of water, testing the dry-matter content of different varieties). Eventually I'd come up with what I wanted, and other people seemed to like them too. Even so, I felt as though I'd barely tapped the potato's potential, so the fact that this series involved chips, mash and roast seemed like a good excuse to take a fresh look at this versatile vegetable.

I drove over to the Norfolk distribution centre of MBM in Little Snoring. (How many times had someone described it as a sleepy little village, I wondered. I decided not to try it out on my hosts.) MBM is one of the biggest suppliers of potatoes in the country and, to judge by the commitment of its staff, one of the best. Peter Pattrick, Tom Dixon and Claire Harrison have a passion for potatoes that at first seems almost comic, but their enthusiasm quickly wins you over. (It's strange that when an Italian waxes lyrical about a tomato it seems fitting and dramatic, whereas vaunting the humble spud only

ANYA TYPE A

PE B

Pink Fir Apple

DESIREE

PURPLE STAR

ANYA

KING EDWARD

Highland Burgandy
Red

BLUE BELLE

gets a laugh. We've no real vocabulary for talking about food in this country; we've not argued and defended and deliberated over the dinner table the way Europeans have. It's surely one of the reasons our cuisine has comparatively little fixed identity or tradition.)

The boardroom table at MBM was covered with crates containing different sorts of potato. The huge variety in shape, size and colour was a sorry reminder of how small the choice is at any local supermarket. Alongside the familiar, golden-globed King Edwards and Maris Pipers were menhir-like Pink Fir Apples and finger-sized Anyas with their pitted skins. Juliette, a smoother version of Anya, lay next to Purple Star – with its purple veining – and the deep-red flesh of Highland Burgundy Red. The names seemed determined to add a lustre of romance to the spud, and often sounded more like exotic butterflies than potatoes: there was a Blue Belle and a Pentland Dell, not forgetting Lady Claire, Lady Rosetta and Lady Olympia. (This naming isn't always successful: BF15 sounds to me more like a fighter-jet than a potato, and the Dutch have created a variety called Arsey which may have limited success in English-speaking markets …)

Before long, Peter, Tom and Claire were trying to convert me to their particular favourites, filling me in on the ducal history of the Highland Burgundy Red or brandishing a Juliette and insisting, 'This'll make a wonderful Joël Robuchon mash.' But there was more to consider here than just varieties. We all donned heavy Day-Glo reflective jackets and stepped outside to explore the equally tricky question of storage.

We were surrounded by pine trees and silence, interrupted occasionally by the yelp of a pheasant. Tom Dixon and I walked between towers of slatted wooden crates towards the metal freight containers where varieties for testing were kept, and he outlined some of the complexities involved in keeping potatoes.

'You've got to remember that a potato's a living thing. Put it in the ground and it'll grow new ones. It's not dead, it's just dormant. And that's how we've got to keep it. To achieve this we

need to consider, first and foremost, the temperature. Keep them too warm and potatoes'll sprout or go bad. Keep them too cold, though, and the starch in them begins to break down into its constituent parts, mainly the sugars sucrose and glucose. Naturally, if you roast potatoes with a high concentration of sugars, caramelisation will occur, browning the spuds and making them bitter. So you need to store them at 7–9°C.'

On shelves running along one side of the container were plastic trays holding new types of potato. 'We're constantly testing new varieties to see if they'll give as good quality as the established types,' said Tom. 'One of the most important considerations is what is known as "dry matter". Although it looks like a solid lump, most of a potato – about three-quarters – is water. The rest is dry matter, most of which is starch. The dry matter is what gives a potato its flavour, and managing the starch content during cooking is what makes the difference between good or bad roast, mash and chips. Floury potatoes have a high dry matter, waxy ones have less.'

Tom told me that many things contribute to the amount of dry matter in a spud: the soil and climate – especially the rainfall – are influential, as are the amount of light and irrigation. Potatoes take on a particular character depending on where they're farmed.

Since dry matter gives a potato more flavour, I was hoping to be able to roast one with a high dry-matter content. So we went over to the labs to see if Tom could find me something suitable by weighing the dry matter of various potatoes on MBM's special scales. He explained that, in order to get an accurate reading, we had to rumble the spuds to remove their skins.

'OK,' I said. 'Let's get ready to rumble.' (I couldn't resist.)

The machine kicked into life – a throaty barrage of noise that sounded like someone had filled a washing machine with rocks and turned it on. Once skinned, the potatoes were placed in a basket suspended from the scales and lowered into water.

Using Tom's matchless advice and his magic scales, I arrived at a quintet of potatoes that held the promise of a good roast and would allow me to experiment with dry-matter content as well. The final five looked like this:

	% dry matter
Lady Claire	21.8
Daisy	21.1
Maris Piper	21.9
King Edward	20.5
Yukon Gold	20.3

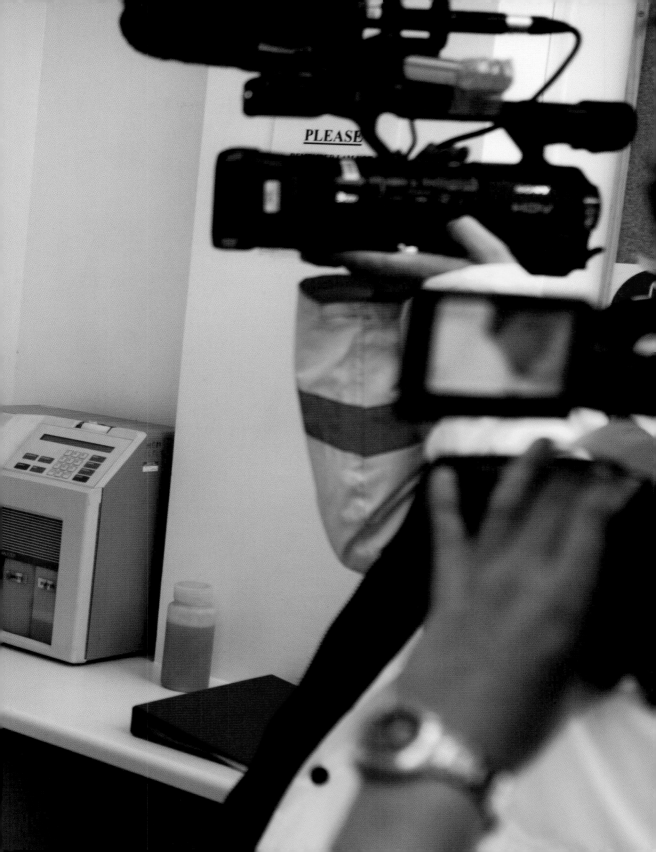

With roast potatoes, as with chips, I was looking for a crust with a delicate crunch, and a fine f centre. I asked two chefs at the Hind's Head, Mary-Ellen McTague and Dominic Chapman, to r the five contenders, then the three of us tasted them.

Lady Claire had a good-looking crust but it was just too tough, even a bit leather didn't give way with the kind of ease you need in a perfect roast potato. It turned out to be first of several to be let down by their crust. Daisy too was tough and chewy on the outside, had a starchy centre. Its flavour was bland and had no character.

Even at first glance, it was obvious that the roasted Maris Piper was in a league c own. The crust had fissured a little round the edges, allowing the oil to penetrate the surface produce a deliciously crunchy, glass-like crust. And so it proved to be. The oil gave the pota real juiciness that was the perfect contrast to the flavourful inside. This was the benchmark others had to beat.

King Edward was close: it probably had a better overall flavour than Maris Piper. B perfect skin is part of the point of a roast potato and the King Edward just didn't have it. There none of the Maris Piper's juiciness, probably because the skin had broken up less. It was altoge chewier – the wrong kind of textural companion to a fluffy interior.

Yukon Gold's crust had gone off-puttingly dark, far darker than any of the others, had a slight bitter note, as though the potato was almost scorched. Since there was virtu nothing to choose between its dry-matter content and that of the King Edward, something else to be at work here. I wondered whether this example of Yukon Gold had developed a high gluc content, perhaps due to bad storage. In any case, the result was a crust with no crunch disaster in a roast potato. It would be Maris Piper calling the tune.

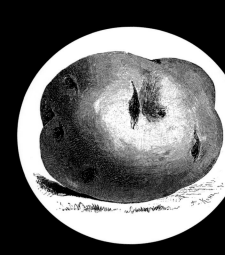

ROAST CHICKEN
& ROAST POTATOES

Serves 4

A raw chicken is about 80 per cent water. Cooking it is basically a battle to hang on to some of that moisture, so that you end up with a deliciously succulent bird. In this recipe, two techniques help achieve that aim: brining and low-temperature cooking.

Brining is a great way of tenderising the flesh and helping it to stay moist at the same time. The salt alters the proteins in such a way that they hold on to moisture more effectively. The result is a much juicier chicken – especially if, as here, some of the bird's own juices are injected back into its body.

The higher the cooking temperature, the more water is lost. (Think of how water leaves a sponge when it's squeezed: heat has a similar effect on protein fibres, causing them to contract and crowd together, forcing out the water between them.) A chicken that has reached an internal temperature of 70°C/160°F will have lost a large percentage of its water. Even at 60°C/140°F, a lot of water will be gone, but this lower temperature manages the best balance of juiciness and a superbly tender texture. It takes a little longer, but it's worth it.

A third technique – inspired by the ducks hanging up to dry in the windows of Chinese restaurants – adds something special to the chicken's texture. Blanching the bird and then letting its surface dry out leads to a marvellous crispy skin when cooked.

My Sunday lunch would team chicken with broccoli and glazed carrots, so I've included recipes for these as well, which can be adapted to other vegetables. The broccoli recipe is also suitable for leeks, green beans and Romaine lettuce, while the carrot recipe is great for many root vegetables – celeriac, swede, parsnips – as well as asparagus.

Special equipment: oven thermometer, digital probe, large tongs, baster with a needle attachment

Timing: This needs to be begun the day before, but mainly in order to sit the chicken in a pot of brine for six hours and then quickly blanch it and leave overnight in the fridge. On the day, the long, slow cooking and resting of the chicken gives plenty of time to prepare the veg *and* mingle with your guests or family.

For the chicken:
1.5kg poulet de Bresse or good quality
free-range chicken
approx. 350–375g table salt
100g unsalted butter
2–3 tbsps groundnut oil
freshly ground black pepper

For the potatoes:
1kg large Maris Piper potatoes
olive oil (enough to fill the roasting tray to
a depth of just under 1cm)
4 cloves of garlic
1 generous bunch of fresh rosemary
table salt

For the carrots:
12 large carrots (about 500g)
50g unsalted butter
table salt and freshly ground black pepper

For the broccoli:
1 large head of broccoli
50g unsalted butter
table salt and freshly ground black pepper

BRINING AND ROASTING THE CHICKEN

1. First, prepare a brine for the chicken. Get a large saucepan or casserole that the chicken can sit in comfortably, and place the chicken in it. Measure how much water you would need to cover the chicken, then weigh out 8 per cent of that volume in table salt.* Remove the chicken and refrigerate. Tip out the water and refill the pot with the same amount of fresh water. Add the salt, then place the pot over a high heat until the salt has dissolved. Leave the brine to cool completely.

2. Meanwhile, remove the chicken's wings at the first joint. Trim away the neck and feet, if present, and discard. Reserve the wings to make a buttery juice for the finished bird (see below).

3. Remove the chicken's wishbone, in order to make carving easier (unless its removal is going to disappoint children who are looking forward to the fun of tugging it for luck!). To do this, lift up the flap of skin covering the neck cavity, and then run the blade of a small, sharp knife along the wishbone on each side of the V-shaped cavity. It can then be eased away from the breastbone and carefully pulled off the chicken.

4. Put the chicken back into the pot of brine. Cover and refrigerate for 6 hours.

5. Remove the chicken from the fridge and pour off the brine. (Brining makes the skin quite fragile, so handle it gently.) Rinse the chicken under running cold water. Return it to the pot and fill with fresh cold water. Leave it to soak for an hour, changing the water every 15 minutes to wash off the salt.

 Generally, grams and millilitres are interchangeable, so if, for example, it takes 500ml of water to cover your chicken, think of this as 500g, then calculate 8 per cent of that and weigh out that amount of salt. (This parity can't always be relied on: where pinpoint accuracy is required – as in the water for the pizza dough – it's best to measure in grams.)

6. Lift the chicken from the pot. Wash out the pot then refill it with fresh cold water and bring to the boil. Fill a large bowl or basin with cold water and ice. Dunk the chicken in the boiling water for 30 seconds. Remove and plunge into the ice-cold water. Bring the pot of water back to the boil and repeat both steps. The skin will now look puckered and slightly webbed.

7. Dry the chicken with paper towels. Place on a cooling rack with a tray underneath. Loosely cover with a breathable fabric such as muslin or even a new J cloth, and leave in the fridge overnight to dry.

8. Preheat the oven to 60°C/140°F, using an oven thermometer to check it. Sit the chicken in a roasting tin and cook until the internal temperature of the bird when probed has reached 60°C/140°F. (This should take about 4–6 hours.) At this point, the chicken will have a pale white, slightly anaemic appearance. It won't look browned.

9. Remove the chicken from the oven and leave it to rest for 1 hour. Meanwhile, roughly chop the reserved chicken wings. Heat the butter in a small pan over a low to medium heat, add the chopped wings and fry until the butter smells nutty and has turned dark brown. Pass the wings and butter through a fine sieve into a bowl. Discard the wings and reserve the buttery juices.

10. To brown the chicken, heat a large frying pan over a high heat for 10 minutes. Add the groundnut oil and, when it starts smoking, the chicken. Use a pair of tongs to turn the chicken so that it browns all over. (Be careful not to burn yourself.) Remove from the pan.

11. Use the baster to suck up some of the buttery juices. Push the needle through the skin, into the flesh of the chicken, and release the juices. Carefully remove the needle and refill. Repeat at several points around the chicken – be really generous with this – after which it is ready to carve.

ROASTING THE POTATOES

1. Preheat the oven to 190°C/375°F/Gas 5.

2. Wash the potatoes thoroughly and then peel them. Reserve the peelings and tie them in a muslin bag. Cut the potatoes into quarters (the quartering's important because it's the edges that get nice and crunchy: that's why reasonably large potatoes are needed for this recipe) and leave them in a bowl under running water for 2–3 minutes (or put in a bowl of water for 15 minutes, changing the water every 5 minutes).

3. Bring a pan of salted water (10g salt per litre of water) to the boil, add the potatoes and toss in the bag of peelings (they contain lots of flavour). Cook for 20 minutes, or until the potatoes are very soft: take them as far as you can without ending up with potato soup. (It's the fissures that form as the potato breaks up that trap the fat, creating a crunchy crust.)

4. Meanwhile, pour the olive oil into a roasting tray (it needs to be large enough to hold all the potatoes in one layer) and place in the oven.

5. Once the potatoes are soft, drain them in a colander and discard the bag of peelings. Give them a gentle shake to roughen the edges and drive off any remaining drops of water.

6. Put the potatoes in the hot roasting tray and roll them around so that they are completely coated in oil. Roast for an hour or so, until crisp and a lovely golden brown, turning every 20 minutes. Add the garlic and rosemary after 50 minutes.

7. Season with salt and serve.

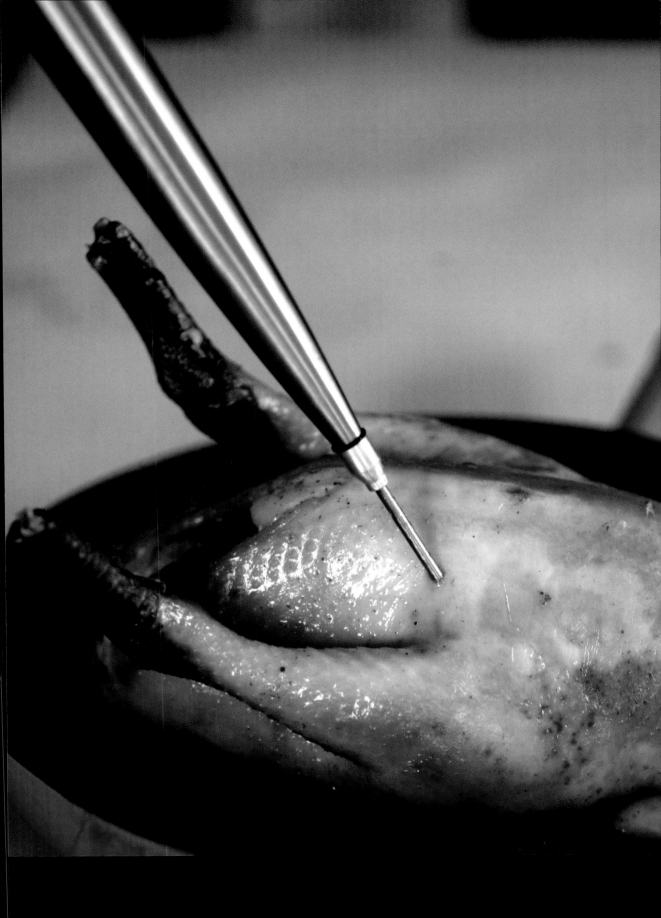

COOKING THE CARROTS

1. Top, tail and peel the carrots, then cut them lengthways into 4 long batons. Keep the pieces together and cut diagonally into chunks.

2. Place the carrots in a sauté pan large enough that they can sit in one layer. Season well, add the butter and cover. Place over a low heat and cook for 30–40 minutes or until the carrots are soft and nicely coated in the butter (which now contains many of the flavour molecules that have leached out of the carrots). Shake the pan regularly to prevent the carrots sticking. If the butter gets too hot and there's a risk of the carrots frying, add a dessertspoon of water.

COOKING THE BROCCOLI:

1. Bring a medium-sized pan of salted water to the boil. Prepare a large bowl of ice-cold water.

2. Cut the broccoli into small florets (as far as possible, they should all be the same size), then drop them into the boiling water, bring back to the boil and cook for 1 minute.

3. Remove the broccoli and plunge into the ice-cold water to halt the cooking process. (At this point the broccoli can be stored in the fridge and reheated – as below – just before serving.)

4. To reheat, put the broccoli in a pan along with the butter, salt and pepper and cook over a medium heat for 3–4 minutes or until the stalk yields slightly when a knife is pushed through. Remove from the heat, adjust the seasoning and serve.

PIZZA

The Neapolitan pizza is a beautiful thing to look at, and extremely substantial to eat; coarse food, to accompany copious glasses of rough wine.

Elizabeth David, *Italian Food*

INTRODUCTION

Elizabeth David was right: pizza is all about beauty and substance. I certainly appreciated the substance when I was young: more than once I did that teenage thing of choosing as many toppings as possible – tuna, anchovies, chilli, artichokes, pepperoni – though I can say with some pride that even then I knew to draw the line at peppers, sweetcorn and pineapple.

Pizza's beauty was less apparent in Britain during my childhood than now. Many were frozen, and came with a half-baguette rather than a dough base. When our local cinema went through a revamp it teamed up with a pizza company and sold exactly that – thick and chewy, with that pre-grated Parmesan which always smelled off-puttingly like vomit. It's quite surprising that pizza survived these travesties. But I guess, at that stage, we bought into the whole cinematic glamour surrounding the pizza, rather than the taste. I know I did. It seemed not Italian but hiply American: the fast-paced take-away culture, the stack of delivery boxes, the freedom of choice. The aspirational allure increased as companies like Pizza Express got in on the act, and I saw what a pizza could be: a splendid evocation of the sun-drenched Mediterranean.

HISTORY

The origins of pizza are fiercely fought over: the Koreans claim its invention, as do the Chinese, whose Historical Society put forward the thesis that *ping tse* – a flat bread made from sweet rice-flour and spices – is the true precursor of the pizza.

However, the word 'pizza' has the same roots as 'pitta', a flat disc of bread that has been baked since at least 2000 BC. The Egyptians invented both leavened bread and the oven, so it's a safe bet that the unacknowledged inventor of the pizza was the first Egyptian who got bored of a diet of pitta and chucked a topping on top.

Over time, of course, pizza has become identified with Italy. The word itself was used as early as AD 997 at Gaeta, a port between Naples and Rome, and by the twelfth century there were varieties from Apulia to Calabria. In the last hundred years, the pizzas of Naples – the marinara (or Napoletana) and the Margherita – have come to be seen as the archetypes. Certainly it is the Neapolitans who, in the late seventeenth century, combined the pizza base with tomato (then generally still viewed with some suspicion, despite being introduced from Peru some two hundred years earlier) to produce what is undoubtedly thought of today as the standard pizza.

Pizza began life in Naples as fast food. Pizzerias were originally simply workshops where the pizzas were prepared and cooked. Salesmen would then wander the town carrying the pizzas on their heads in a *stufa*, a round metal container with shelves. They also carried a *lanzuno*, a small foldable table. If they made a sale, the *lanzuno* would be whipped out and the *stufa* set upon it while negotiations took place. The last – and therefore coldest – pizza was usually sold at a knock-down price. (In a region as poor as Naples, such financial compromises were commonplace: you could even buy a pizza on credit, giving you seven days to find the money somehow, anyhow.)

The purchased pizza would be folded in half, then half again, and eaten from the point outwards. Here was a perfect food for the busy working man: no knife and fork needed, and the dough doubled as a plate. The Neapolitan fishermen sought it out when they returned from work and needed something quick and light to eat straight away, and so they gave their name to the first classic Naples pizza, the marinara.

From here to a pizza named after a queen seems quite a leap. And it's true that pizza was considered a platter for the poor until 11 June 1889, when King Umberto I and his wife, Queen Margherita, requested to taste the local speciality. Raffaele Esposito of the pizzeria 'Pietro ... e basta così' was summoned to the Capodimonte Palace, where he offered up three types of pizza: one with small fish (*cecinielli*), one with olive oil and cheese, and one with tomato, mozzarella and basil.

Pizzeria Pietro has since changed its name to Brandi, but it still proudly displays the queen's response to her first taste of pizza. On headed notepaper, the head of the Servizi da Tavola della Real Casa (the Royal Household Culinary Service) declares that the pizzas 'were found to be very good'. From that point on, the pizza with tomato, mozzarella and basil became known as the Margherita – the queen of pizzas – patriotically decked out in the green, white and red of the Italian flag. And with royal blessing, of course, the pizza was finally accepted by the local bourgeoisie.

Pizza remained a Neapolitan speciality, however. As late as the 1970s it was still largely unknown in the north of Italy. For its current status as a truly international food, we have to thank American fast-food franchises.

Italian immigrants and American soldiers stationed in Naples during the Second World War had taken the pizza to the States, at about the same time as the McDonald brothers began introducing assembly-line production methods into the restaurant business. Several chains hit upon the idea of marketing 'ethnic' food in the same way, and suddenly Tex-Mex and pizza joints sprang up all over the place. By 1970 Americans were eating two billion pizzas annually, and exporting their version of the Neapolitan pizza throughout the world.

Of course, the American pizza bears only a passing resemblance to its Italian cousin. With its light, elastic crust and deliberately sparse ingredients, the Neapolitan pizza can come as a surprise. Eisenhower certainly thought so, and caused a diplomatic incident when he said he'd tasted better pizza in New York than Naples.

I had no intention of causing another diplomatic stand-off. Most great chefs, food critics and cookbook writers still insist that Naples is the place for pizza. If I was to have any chance of creating a decent pizza, I had to go there and see for myself.

THE QUEST FOR THE BEST

• The Secret of San Marzano •

In *Treasures of the Italian Table*, Burton Anderson notes that, 'It has been said that if Naples had managed to patent the pizza it would now be among Italy's wealthiest cities instead of one of its poorest.' Perhaps that is why, a little late in the day, the Neapolitans are trying to protect their product against pale imitations (to say nothing of the viler variants that have been foisted upon us, such as Pizza Hawaii with its chunks of tepid pineapple). The Associazione Vera Pizza Napoletana has drawn up a code that regulates every aspect of preparing the proper pizza, from the exact heat of the oven to the techniques employed to knead the dough. The grade of flour, the types of cheese, the kinds of tomato – each part of the process is specified in minute detail. And there are now moves to get the Neapolitan pizza included in the list of products recognised by the EU as traditional specialities, and effectively copyrighted as such. This might seem heavily traditionalist, and counter to a spirit of adventure, but to me it was very encouraging. Although I could never hope to emulate the lengthy apprenticeship of the *pizzaiolo* (pizza-maker), here at least was a blueprint for the perfect Margherita and marinara. Surely this was a short cut to success. I flew to Italy full of confidence.

The Italians are passionate about their food. This was borne out almost as soon as I touched down in Naples. In the bus from the airport the driver began arguing about the best pizza, insisting that the Neapolitan product was superior. 'It's the way the *pizzaiolo* works the dough,' he declared, 'and the silkiness of the mozzarella, the juiciness of the San Marzano tomato.' For Italians, food is not just the stuff of life but an everyday drama, a ritual to be enacted and enjoyed,

a communal celebration. This is part of what makes their cuisine great, but the mythical status accorded to much of their food makes it almost impossible to separate fact from fiction. Marco Polo, for example, is credited with the discovery of many foodstuffs, even though the dates often deny this. Similarly, people claim the Margherita was invented for the queen, yet it pre-dates Raffaele Esposito's excursion to Capodimonte. In Italy, it seems, the bigger and better the story, the more it has to be taken with a large pinch of salt (any kind: the Associazione offers no stipulations here).

So it was with a mixture of excitement and trepidation that I set out from the headquarters of Solania, one of the top producers of canned San Marzano tomatoes in Italy. My bus driver wasn't alone in his esteem for the San Marzano: almost every Neapolitan I met said it was the best tomato for pizza, and I'd come across several Italian chefs who were gripped by nostalgia at the mere mention of its name. The celebrated Marcella Hazan says that the authentic flavour of Naples pizza owes much to the San Marzano. Could it possibly live up to the hype – or would it turn out to be just another story?

Our simple trip to the tomato fields was, of course, turned into ritual and drama. By the time we had bumped our way down the rutted track at the end of our journey, we were part of a motorcade that included members of the Italian press (Solania's general manager had a keen eye for any publicity opportunity) and a local government dignitary. The pomp and circumstance seemed at odds with the rustic setting: the fields spreading out haphazardly, like allotments, with tumbledown huts and sagging netting attached to staves.

If you could bottle romance alongside the product, the San Marzano tomato would undoubtedly be the most delicious in the world. The fields lay in a wide valley between the steep green ridges of the Picentini and Lattari mountains. In the background loomed the stubby peak of Vesuvius, familiar from hundreds of photographs, paintings and engravings – the inescapable, brooding symbol of Naples. Occasionally a tiny Piaggio van trundled past, its flatbed stacked with sheaves of freshly washed rocket, but most of the time the only sound was the low moan of wind. At midday the church bells rang out the *mezzogiorno*, as they have for centuries.

The fieldworkers, too, looked as though they had stepped out of an old photograph – especially the women, who wore brightly patterned aprons over shapeless dark skirts. Both sexes had close-cropped hair and weather-beaten brown faces that signalled a lifetime spent working out of doors. They were all old: the San Marzano is a notoriously delicate tomato – it needs constant, careful tending (*com' un bambino* – like a child) and the harvesting has to take place by hand; it's back-breaking work, and the young simply aren't interested.

This isn't the only factor jeopardising the tomato's future: over time the soil has lost much of its ability to hold water and now needs an elaborate system of pipes and irrigation to support it. This worsens the fragile economics of a fruit that's difficult to grow, and already there is strong competition in the area from hardier varieties. A hybrid has been developed from Chinese seeds: the tomatoes give a higher yield but they're not the pure San Marzano. Locals contemptuously dismiss them as 'Chinese balls', but you can see that the bravado hides a certain anxiety.

Despite their hardships, the workers were incredibly welcoming, and eager for us to try their tomato. From somewhere they conjured up rough chunks of fennel bread, a bottle of extra virgin olive oil and a jar of salt. Stemfuls of *peperoncini* – small round chillis with a purplish tinge – were wrenched from the ground. There was even a bottle of rough red wine that had to be levered open with a hammer and screwdriver. A plastic crate was up-ended to serve as a table. Someone cut open a tomato and held it out to me. '*Vai, vai. Mangia.*'

I was about to get my first taste of the fabled San Marzano.

What can I say? The tomato's elongated shape – like a fat teardrop – sat satisfyingly snugly in the hand; it filled the palm and it felt good, firm but fleshy.* It looked good, too, with its instantly recognisable *pizzetto*, or small pointed pimple, at one end. But the taste? It wasn't what I'd hoped for – it was fresh-tasting, sure, but I've had more sweetness and flavour complexity from a cherry tomato. (And before you start thinking that I'm just a fussy chef who's spoilt for choice, this wasn't only my opinion. I took a bunch of San Marzano back to my restaurant and everybody felt the same. During my time in Italy I bought bags from several greengrocers, hoping for an epiphany, hoping to have my verdict overturned. It never was.)

Masking my disappointment from my generous hosts, I chatted with the government representative, Francesco di Pace, and Laura, Solania's PR, trying to discover the secret of the San Marzano tomato. Italians are fiercely protective of their local produce but they're also intolerant of anything but the best. There had to be a reason why they prized this tomato above all others.

They told me that the San Marzano is a 'dry' tomato: the low water content means it doesn't over-dampen the dough, causing the base to go soggy. (After all, in Naples the ovens are so hot that a pizza is only in there for a couple of minutes at most. That's nowhere near enough time to dry out the tomatoes.) And it turned out that Vesuvius isn't just a picturesque backdrop to the fields: its volcanic content feeds the soil, producing a fruit that is low in acid and low in pectin (the jelly-like substance that helps reinforce plant cell walls, much as cement surrounds the iron rods that run through the walls of a building).

Finally, I thought, we're getting somewhere. Acid and pectin play a significant part in the canning process: a high concentration of both can lead to a toughened tomato, as the acid binds to the pectin and hardens it. (A similar process happens in jam-making: we add acid to the fruit so that it reacts with the pectin to give a denser, drier structure.) Maybe this was the secret of the San Marzano – maybe the balance of pectin and acidity meant its perfection manifested itself only after canning, producing a soft, moist tomato that broke down particularly easily. I'd have to go to some pizzerias and find out.

• A Pizza the Action •

Where better to start than the most historic pizzeria of all? Pizzeria Brandi is in a narrow cobbled alley in the Chiaia district. A stone plaque on the wall declares that pizza Margherita was born here:

QUI 100 ANNI FA
NACQUE LA PIZZA MARGHERITA
1889–1989
BRANDI

Some people had told me that the secret of the San Marzano depended on that shape, that the key to its success was not gastronomy but economy. Increased use of the San Marzano coincided with the growth of the canning industry, and its shape meant you could fit more in a tin. In Italy, no one could confirm this. It was a secret that stayed secret.

The place is steeped in history. In the small front room, open to the street, old wine bottles line the shelves and every inch of wall space is covered with photographs. There are kings and queens, government ministers and even Chelsea Clinton, though the real royalty seems to be Luciano Pavarotti, who smiles stiffly at you from all sides.

In the kitchen, copper pots hang on hooks and there are several examples of old *stufe* proudly emblazoned with the pizzeria's name. The huge dome of the oven is tiled in blue and white, like the onion dome of a Russian Orthodox church. Before it, clad in white like priestly acolytes, the chefs went about their business. A dusting of flour had settled on all of them, making them look older than they really were.

On fact-finding trips like this, it's best not to build up your expectations too much because they are often overturned. It's frustrating and exciting in equal measure – going back to the drawing board is often the springboard to a better idea. I'd been wrong-footed by the fact that the San Marzano, although delicious, didn't live up to its reputation. And at Brandi I was disappointed to discover that they sieved the tomatoes before putting them on the pizza base. Suddenly my image of the *pizzaiolo* appreciating this tomato because it could be easily squeezed and crushed by hand seemed utterly fanciful.

Even the pizza wasn't quite what I'd hoped for. I liked the use of provola cheese, which gave it a smoked character that is often absent from the Naples pizza due to its short cooking time, but in general the dough was thick and the taste nothing special. I'd flown across Europe for this, so perhaps my expectations were unreasonably high, but I couldn't honestly claim it as the perfect pizza. I asked our driver, Dario, what he thought, and got cautious approval, so I pressed further.

'You live in Rome. How does this compare with the Roman pizza?'

'Oh, the pizza there is disgusting. Too crispy – a nothing! Naples is the only one …'

Great! I thought. Here was the opportunity for some inside information from someone I knew would be straight with me. Now I'd get to the bottom of what made Naples pizza the best.

'… But I don't really eat pizza. I don't much like it,' he finished abruptly. It put my quest for perfection in perspective. There were as many pizza points of view as there were people to eat it (or not eat it).

The taste at Brandi might have been a bit of a let-down, but it was still an instructive experience. The pizzas were certainly authentic: the marinara relying for its flavour on tomato, garlic and oregano; the Margherita swapping garlic for basil and mozzarella. Nothing else. I was reminded of pizza's origins in pitta and reflected that not much had changed. With so few ingredients, pizza was still basically a flavoured bread. There was so little to disguise it that the quality of the dough was paramount. I had begun my Italian journey of exploration with the San Marzano tomato because it was the very last day of the harvest. Now, I decided as I walked away from Brandi, I had to investigate the start of the pizza process. I needed to visit a flour mill.

• Flour Power •

The next morning, when I arrived at the Caputo mill on Corso San Giovanni, the first delivery of wheat was thundering in on a huge Fiat truck covered by a tent of blue canvas. It pulled up on the parking plate and the driver jumped down. With a long pole he knocked out the bolts holding the flaps on one side of the truck. The resounding clang of metal on metal was drowned by the sound of hundreds of kilos of wheat avalanching through a metal grid in the floor. As the deluge slowed, the parking plate tilted upwards through 45°, like something out of *Thunderbirds*, to pour the remaining wheat into its underground silo. This is the raw product from which the Caputo brothers make what is reputedly one of the best pizza flours in Italy. I wanted to find out how they did it.

Antimo Caputo Srl has been on the same street, and in the same family, since 1925. It was established by Carmine Caputo, the grandfather of Carmine and Eugenio, who now run the company along with Carmine's son, Antimo. This continuity might seem unusual to us in Britain, where relocation and high turnover are the norm, but it's part of what ensures the quality of Italian food. Italian businesses are often handed from father to son, and they take their legacy very seriously.

Eugenio escorted me from the delivery bay across the hacienda-style courtyard, dodging busy fork-lifts, and led me up three flights of stairs to the top of the mill. The din outside was nothing compared to the roar of the sieving room. Here, what looked like gigantic school lockers suspended on rods shook back and forth with a relentless, dizzying energy. These were the sieves. Even before reaching these, Eugenio explained, the wheat underwent several processes: it was tested for quality and cleaned of impurities before being passed through break rolls that split it open ready for separation.

Wheat consists of bran (the outer skin) enclosing the germ (the embryo which, in the right conditions, will grow into another plant) and the endosperm, which is mainly starch and acts as a food store for the embryo. The huge sieves before me were vigorously separating wheat into these three constituent parts. It's the sieved endosperm particles – known as 'granita' or 'semolina'* – that produce white flour. Sieving takes place after each rolling, and each time the granita is removed, leaving the rest to go through the whole process again.

After a while the noise and motion became hypnotic, disorientating. Even the floor tremored constantly. I was beginning to imagine what it would be like if one of the machines broke free of its slender rods and catapulted forwards, so it was a relief to leave the sieving room behind and go down one flight to the milling room.

The smell hit me as soon as the doors opened. The pleasant, creamy smell of a freshly opened bag of flour. It took me back to childhood memories of home-baking – so much so that I almost expected the workers here to be dressed in a black suit and bowler hat, like the Homepride man, rather than their usual brown overalls and jaunty white cap. Above me was a forest of pipes, branching and criss-crossing, feeding into the square grey Buehler reduction rolls that grind the endosperm to a fine powder. 'We mill up to twenty-two times,' Eugenio told me. 'The first and second millings are the finest and these are for pizza flour. Later millings have more bran particles, and are used for other types of flour. And we can add in some of the bran or wheatgerm to produce brown or wholemeal flour. It's a little like the pressings of olive oil. The quality and character changes each time you put it through the machines.'

We walked down one more flight to the packing room – a W. Heath Robinson tangle of pipes, cogs and conveyor belts. Paper sacks stamped CAPUTO and striped with different colours according to flour type were stacked in tall towers around the room. When these were fed into the machines I was pleased to see that their filling echoed the rising process itself: mechanical guiders up-ended the flattened sack in front of a chrome nozzle, whereupon it ballooned into a rounded shape before travelling on, now full of flour, to a chute through which it would abruptly disappear into the warehouses below – eagerly awaited by those busy fork-lifts.

My last stop was Caputo's laboratory. I wanted to know what was so special about

 Not to be confused with durum wheat semolina, which is entirely different.

Caputo flour. 'Making the flour for pizza is a very complex business,' said Eugenio. 'It has to have good water absorption so that the dough rises evenly and has a good texture. It must not be too high or low in protein because that will affect the elasticity of the dough. Ideally the flour should have 55 per cent absorption and 13 per cent protein. We do tests on our wheat and flour every day to make sure that they do all these things. And we source our wheat from many different places – Manitoba, Lithuania, Kazakhstan – and monitor and test and mix it together because the quality changes all the time. Bad weather has meant that Manitoba wheat is not so good this year, and we have had to replace it with another. It's important, too, that care is taken not to crush the wheat too much during milling, as this harms the protein, which then affects not only the elasticity but also the lightness and flavour of the dough. Not so good for pizza!'

This care and consideration is perhaps the key to the Caputos' success and reputation. They even arrange for their flour to be tried out regularly by pizza-makers to ensure consistent quality. 'Most of the pizza is dough,' observed Eugenio. 'Only that. It has to have that special flavour, that strong taste. The flour must be soft ... but with a texture, a roughness to it. You in Britain mill your flour much softer than we do, and so you don't get that flavour.'

Well, I wanted to get that flavour. And it seemed that the most likely way to achieve that was to use not just '00' flour (which the Associazione considers essential for a good pizza) but Caputo '00'. As I packed flour sacks into the car I asked Eugenio whether he had any advice on how to make the perfect pizza.

'The only way is to go to a pizzeria, watch the *pizzaiolo*, watch what he does. And then have a go yourself. And if you're still having trouble after that, you can always give me a call.'

I thanked him and said goodbye, tucking the business card bearing his phone number into a safe place in my wallet. I reckoned I might need it.

• Presidential Pizza •

'The only way is to go to a pizzeria ...' It seemed like good advice and, besides, it was lunchtime. I went to Il Pizzaiolo del Presidente on Via dei Tribunali in the Duomo district.

I had visited Brandi because of its history, but I visited Il Presidente because of its gastronomy: one of Italy's top food critics had told me that if I wanted to eat perfect pizza this was the place.

I liked Il Presidente immediately. It has a brisk, business-like air. The kitchen is right at the front of the restaurant, with a glass counter looking on to the street from which you can buy pizza without setting foot inside – a reminder of pizza's origins as fast food for the working man. I squeezed past the kitchen and went downstairs to a bright room with exposed brickwork and a vaulted ceiling. Once again, the walls were covered with photographs, though this time most featured the pizzeria's charismatic owner, Ernesto Cacialli, at various pizza festivals around the country, wearing the red neckerchief of the *pizzaiolo*. There were no pics of Chelsea Clinton; instead her dad grinned down at me. He ate pizza here during the 1994 G7 summit and the pizzeria was promptly renamed in honour of his visit.

From the photos it was evident that Ernesto is a great roving ambassador for pizza, and his spirit spills over into the atmosphere of the restaurant: lively, noisy, energetic. There's no menu, you simply negotiate with the waiter for what you want on your pizza. My request was simple: I wanted the two classics, marinara and Margherita; then, if possible, I wanted to have the opportunity to watch a *pizzaiolo* at work and maybe have a go myself …?

When they arrived, the pizzas looked very promising. The *cornicione* – the unadorned dough around the edge of the pizza – was narrow and attractively charred in places. Given the brief oven time, I wasn't sure how Ernesto had managed this, but it added an extra flavour dimension to a terrific pizza. The tomatoes had both fresh and cooked notes (I was pleased to notice later that they weren't sieved but lightly crushed, so there was still hope for my canning theory). I was sure I could also taste some provola in there – that deliciously smoky, almost meaty flavour – although when I asked the waiter about this, he got a rabbit-in-the-headlights look and started to edge away from me. Was it a trade secret? Was provola banned by the Associazione? Or was there some other reason for such behaviour? Maybe I'd mangled the Italian language so much that, instead of asking about cheese, I'd said something that could frighten and repulse waiters? It was impossible to tell, although I was to discover that a shroud of secrecy often surrounds unexpected areas of Italian cuisine: whenever I stumbled across one I was given the verbal runaround until the cameras were turned off and I gave up. Perhaps it's a way of keeping the myth and romance going.

Provola may or may not have been a secret, but Ernesto didn't hold back in sharing his expertise. Although we'd arrived in the middle of service, he took the time to show me how he made a pizza base. The dough was flattened by hand into a rough disc and then turned and worked with the fingertips. Once it had the right shape Ernesto held the base in his right hand and, with his left, flapped and turned it until the disc had stretched, elongated and thinned to just the right size and thickness. He made it look easy, but as soon as I had a go I began to understand how a losing contestant must have felt during one of those impossible tasks on *The Generation Game*. I couldn't get it to work, couldn't get the rhythm going. No *pizzaiolo* was going to lose sleep over my performance.

Using the long-handled paddle – known as a 'peel' – to move the pizza in the oven proved no easier. The aim is to cook the pizza evenly. To this end, Ernesto wielded the peel with the dexterity of a test-match batsman, giving the pizza a number of quarter-turns without shifting its place in the oven (which is vitally important because the stone floor will be hotter around the pizza than under it; shift the pizza to the left or right and you burn the base). His pizza came out looking like it should; mine came out looking like an unmade bed, the dough gathered and ruckled in places, the topping erratically scattered. Clearly I was going to have to work on these skills.

• A Water Fountain in the Villa Communale •

After lunch I had a rendezvous in the Piazza Vittoria. So I returned to the car to sample another unforgettable Naples experience: driving through the city.

Braking distance and lane discipline are mere memories. Drivers switch lanes abruptly whenever there's an opening and hit full throttle as soon as they can see three feet ahead of them. Each car stutters along the tarmac in a stop–start–swerve pattern, veering past the swarm of Vespas that weave in and out at breakneck pace, and accelerating past any pedestrian unwise enough to try their luck at crossing. It's survival of the fittest – or at least the fastest. Several times we left the road altogether and hurtled down the tramtracks instead. 'Is this legal?' I wondered aloud as a tram loomed increasingly large in the rear-view mirror. But the bored look on the faces of policemen we passed suggested this was normal.

This time my destination was the Villa Communale, a large park by the coast with broad avenues bordered by scraggy palm trees. I'd come to visit a drinking water fountain. And I'd come armed with two nifty pieces of technological hardware: a pH meter to test the acidity of the water, and a conductivity meter to establish how hard or soft it was.

Heston the mad scientist going too far? Certainly some of the locals seemed to think so, eyeing me dubiously as they bent to take a drink while I dunked what looked like a TV remote control into a plastic beaker of water. However, scientists have determined that the chemical composition of the water used when making dough will affect its behaviour. And, although they use different words, Neapolitans agree with them. They declare that water is what makes their pizza so perfect – the water of the Serino aqueduct, which is so soft and light that it makes for superior dough. Since the Serino aqueduct supplies only a small part of the city, there's a certain amount of myth-making involved. I wanted to strip away the myth and find out whether Naples water really was perfect for pizza.

Making dough relies above all on one thing: the formation of gluten, a kind of super-protein with the characteristics we recognise in dough – plasticity and elasticity. Gluten is made up of two proteins in flour: gliadin and glutenin. When water is added to them and the mixture kneaded, the proteins stretch and spread out, like tentacles, gradually intertwining to form a complex, tensile network.

Water's constituents affect the strength of this network. First, high acidity interferes with the proteins' ability to form bonds, resulting in a dough that's not stretchy and that snaps when pulled apart. (Conversely, too alkaline an environment encourages the bonds, creating a dense, brick-like dough that's impossible to work with.)

Second, harder water produces a firmer dough. Water is very good at dissolving other substances, the two most common of which – depending on where your tap water originally comes from – are salts of calcium and magnesium, which crust up in your kettle to form a fur and dull the vibrant green colour of vegetables during cooking. They also have a cross-linking effect in dough formation, helping to chemically join the molecules in strong bonds. So too much calcium and magnesium has the same effect as too much alkali, producing a tough, inelastic dough. I was curious to see how the fabled Naples water measured up on the meters.

The pH scale runs from 0 to 14. The pH of neutral water is 7. Anything above this is increasingly alkaline (ammonia measures 11.9); anything below is increasingly acidic (lemon juice is 2.1). Trying to look nonchalant before the suspicious gaze of several old men on the bench opposite, I lifted the pH meter out of the beaker of water. The read-out was 7.2, which seemed to me pretty perfect for pizza dough: near neutral but with just enough alkaline content to strengthen the gluten network a little.

I put the pH meter away, plucked the conductivity meter out of my pocket and popped it into the beaker. (By now the look on the faces of the men opposite had shifted from suspicion to downright hostility.) The digital screen flashed out 0.9 and I multiplied this by 1,000 to get a reading in microsiemens of 900. Since the maximum was 2,500, this showed that Naples water had the suitable softness for pizza dough. The Neapolitans were right: their water was indeed soft and light.

• Da Michele •

It was fast getting dark but there was another pizzeria in Naples that intrigued me because its min-imalist menu – it serves only the marinara and Margherita – seemed to reflect the purity and sim-plicity of the original Neapolitan pizzas. So we drove (and swerved and slalomed) over to Via Cesare Sersale, where the Pizzeria da Michele has been serving up its twin attractions since 1870.

By the time we arrived, night had fallen. Already a crowd had gathered outside. They had all taken a numbered ticket from the dispenser and awaited their turn at the tables. Few talked; most gazed expectantly through the narrow doorway, as though mesmerised by the glow of the brick oven – or faithfully anticipating that they were about to eat the perfect pizza.

Where Brandi is stately and Il Pizzaiolo del Presidente is no-nonsense modern, Da Michele has more of a 1930s feel. Its two small, high-ceilinged rooms have green and white tiles from floor to dado rail. The customers sit at marble-topped tables while sepia portraits in dark wood frames gaze down upon them. High in an alcove sits a statuette of Saint Anthony.

While talking to Eugenio Caputo in his flour mill I had become increasingly convinced that good dough was the key to pizza, so although I would enjoy tasting the toppings, it was Da Michele's dough that I really wanted to try out.

It didn't disappoint. It was delicate and light, with a nice slightly charred character. And the flour really did seem to give it a special taste. Before coming to Naples I'd have dismissed such a claim as fanciful romanticism, but it turned out to be true. The dough had a particular flavour, and I'd have to try to capture that back at the Fat Duck.

That was going to be a big challenge, bigger maybe than what went on top. Already I had a few ideas about that – perhaps using a combination of provola and buffalo mozzarella to get both a stretchy cheese and that wonderful smoky note. By exploring the city and eating in places with very different styles, I'd picked up a lot of tips. But what I'd learned above all was how com-plicated the process was that shaped something as apparently simple as pizza. I'd encountered obsession and sleights of hand, myths that turned out to be true, vital techniques and subtle nuances. It had become much more than just a few ingredients, and it was going to be tricky translating that into what I wanted. The possibilities kept multiplying before me, like a funfair's hall of mirrors. I hoped the joke wouldn't be on me.

• Pizza School •

Drive up and away from the Bay of Naples and it's another world. For centuries the rich have chosen to live high up here in the hills, rising above the ravages of plague and the harsh heat of summer, and with spectacular views across the azure bay and moody Vesuvius to boot. The wealth shows: the streets widen into generous boulevards, beyond which I caught glimpses of vast apart-ment blocks, painted in hectic lemons and pinks that offset the deep greens of the roof gardens with their elegant furniture.

Enzo Coccia's Pizzeria La Notizia, however, is a simple place – a small, brightly lit room with space for perhaps thirty customers and a TV in one corner. The walls are dotted with reproductions of antique prints: the Teatro San Carlo; fishermen by the Gulf of Naples. It's a welcoming, practical place, and I could it imagine it was a favourite with local families, eager to catch an early dinner together. However, I wasn't here to eat but to learn, because Enzo also runs a small pizza-making school.

Pizza-making is in Enzo's blood. His father, Antonio, owned Pizzeria Fortuna near the Piazza Garibaldi and handed on his passion to his son, for Enzo is an apostle of pizza. In addition to revealing the secrets of the *pizzaiolo* (I could see young men of various nationalities in his kitchen, effortlessly twisting and flipping dough on their forearms to stretch it into a workable pizza base), he has invented cartoon characters for wheat, tomatoes and mozzarella, in an effort to educate kids about their food. When he realised I was interested in more than just the basics, his eyes lit up. As I asked questions about temperature and protein content and rising times, he sprang into action, scribbling diagrams and grabbing scales, shaving slivers off a block of yeast, filling the air with its malty aroma. He was so excited that he would often cut in before the translator had finished the previous sentence. Here was someone as fired up by the technicalities of his trade as I was. Enzo was *simpatico*. If anyone could help me master the intricacies of the perfect pizza, it was him.

As if to confirm my impression, Enzo asked to change before the filming started. He returned in full *pizzaiolo* regalia: beautifully laundered whites and the traditional red neckerchief. This was clearly going to be the full monty – or perhaps, since we were in Naples, the full Capodimonte.

Enzo hauled out a small square wooden trough with handles at the four corners. Into this traditional mixing bowl went the best part of three litres of ordinary tap water at room temperature, plus about 150 grams of salt.

'How important is salt for the taste of the dough?' I wanted to know.

'It improves the taste, but you've got to be careful because it slows the rising and too much will make the dough too compact and difficult to work with.'

He sliced off 8 grams of yeast and told me to dip it in the water and rub it between finger and thumb until it dissolved. Then I added flour – Caputo flour, I was pleased to notice – in great scoopfuls while Enzo stirred it with his hand. '*Vai, vai. Mette farina*.' Another scoopful. '*Vai, vai*.' And another, until the mixture became less liquid and Enzo began advising just a sprinkle of flour each time, aiming for exactly the right consistency.

'OK, it's ready,' he declared eventually. 'Take off your watch, roll up your sleeves. Work with me.'

Normally, kneading is now done by machine: it makes no difference to the outcome (it's even sanctioned by the Associazione) and cuts kneading time from forty to twenty minutes, though you still have to oversee the whole process rigorously, in case more flour is needed. We, however, were going to do things the traditional way. Enzo and I stood either end of the mixing bowl, and went at it.

Enzo demonstrated a kind of up-and-down rhythm. 'This is to make sure that the dough is soft, elastic, uniform and – most important of all – that it has plenty of air in it. All of this activity is to get air into the dough,' he said. 'Like this: *uno, due, uno, due*.' I thought he was suggesting giving it the old one-two, like a boxer, and started pummelling, but he reined me in. 'Strong but slow. You don't have to fight it.'

We walked our fists along the dough towards the centre, then folded it and began again. At intervals, Enzo would pick up the dough and hold it out, as though showing off a baby – testing the feel and consistency, how loose a shape it made as it hung. Then he'd flip it over on itself and return it to the bowl. '*Un poco di farina*,' he'd announce, and off we'd go again.

'Enzo, how come on my side the dough's all sticking to the bowl but on your side it's not doing that at all?'

He laughed. 'Maybe you're not working hard enough ...'

Despite this, the dough gradually became softer, whiter and more resistant to our fists. It must have been exhausting work in the old days before machines, especially if you had to do it every day. Although I train in a gym, by the time Enzo judged the dough ready for the next stage I'd really broken out in a sweat. I decided that if a kneading machine was OK with the Associazione, then it was OK with me. That's what I'd use in Bray.

All the hard work had been to good purpose. The dough sat on the table, dense and plump, like a small pillow. Enzo grabbed a scraper and severed it neatly in two. The cut face looked like the moon's surface, cratered and pock-marked, evidence that there was plenty of air in there. (This would give the pizza base its lightness: in the heat of the oven the air would try to escape, rising up and giving the base that characteristic bubbled texture.) He looked happy with the result, which meant I was too, though I knew that the next job was another of those that looks easy when done by an expert but is in fact very tricky indeed.

In one swift movement Enzo cut a long thin strip from the dough, grabbed it between thumb and forefinger as though holding a snake, and worked the dough with his other hand until, magically, a small white globe of dough seemed to grow out of the top of his fist. A firm final squeeze and he separated it from the rest of the dough and placed it – by now about the size of a large bread roll – on a tray. A minute later there were fifteen of them, tidily ranked in three rows.

My first attempt spoiled this symmetry – it was smooth and round all right but barely larger than my palm – but gradually, under Enzo's patient guidance, I got a feel for the character of the dough and produced my own neat row of balls, though I was never going to match his speed.

The trays would be left to rise for anything between four and eight hours. (Before even mixing the dough Enzo had checked the weather for humidity, assessed how much moisture the dough might take up, and adjusted the amount of yeast accordingly. This is part of the art of the *pizzaiolo* that can't be learned. Over time Enzo has developed an instinct for how much is needed, and knows exactly how long it will take to perform its task.) Eventually, the dough balls should have increased in size by about 50 per cent, spreading outwards rather than up, until each ball is just touching its neighbour. The dough will be much softer than at the start of the rise, as carbon dioxide does its work, moving from the yeast cells into air pockets in the dough and inflating them. It's then ready to make pizza.

With all this care and attention, Enzo's pizzas rivalled anything dished up by more famous places: the dough was deliciously savoury, the tomato moist and characterful. Long after I should have left to catch the flight home, Enzo was expertly presenting pizza after pizza for me to taste. Eventually I had to insist, regretfully, that it was time to go. His parting words were, 'For the perfect pizza you need water, flour, yeast, salt – and a little love.' Well, I loved cooking and I'd just received a master-class in handling the ingredients. I hoped it would be enough.

The film crew and I got to the airport just in time. But Naples had one last surprise, one last reminder of the theatre, spectacle and generosity that surrounds food here. It was my daughter's birthday that night and so I had asked my friend Enzo Caldarelli if he could get me a cake to take back to Britain. As we queued at the check-in, he arrived, breathless, in a dark suit, white shirt and wraparound shades, like a hitman from *Reservoir Dogs*. 'Heston, *aspetta*! Wait!'

Wait we did, nervously eyeing the clock ticking towards the time when the gate would close. At last two men arrived pushing trolleys piled high with handmade biscuits, cellophane-wrapped lemon desserts and cartons of mozzarella. They were followed by Pasquale Marigliano, one of the best pastry chefs in Italy. His whites still had a dusting of sugar on them and he was carrying an impressively large cake box.

We set aside what we could carry on to the plane, but that still left an awful lot of food on the trolley. And so, as onlookers stared, we ripped open cellophane and polystyrene and had a final taste of the best Italy has to offer. It was a fitting end to the trip.

And my daughter loved the cake.

• Off the Scale •

While I was in Italy, in addition to my pH and conductivity meters I'd carried another neat bit of kit: a thermometer that went up to 500°C. It hadn't been easy to come by: conventional oven thermometers don't go anywhere near this high because there's nothing in the kitchen that requires that temperature. But the Naples pizzeria is an entirely different ball game. The oven takes little more than a minute to cook a pizza, which gives you some idea of the tremendous temperature involved. The Neapolitans may not have experienced the volcanic heat of Vesuvius since 1944, but their ovens are real furnaces!

Of course, this has a dramatic effect on the taste and consistency of the pizza itself. For one thing, the brief cooking time means the tomatoes remain moist and runny, retaining an intense tomatoey flavour rather than acquiring the thicker, jammy character of their British counterparts. In order to produce a truly authentic pizza, I'd have to replicate that kind of heat, so I wanted to know what temperature I was aiming for.

When I'd first tried out the thermometer in Da Michele, I thought the equipment was on the blink. The digital read-out raced through the 300s and 400s before feebly flashing out 'error'. But at La Notizia the same thing happened and I realised it wasn't the machine that was at fault: the oven was simply too hot to handle. It topped 500°C.

The thermometer may not have given me an accurate read-out, but it did tell me one thing: I would have to either make my own pizza oven or do something fairly unconventional to a conventional oven.

• Dough Boys •

Naples had shown me that dough was the key to pizza. Just as a good pasta provides fundamental flavour to the dish it graces, so the pizza base is more than a backdrop to the toppings, or the ultimate biodegradable plate. It provides the underlying taste of any pizza, and so I had to come up with a dough delicious enough that you could eat it on its own.

Neapolitans would say that achieving this was simple – just use Caputo flour! I suspected they were right but I wanted to see for myself; besides, Enzo's dough-making techniques were all about feel and touch, and I wanted to get in some practice. I enrolled the help of Chris, my research chef, and we each made a batch of pizza dough – me using Caputo while he used standard, superfine plain flour. We'd check out how they responded to kneading then cook them and taste the results. At the very least we'd gain some idea of how much flour type influenced dough behaviour.

I had a vague fear that, back in Bray, I wouldn't be able to summon up what Enzo had taught me. But it turned out that, like riding a bike, it was knowledge that didn't really leave you. As I placed the dough on the table, marched my fists up and down it, then folded it over and started again, my muscles seemed to relax into a familiar rhythm. The manual-labour pleasure that is part of working in a kitchen took over.

Although the rhythm was familiar and I was no longer a newcomer to the process, I still found the thirty-minute push 'n' pummel a real workout. I'd been wondering if I would recognise the precise moment when the dough was ready. As perspiration began to bead on my forehead I decided I should probably patent a Sweatometer: clap the electrodes to your forehead and start kneading; a red light would tell you the dough was ready once you'd worked up enough of a sweat.

Chris, I was happy to notice, was finding it no easier. We stood side by side, hunched over the polished black granite work surface, silently rucking and knuckling the dough. Chefs are, by nature, a competitive bunch. We both affected a nonchalance that was hardly backed up by our reddening faces and ragged breathing, and then redoubled our efforts. I tried to remember the texture of Enzo's dough. Mine was still too soft, too flaccid. It needed to gain more body and acquire that cratered, aerated texture. Gradually it became springier. I held it at arm's length and let it hang there, to check elasticity.

'I've got bubbles,' I called out like a boastful schoolboy, even though I'd started fifteen minutes before Chris. The dough was now white, smooth, tensile. I sliced it in two with a knife and examined the cut face. It was riddled with bubbles – real Enzodough. 'Are you ready, Chris?'

'I'm almost done.'

From the look on his face, he was almost as done in as I was. But we had two pillows of dough to show for it. They had to rise for about eight hours, but we twisted pieces off to taste right away. Already there was a marked difference: the Caputo flour had a strong toasted bread-crust flavour that the other couldn't really match.

'The insipid one's yours, Chris,' I said. 'Enzo told me that for dough you need five ingredients: water, flour, yeast, salt and a little love. Maybe you didn't put enough love in …'

Professional that he is, Chris didn't rise to the bait. 'I'm amazed at how noticeable the difference is between the two, even now. It'll be exciting to see how they bake off and taste after that.'

But before that happened we had one other test: we wanted to compare hand-kneaded dough with machine-kneaded. We used one type of flour, one recipe, one rising time, and the results were as unexpected as they were extraordinary. After rising, the machine-kneaded dough balls had spread and softened on the tray until they touched one another. They were at least 50 per cent bigger than the hand-kneaded, which sat stingily separate, looking more like large cookies than dough balls. I could not only feel the difference – the machine-kneaded were far springier and more elastic – I could see it. The machine version was speckled with airholes that would easily spread cooking heat throughout the crust and expand to give that characteristically Neapolitan bubbled surface. Chris and I held and stretched out examples of each – like two wives in a washing powder commercial comparing shirts – but it was already obvious which way we'd be kneading our pizza dough. So many times in this series I'd ended up recommending a slower, less mechanised approach; it was quite refreshing to be able to advocate a technological advance that was not only quicker and easier but also better for the end product. Maybe I wouldn't need the Sweatometer™ after all.

• In the Can •

It had sat on the shelf for weeks, tempting me with its vibrant primary colours and the promise of what was inside. I had resisted manfully, and now the moment had come when I could let the genie out of the bottle, or in this case out of the can: I was going to compare the famous San Marzano tomato with a number of other varieties to see if canning gave it a superior texture or flavour.

I lined up Solania's San Marzano alongside cans of peeled plum tomatoes from Sainsbury's, Tesco, Waitrose, M&S and Napolina. In Naples pizzerias most chefs take tomatoes straight from the tin and crush them by hand before popping the lot on the pizza, so I did the same and tasted the results.

Things got bloody almost as soon as I began. I misjudged the first squeeze and ended up with my chef's whites covered in red, as though I'd secured a walk-on part in a splatter movie. Proceeding more gingerly, I squashed each tomato into a bowl then speared some on a fork and chewed, trying to discern its characteristic flavours.

A couple were far too liquid: they would never dry out sufficiently during a ninety-second cook, no matter how high the heat. The pizza base would be drowned. What I was looking for from the others was the right balance of flavour and acidity. If the flavour is bland, the acid dominates, giving an unpleasant taste in the mouth. If, on the other hand, there's a big fruity flavour, then the acid does a valuable job of cutting through the sweetness. The San Marzano definitely had the best balance: the canning had concentrated its taste (the heat involved in the canning process effectively cooks the tomatoes, giving them some of the flavour dimensions of oven-roasted tomatoes) to produce something sharp but sweet. It was the taste I remembered from Neapolitan pizzas.

Yet both M&S and Waitrose peeled plums could give it a run for its money – a big consideration given that San Marzano tomatoes are difficult to get hold of in Britain and can cost up to six times more than a supermarket brand. I was sure that I could get equally good results using a tin of M&S tomatoes. But could I get better results going down a different route altogether? When I'd visited the tomato fields beneath Vesuvius I'd discovered that the San Marzano was less flavourful than other tomatoes I'd tasted. I decided to try pressure-cooking some of those to see if they'd add something extra.

Mozzarella-tasting turned out to be a similar experience. In Naples airport I had eaten some of the best mozzarella I've ever had: a smooth, creamy, melt-in-the-mouth texture allied to a rich depth of flavour and just a delicate hint of acidity. I arranged for Enzo Caldarelli to send some over to my development kitchen: I wanted to blind-taste it against the best I could obtain in Britain – Blissful Buffalo, Mandara and Garofalo Mozzarella di Bufala Campana – to find the right cheese for my pizza.

Maybe I had just got lucky, or maybe mozzarella's one of those things that 'doesn't travel well': Enzo's next batch had none of the same magnificence. It was still very good, but so was Garofalo, which is a lot easier to get hold of. In some ways this was a relief, as I already felt a little guilty about the hoops I would be putting home cooks through as they scoured the country for Bresse chickens, artisanal pasta and Japanese brown rice malt syrup. I was glad to be able to recommend something that might be picked up in a shopping trolley rather than via website.

The EU pizza copyright proposal specifies an oven-surface temperature of 485°C and a cooking time of between sixty and ninety seconds. As I've said, this speedy, high-temp approach has a profound effect on the end result: one of the reasons British pizzas tend to taste different from the Neapolitan version is that the pizza ovens here often peak at a far lower temperature and thus take five minutes to cook, which changes the character of the dish.

So my goal was a sixty-second pizza, and to achieve it I'd need to make an oven as hot as I possibly could. I bought a proper *pizzaiolo*'s peel and a smart, boxy, brushed-steel Gaggenau cooker, and set to work.

I was all for disassembling the thermostat and bunging in a few anthracite coals to whack up the temperature, but when people suggested it would melt the seals and crack the glass it seemed sensible to devise an alternative.

How else could I buck the oven's top temp? I programmed 300°C into the oven and placed a pizza stone inside. Once the LCD told me I'd got to 300, I turned off the oven and turned on the grill. As expected, that extra burst of heat upped the temperature rapidly. I checked the fast-paced scramble of the temperature gun's read-out: 320 ... 353 ... 370. That's where the thermostat lost our game of 'Chicken', shutting off the grill to cool things down. But the pizza stone would retain the heat for a while, and I could turn on the grill again in a minute for a final blast.

It wasn't 485°C but it was a start. With a temperature gun and split-second timing, we had a small window of opportunity during which we could cook a pizza base at a reasonably high heat. Chris grabbed the peel, I clutched the temperature gun and we waited – like sportsmen ready for the off – until the heat reached 370°C again.

'GO!'

Dough disc was scooped on to peel I flipped open oven door in it went with a shove and jerk on to stone and *slam!*

The door was shut. We all stared through the glass – me, Chris, the director, the cameraman, the researcher – waiting to see what would happen, willing it to work.

The dough bubbled up just like a Naples pizza before puffing out like a poppadom – time to take it out. It had been in there for ninety seconds.

It looked great, nicely browned in places and retaining a lightness of structure. And it tasted great, too: the distinctive sweet, toasty bread flavour I remembered from Naples. I still had to get the topping right, but already the dough base seemed to me to be really authentic.

Intoxicated by success, Chris and I flipped one dough base after another into the oven, testing the cooked taste of hand-kneaded dough against machine-kneaded. As expected, machine-made had the edge: the more generous rising meant bigger bubbles that made for a less dense, more elastic texture. It had the crisp crust and tender interior of a genuine Naples pizza. Technique and ingredients were starting to come together. It was all very exciting.

Later, it momentarily became even more exciting when we discovered that the oven's cleaning cycle actually went up to 470°C. Problem solved! We'd got access to the temperature we wanted and there couldn't be any danger of the glass door cracking or the seals melting because the oven was designed to handle that kind of heat. We were on track at last for the sixty-second pizza ...

Except that the Gaggenau's door automatically locked during cleaning. Technology isn't always your best friend. The perfect recipe was still a few hurdles away.

UMAMI: THE FIFTH TASTE

There's a fundamental difference between taste and flavour. Crudely speaking, we taste with our mouths but we discern flavours with our nose (via an olfactory bulb situated behind it). If this seems counter-intuitive, put onion purée and apple purée in bowls and don a blindfold. Pinch your nose while eating from one of the bowls and see if you can guess whether it's onion or apple. The chances are you'll find it impossible to distinguish one from the other until you stop pinching your nose. This is because flavour is registered by the olfactory bulb as flavour molecules pass up into it. When we pinch our nostrils, denying air to the olfactory bulb, our brains can't decipher the information received.

The olfactory bulb can distinguish between thousands of different flavours. But the mouth can only distinguish five tastes. (That's why wine-tasters spend more time sniffing than swilling.)

At least, that's the current thinking. But this is an exciting branch of science in which new discoveries are being made all the time: scientists only recently established that we have more than 600 genes that can register flavour – double the previous estimate. There is still debate over whether the concept of five tastes is too simplistic: for the bitter taste alone, for example, there are more than twenty receptors, which respond to different things and in different combinations. And some scientists are pushing for fat to be identified as a taste.

Even the fifth taste was only discovered in the last one hundred years. Up until then, scientists had only formally recognised four tastes distinguishable by the tongue: salty, sweet, sour and bitter. But Professor Kikunae Ikeda of the University of Tokyo became interested in the brothy, savoury taste generated by *kombu*, or giant kelp, which grows up to thirty feet long off the northern islands of Japan and has been flavouring their food for at least a thousand years. In 1908 he discovered that the savoury taste was caused by the presence in *kombu* of glutamic acid, and decided to name that taste 'umami' (which translates roughly as 'delicious'). Since then, scientists have discovered several other substances in food that provide the umami taste: inosinate (which is present in bonito and many meats), guanylate (more abundant in plants: shiitake mushrooms have high concentrations) and adenylate (which occurs mainly in fish and shellfish).

Ikeda went on to develop a new flavouring based on glutamic acid. In 1909 he marketed monosodium glutamate (MSG), which has since been readily accepted in Asian countries (where it appears in kitchens much as salt would, in fine pale flakes in a jar) but has provoked concern in the West. A phenomenon known as 'Chinese restaurant syndrome' (CRS), the effects of which include dehydration and headaches, is thought to be caused by MSG.

Admittedly, monosodium glutamate's acronym has done it no favours, making it sound especially synthetic and unnatural. But the truth is that the scientific tests which led to the identification of CRS were unrigorous, and more recent tests have found that earlier conclusions were largely without foundation. Food writer Jeffrey Steingarten made a succinct defence of MSG in the title of his essay 'Why Doesn't Everybody in China Have a Headache?' This might seem flippant, but many people who consider MSG harmful wouldn't think twice about putting ketchup on their chips or adding a stock cube to their sauce, both of which are rich in umami.

What's all this got to do with pizza?

Although umami was identified in Japan, it's not an Eastern phenomenon. It is present in all kinds of foods familiar to us: anchovies, bouillon, bouillabaisse, gumbo, soy sauce, ketchup, Marmite and those pizza staples, Parmesan and tomatoes. (Try this next time you have a really ripe tomato: take a bite of the outer flesh on its own, and then of the stuff around the seeds. There'll be a big difference in taste, and it'll be the inner part that gives the big, savoury, meaty mouthfeel. That's umami. As you can probably tell, this is a subject close to my heart. Reading University recently awarded me an honorary D.Sc. degree, which I'm very proud of. The first research paper to which I'll contribute as a doctor explores precisely this concentration of umami compounds in tomatoes, and the factors that might affect it.)

What is more, in combination the umami chemicals have a magnified effect: if you add a food rich in glutamic acid to another that has, say, traces of inosinate, the umami taste is massively intensified. This plays a huge part in the recipes in this book. Put mushroom ketchup on a steak, simmer meat and tomatoes in a Bolognese, add Parmesan to a Margherita, and you get a taste explosion!

PIZZA
MARGHERITA

Serves 5

By pressure-cooking and oven-drying tomatoes, I managed to get the big, meaty umami taste I'd been looking for, and using a smoked salt captured that provolone touch, but the key features of this pizza are still heat and dough.

Making dough involves a number of conflicting demands: the longer it's left the more its flavour develops, giving that wonderful yeasty, bready note. But, over time, the gluten loses its elasticity and becomes wet, flabby and difficult to work. The answer to this dilemma is a pre-ferment: a small amount of dough, prepared for its flavour, which is then added to a larger amount of dough that still retains its extensibility. The best of both worlds!

It's essential to get the heat above and below the pizza as hot – and as even – as possible. The secret is a heavy cast-iron frying pan, which can get much hotter than a ceramic pizza stone and holds that heat for longer. Whack the grill on full for a while, put a preheated pan under it and you've got yourself a very serviceable pizza oven that should cook a Margherita in a couple of minutes. The speed's vital because the character of the ingredients changes with a longer cooking time. It might take a bit of experimentation to get it just right, but after that the pizzas will come fast and easy – an authentic home pizzeria, especially if you've got hold of a pizza peel for that final Italian touch.

Special equipment: food mixer, pressure cooker, cast-iron frying pan (at least 26cm in diameter: large enough to accommodate a pizza on the base), short-handled pizza peel (optional)

Timing: Making pizza dough is as easy as making bread – a matter of a few minutes' mixing and a few hours' proving (rising). You need to start a day in advance, but only so the pre-ferment dough can prove overnight. Peeling, cutting and deseeding the tomatoes takes a while, but after that there are no complicated cooking techniques: they can be put in the oven or pressure cooker until done. (And you can do it all the day before, to stagger the workload.) The pizza itself is incredibly quick. Once the pan is hot enough and the dough ball has been flattened out, it takes only a couple of minutes to put on the toppings and cook the pizza.

For the pre-ferment:

150g pizza flour (such as Caputo, or a
flour with a medium-to-high protein
content – about 12% – such as Alimonti
Organic '00' pasta flour)

$1/4$ tsp malt syrup

85g cold water (here it's important to
weigh the liquid in grams rather than
using a measuring jug, for accuracy)

3.5g fast action bread yeast ($1/2$ sachet)

$1/2$ tsp table salt

For the dough:

350g pizza flour

$1/2$ tsp malt syrup

195g cold water

7g fast action bread yeast (1 sachet)

1 tsp table salt

pre-fermented dough (see above)

For the tomato toppings:

45 large cherry tomatoes, on the vine
(about 1kg)*

2 large cloves of garlic

20 fresh basil leaves

20 fresh thyme sprigs

2 fresh bay leaves

extra virgin olive oil

1 tsp unrefined caster sugar

table salt and freshly ground black pepper

For each finished pizza:

1 ball of prepared pizza dough

50g tomato sauce

10 oven-dried tomato halves

125g buffalo mozzarella (such as Garofalo
Mozzarella di Bufala Campana), drained

4 fresh basil leaves

extra virgin olive oil

smoked sea salt

PREPARING THE PRE-FERMENT

Flours vary, hydrating at different levels. If,
at the end of mixing, the dough is still too
crumbly, add a little extra water and mix a
little longer, so that it forms into a cohesive
ball. Conversely, if it still seems 'wet' at the
end, add a little more flour.

1. Tip the flour into the bowl of a food mixer.
Using the dough hook, begin to mix on the
first (lowest) speed.

2. Stir the malt syrup into the water, then pour
the liquid into the flour. Mix on the first speed
for 3 minutes, then stop the mixing and allow
it to rest in the bowl for between 10 minutes
and 1 hour. (An hour is best, if the time is
available. It improves the flavour of the dough
and its stretchiness.)

3. Add the yeast and salt and mix on the
second speed for 7 minutes. (If, halfway
through this process, the dough does not look
like it is coming together, stop the mixer and
scrape the flour from the sides of the bowl.)

4. Transfer the dough to a large, clean mixing
bowl and cover tightly with clingfilm to prevent
a skin forming on the surface. Place the bowl
in the fridge and leave to ferment for 12
hours.

 As with all recipes in this book involving tomatoes, it's very important thay they are ripe and of good quality. It's equally
important they're not stored in the fridge: low temperatures actually kill off the flavour of tomatoes.

MAKING THE DOUGH

1. Tip the flour into the bowl of a food mixer. Using the dough hook, begin to mix on the first speed.

2. Mix the malt syrup into the water, then pour the liquid into the flour. Mix on the first speed for 4 minutes, then stop mixing and allow it to rest in the bowl for between 10 minutes and 1 hour. (As with the pre-ferment, an hour is best.)

3. Add the yeast and salt and mix on the second speed for 4 minutes.

4. Stop the mixer. Add the pre-ferment to the bowl and mix for 4 minutes on the second speed.

5. Remove the dough (it should pull away cleanly from the sides of the bowl: if it doesn't, try adding a little more water and mixing for a further 2–3 minutes). Place it on clean work surface, shape the dough into a log and then cut into 5 pieces, each weighing about 150g.

6. To make the dough balls, first place your palm down on a work surface then arch it up into a kind of claw shape. Place a piece of dough within it. Move your hand round and round – your fingertips should be touching the work surface and your palm pressing gently on to the dough. This motion will form perfectly round balls – the more round your dough is, the better the shape of the pizza base – and, more importantly, it doesn't squeeze the air out of the dough.

7. Place the balls on a plastic tray that has been brushed with oil (or a baking tray lined with oiled clingfilm), leaving at least 4cm between each ball. Cover well with a large piece of oiled clingfilm. Leave to prove for 2

hours in a warm place (or refrigerate for 12 hours). The dough balls will double in size and should look moist, light and airy.

MAKING THE DRIED TOMATOES AND TOMATO SAUCE

1. Preheat the oven to 110°C/225°F/Gas $^1/_4$. Bring a large pan of water to the boil. Fill a large bowl with ice-cold water.

2. Pull the tomatoes off the vine, reserving the vines. Remove the cores with a paring knife. Blanch the tomatoes by dropping them into the boiling water for 10 seconds and then carefully removing them to the bowl of ice-cold water. Take them out of the water immediately and peel off the split skins. (If the tomatoes are not ripe enough, make a cross with a sharp knife in the underside of each, to encourage the skins to come away. They can be left in the hot water for an extra 10 seconds or so, but it's important that they don't overheat and begin to cook.)

3. Cut 25 of the tomatoes in half vertically. Scoop out the seeds and membrane.

4. Place the tomato halves in a bowl and drizzle with olive oil. Toss the tomatoes in the oil and then, using a slotted spoon, transfer them to a baking tray lined with tinfoil, cut side up. Slice the garlic and place a slice on to each tomato half. Tear the herbs and scatter over the tomatoes, along with a drizzle of olive oil. Season with salt and pepper and sprinkle over the sugar.

5. Cook the halves for approximately 2–3 hours (the ripeness of the tomatoes can make a big difference to the cooking time), turning them over about halfway through cooking. When they are ready, the tomatoes will have shrivelled slightly and turned a deep, vibrant red, but they should still be moist rather than 'sun-dried'. (If, during cooking, some appear to be drying more than others, remove them from the oven early.) Allow them to cool, pick off the garlic and herbs, and store the tomatoes in a container, covering them with extra virgin olive oil.

6. Cut the remainder of the blanched tomatoes into eighths and place in a sieve over a bowl. Sprinkle over 1 teaspoon of salt and leave until 5–6 tablespoons of tomato juice have collected in the bowl.

7. Place the tomatoes and their juice in a small pressure cooker. Put on the lid and cook over a high heat at full pressure for 12 minutes.

8. Remove from the heat and leave to cool. Once cool, remove the lid and place the tomatoes back on the heat. Cook over a high heat, stirring frequently, for 10–15 minutes or until there is very little liquid left.

9. Leave the sauce to cool again, then tip into a container. Add the reserved vines (plus any extra that are to hand) and cover. Leave at room temperature if cooking the pizzas straight away, otherwise store in the fridge for up to 24 hours. (The vines seem to contain a lot of that wonderful fresh tomato smell. Adding them here allows that aroma to permeate the sauce. It's a technique that can be used in other dishes – try orange, lemon or mandarin leaves – bearing in mind that the leaves may be heat-sensitive, and so are best added to slightly cooled ingredients.)

ASSEMBLING THE PIZZA

1. Preheat a cast-iron frying pan over a high heat for at least 20 minutes. Preheat the grill to the highest temperature possible. Generously flour the work surface and a baking sheet or pizza peel.

2. To shape the pizza base, first put a ball of dough on the floured surface. Then place your fingertips 1.5cm in from the edge and push down as you move the ball around in a clockwise direction. Continue pushing and turning until a rim (the *cornicione*) forms that will ensure the sauce collects in the centre of the pizza.

3. To finish, place the palms of your hands on the dough and gently stretch it in opposing directions. Rotate the pizza through 90° and repeat this action. Continue to rotate and stretch until the pizza is some 20–25cm in diameter. (Make sure it's not bigger than the base of the frying pan!) If you're gentle, this process should preserve the circular shape of the pizza. Be careful not to squash the rim or leave a dome in the centre.

4. Carefully lift the pizza base on to a baking sheet or pizza peel. Spoon the tomato sauce on to the centre of the pizza and swirl it outwards in a circular pattern to cover the dough thinly, making sure you don't spread it over the *cornicione*. Scatter the oven-dried tomatoes on top. Tear the mozzarella into chunks the size of a gobstopper and dot over the pizza. Finish with a generous drizzle of olive oil and a sprinkling of smoked sea salt.

5. Remove the frying pan from the hob, turn it upside down and place under the grill. (It needs to be very close to the grill but with enough space left for the pizza to rise slightly: you don't want the topping to end up stuck to the grill's element.) Let it heat up for several minutes before carefully sliding the pizza on to the base of the frying pan. (This must be done while the pan is under the grill, so as not to lose valuable heat.) Cook for 90 seconds or until the dough has cooked and turned golden brown and the mozzarella has melted and started to bubble but not brown. Add the basil leaves and serve.

BANGERS

& MASH

These goat sausages sizzling here in the fire –
We packed them with fat and blood to have for supper.
Now, whoever wins this bout and proves the stronger,
Let that man step up and take his pick of the lot!

Homer, *The Odyssey*

INTRODUCTION

It's easy to see why the sausage is viewed with such affection. Like a goodwill ambassador, it can be all things to all people – a supremely adaptable foodstuff that crosses cultural divides. From the vibrantly spiced thin red merguez to the coarse, garlicky Bierwurst, from the coiled Cumberland to the hot paprika of a chorizo, the sausage effortlessly takes on the history and resources of its sur-roundings. My own tastes reflect the sausage's multiple personality. My father grew up in South Africa and we took holidays there. I often find myself hankering after a boerewors, the spicy South African sausage flavoured with coriander. And twenty years of French cuisine have left me with a passion for that cured, rustic, intensely flavoured homage to the charcutier's art: the Toulouse sausage. If variety is the spice of life, then the sausage must be one of life's true pleasures.

What other food suits all times of day and all seasons? It can happily be eaten for breakfast, lunch or dinner; served up hot and sticky to counter winter's chill; or bunged on the barbie for a chargrilled alfresco experience. Probably my first memory of cooking is camping in the garden and roasting a sausage over an open fire. It was a standard, shop-bought banger – unpleasantly squidgy as I pushed it on to the stick – and ended up absolutely charred. But it had been an adventure and I'd done it myself, so to me it seemed delicious. I prefer my sausages a little less burnt now, but that chargrilled note is still very important to me. Give me that with ketchup and potato that has been pressed with a hand-masher – curling into fat shapes, like plasticine through a mould – and then topped with cubes of butter with the cold of the fridge still on them, and I'm as happy as a little boy.

HISTORY

• Sausages •

As the quotation from Homer shows (though I'd not considered goat as an ingredient; maybe it was an idea worth exploring …), sausages have been a part of our culture – and highly prized as such – for a long time. A sausage-seller appears in Aristophanes's satirical play *The Knights* (424 BC), where his skill in mincing meat makes him a suitable candidate for politics, where he can mince words instead. Seneca noted that the sausage-seller's call was part of the cacophony of street cries in ancient Rome, and in Petronius's *Satyricon* the description of Trimalchio's feast includes sizzling sausages on a silver gridiron with Syrian plums and pomegranate seeds placed beneath it.

The sausage had clearly already become a feature of everyday life – so much so that *Apicius* contains several recipes for sausage. (For example: 'Grind pepper, cumin, savory, rue, parsley, seasoning, bay berries and *liquamen* [salted fish sauce, possibly similar to Thai *nam pla*]. Mix with finely chopped flesh, grinding both together. Mix in *liquamen*, whole peppercorns, plenty of fat and pine nuts, and carefully force into an intestine stretched thinly, and hang up to smoke.') Undoubtedly, its versatility played a part in this ubiquity: a well-spiced sausage could disguise dubious or unusual cuts of meat, and its handy packaging made it good food for soldiers on the march. The sausage may have invaded north-western Europe alongside conquering armies. Certainly by the third century AD the sausage figured in cuisine in Britain. Excavations of the Roman town of Verulamium (St Albans) have unearthed the remains of what appears to have been a sausage factory.

The sausage's origins reach back beyond Rome and ancient Greece to coincide with mankind's ability to furnish itself with meat on a regular basis: as soon as there was a surplus, people were thinking of ways to preserve it. The pig was domesticated early – about 5000 BC in Egypt and China – and the art of cutting up meat, salting it and putting it in a casing was one of the first methods of preservation. The pork sausage is the brainchild of these two historical facts. (The word actually derives from the Latin for 'salted': *salsus*.) And although the term 'sausage' covers a wide range of objects – there have been fish sausages since antiquity, Glamorgan sausages contain cheese and leeks, and there are seventeenth-century records of mutton-and-oyster sausages – the pork banger has remained the most popular (and accounts for 83 per cent of all sausages eaten in Britain each year).

Despite its wide and long-standing acceptance, the sausage has had a chequered history. Emperors Constantinus I and Leo V both banned sausages because they contained blood (the consumption of which was forbidden by the Bible) and because their shape inevitably associated them with pagan phallic rites. However, the sausage's reputation has probably been harmed more by the very thing that brought it increased popularity in the nineteenth century: mass production. The urge for quantity all too often led to a drop in quality: cheaper cuts of meat, larger percentages of fillers like rusk or cereals, the parts of the animal that had no other commercial use, artificial flavours and preservatives – all could be hidden beneath the sausage's pink skin. This downward trend led to the 'economy' sausage, which might contain 30 per cent pork fat, 20 per cent recovered meat (often including skin, rind, gristle and bone), 30 per cent rusk and soya, 15 per cent water and 5 per cent E-numbers. Now there's a sausage worth banning. No wonder Otto von Bismarck observed that 'Laws are like sausages. It's better not to see them being made.'

Of course, the unsung heroes of the sausage industry are the butchers who stayed loyal to a quality product despite falling sales. But the public saviour was an unlikely one: in the mid-1980s the famous society photographer Norman Parkinson created his own Porkinson's banger and teamed up with Saatchi & Saatchi to persuade the nation back to its senses. (It was served on Concorde and marketed as the world's first supersonic sausage!) By 2005, a hefty 189,000 tonnes of sausages were being eaten in Britain – 17 per cent more than in 2000 and directly attributable to better quality meat and a wider range of ingredients. This is the way the story ends, not with a whimper but a banger.

THE QUEST FOR THE BEST

She had a vague impression of … the hissing and delicious smell of sausages, and more and more and more sausages. And not wretched sausages half full of bread and soya bean either, but real meaty, spicy ones, fat and piping hot, and burst and just the tiniest bit burnt.

C. S. Lewis, *The Silver Chair*

• Getting the Lowdown in Ludlow •

I wanted to create a bespoke banger, one that really captured the taste, texture and feel of a fine sausage. To do so, I needed first to talk to the experts and get their advice on how it was done. If only there was a way I could meet up with a number of master butchers who were competing to produce the best sausage they possibly could, I thought. If only I could pick their brains, then talk to members of the public about what they thought of the butchers' offerings and of sausages in general …

As it turned out, I could do exactly that – in Ludlow in Shropshire.

Ludlow is an impressive place. With its tottering, half-timbered Tudor houses and its solidly built red-brick mansions, it must be one of the most picturesque towns in England. And its inhabitants are enthusiastic about their food. The town has several Michelin-starred restaurants (including Claude Bosi's wonderful Hibiscus), and every autumn it's the backdrop for a spectacular Food & Drink Festival. As well as showing off local produce and suppliers, the festival explores every aspect of food. This year there were pudding tastings and a pork pie competition, workshops on perry-making and black pudding, demonstrations of Veronese cookery, a fresh herb market, and even a waiters' race. It was all very tempting, but I couldn't be distracted. I had come to Ludlow

 The term 'banger', which is now an affectionate nickname, is in fact a reminder of the sausage's dodgy innards: during the Second World War the high water content of sausages meant they could be a real flash in the pan – exploding as the water turned to vapour and expanded, bursting the casing.

with one aim in mind: to go on the Sausage Trail.

Each year, Ludlow's five butchers create a new sausage for the festival. By the imposing remains of the town's castle (a reminder of a time when, as a border town, Ludlow's skirmishes might centre on more serious matters than sausage manufacture), you can buy a ticket and voting form, which gives you the opportunity to try all five sausages and then vote for which you think is the best. The banger with the most votes is acclaimed the 'People's Choice'.

I paid my two pounds, received my ticket and a map showing me the whereabouts of the competing butchers, and joined the long queue forming before a small marquee on the High Street.

Mike Wall and his team were neatly turned out in red pinstriped aprons, and they had a long trough of sausages on the go. 'For the competition,' he told me, 'the biggest problem is thinking up new flavours. Last year we came up with a Thai sausage that won us a prize. Usually I'll have an idea, try it out on the lads in the shop. If they like it we'll ask the opinion of some of our customers – see if they say "That's fantastic" or "Yuck".'

'So what's the idea this year?'

'Pork with beer mustard. It's rare-breed meat – Gloucester Old Spot from local farms – and natural sheep's casing. What do you think of it?'

It was juicy, firm-textured and full-flavoured. The casing broke apart just right as I bit into it. Of course, it was breakfast time, I was hungry and it was the first sausage I'd tasted, all of which probably made me a less than impartial judge, but it seemed excellent. 'That's great. Really tasty. It's nicely peppered.'

'That's the mustard and beer mustard doing their job,' Mike said. 'I don't think it's over the top, though. There's only so much you can do with a sausage. Go too far and it ends up being something else.'

He mainly used cuts from the shoulder, along with some from the belly to provide fat. 'We don't do any curing before mincing. And the meat has to be absolutely fresh – there's no ageing involved. Three or four days old and it needs to be used. After which there's probably a week's shelf-life for the housewife.'

One thing that surprised and interested me was that he used 20 per cent filler. I'd been contemplating making a filler-free sausage, assuming that would give a meatier experience, but in Mike's skilful hands the filler appeared to add something important: a more interesting and varied texture, a kind of welcome roughness rather than smooth homogeneity. It would be interesting to see how the other butchers' offerings compared.

Mike Wall had told me he was born and bred a butcher. And he wasn't kidding – he was born in an upstairs room of the family's shop opposite. He knew his stuff, so before I moved on I wanted to cadge his top tips for making a great sausage.

'The quality of the meat is absolutely essential. And the same goes for the seasonings, which have got to be well balanced. On top of that, there's the skin. You've got to use natural casings from an animal of the right age. Older animals are too tough, and nobody likes a rubbery sausage skin.'

With that caution ringing in my ears, I made my way round the other butchers. The differences of opinion and approach made the task of creating my own sausage all the more daunting. Fresh herbs or dried, leg meat or not, rare breed and free-range or not, spiced-up or spice-free – each butcher had a different take. (One even happily admitted to using an E-number as a preservative!) At least I made headway on the question of filler: I tried a 100 per cent meat

sausage and it did indeed seem blander in texture, too uniform to really grab the attention of the tastebuds. I'd learned a valuable lesson here and had a hunch disproved.

The final stop on the trail was Andrew Francis's shop, tucked into a corner of Ludlow's market square. It had a very traditional air: two rabbits were hanging up outside, fur and all, and green-framed chalkboards announced the day's offers – *Pickled Brisket*, *Salted Silverside*, *Ox Tongue*.

The white marquee outside the shop was doing a roaring trade. 'How come you've got the longest queue? What's the secret?' I asked Andrew as he cooked.

'Perhaps they're starting here and working their way down the hill. No – best sausage, that's what it really is! I'm using an old English recipe for pork and mixed herb. The pork's rare-breed Tamworth: all lean prime shoulder which has the fat you need to keep it moist and tasty. And the casing is natural lamb – none of that artificial stuff; it's the real McCoy, that is, a recipe handed on to me by the butcher who had the shop before me.'

'Is the age of the animal part of what makes a good casing?'

'The age is crucial. Spring lambs are small so you get a small sausage with a skin that tends to split. Mutton, on the other hand, is basically hard and chewy. Animals between four and twelve months old are best.'

By now, the next batch of Andrew's bangers was ready. He handed one over. 'There you are. Fresh off the barbecue. Don't burn yourself. Now, what's the verdict?'

There was a gleam of competition in Andrew's eye as he asked. It was a lovely sausage, with a nice meaty taste. 'It's important that it's not too spicy,' he told me. 'You want the pork flavour to come through. It needs to be a pleasant sausage for everybody, young and old alike.'

Judging by the numbers milling round his marquee, Andrew had achieved that goal. The queue contained all sorts: men in Barbours and green wellingtons, harassed mothers with prams, kids getting a kick out of following a map and getting it stamped at each location. It was inspiring to see such enthusiasm for food among such a range of people. Maybe Britain really was shrugging off its past reputation as a culinary no-go area. The ingredients for all the sausages I'd tasted had been sourced locally: a great advert for what was on the doorstep and how much better it was than its mass-produced counterparts. I came away from the festival full of enthusiasm not just for sausage-making but for the future of food in Britain. At last we were acknowledging and appreciating the quality of our produce – and supporting, encouraging and eating it too.

• From Tasting to Testing •

After lining up for the Sausage Trail, it was time to line up the sausages for the Sausage Tasting.

This was not to be a competition. My head chef (Ashley), my pastry chef (Jocky), Chris and I weren't expecting to crown our own 'People's Choice'. We were looking to find out what were the qualities that made the Great British Banger. Even in Ludlow it had become clear that this was a subject of debate: people in the queues agreed that a great sausage must be juicy and densely textured, but they were divided over spicing in their sausages; I also talked to several who insisted that a good banger must be filler-free and yet, as it turned out, their favourite did contain filler. Obviously the sausage's simple, compact shape hid a number of complex considerations. To sort out what went into perfect sausages, we would really have to get under their skin.

In the development kitchen at the Fat Duck, forty sausages rested, plump and pink, on the work surface, as though four fat-fingered pianists were about to embark on a complicated piece of music. We had sourced the sausages from many places. There were several examples from each of the major supermarkets, generally advertised as 'traditional', 'classic' or 'old English' – encouraging evidence of how much we now expect a better bit of banger for our buck. We had included the standard offerings from each of our five butchers in Ludlow, and from other specialists, including Norman Parkinson's supersonic sausage.

This was not the time for a fry-up: browning a banger gives it a lot of meaty flavour and enhances its juiciness. It can disguise a substandard sausage, and I wanted the test to be as rigorous as possible. So we vacuum-packed and labelled the lot, and put them in a water bath for one hour at 60°C. After which, like kids at Christmas, we opened our parcels and tried them out.

We chewed on slices and, like forensic specialists, prised open the meat and picked at the casings. Each of us took notes on the texture of the casing and the meat itself, on the juiciness and flavour, on the overall delicacy – whether it burst satisfyingly as you bit into it.

It was a strange experience, but an instructive one. I had spent ten years thinking about and preparing food, and then being judged on it; this was the first time I'd swapped the chef's hat for the critic's pen. What was immediately apparent was what a wide range of product goes under the name 'sausage'. Here, indeed, were the good, the bad and the ugly. There were gutsy little numbers containing offal that tasted delicious but were too far removed from what we thought of as the classic banger. Similarly, some had been seasoned to the point where they tasted positively exotic. The spice was nice, but again not what we were looking for. Only one sausage was so unpleasant and gluey that it was unswallowable, but there were others that had a definite aroma of biscuit tin – as though they'd used Rich Tea as a filler – or that tasted of cheese and onion.

Weeding out the bad and the ugly was easy. Choosing which sausages captured something of the perfect banger and could be used as a template and inspiration for making our own proved much harder. We swapped notes and whittled the choice down to ten, which we then cooked, and tasted, again.

Even at this stage there was disagreement: a couple were too strongly flavoured or herby, and one was so dough-like that we couldn't understand how it had got this far. But eventually we found a sausage that we felt incarnated the qualities of the classic British banger: full of flavour, dense but not overly so, with a nice rough texture that didn't go too far in the direction of charcuterie-like individual chunks of meat.

On camera, while blind-tasting, I'd suggested this might be a mass-produced sausage that none the less managed to tick all the boxes, as though a checklist had been involved in its creation. It's possible that there was, for it turned out to be the Porkinson's banger, which had had the might of Saatchi & Saatchi behind it. Had focus groups and ad planning gone into finding out what exactly makes a banger a banger? In the end it didn't really matter: this was the sausage that best captured what I expected in a banger; this was the sausage that gave me the most signposts towards what I wanted to incorporate in my own sausage.

Balance, it turned out, was the key. In making a sausage, there are a lot of variables to be taken into consideration: the texture must be meaty but not too chewy, the seasoning fresh but not overpowering. The meat needs to be tightly packed but not homogeneous or mousse-like. Originally I had thought a good sausage would need 100 per cent meat, yet I'd learned that the filler can add something – a chunkier, more interesting texture (though this depends on your choice of filler: many of the sausages ended up too starchy, too dry). The salting was important – the best examples all had a slightly cured note – and the casing crucial to a sausage's success: anything too tough made you feel as though you were chewing a plastic bag, no matter how delicious the rest of the sausage's contents.

All of these things contributed to the rounded flavour and 'natural' taste that seemed to be the keynote of the best sausages we tested, the ones that let the flavour of the meat come out. (That natural aspect is often the downfall of commercially produced sausages. Anything too processed has an artificial character: you can taste the nitrates used for preservation.) And Porkinson's banger was the sausage that best performed that balancing act. Though I had a few ideas of my own (perception of juiciness, it seemed, was all-important in a proper banger; I'd realised I needed to make a sausage dense enough to get the saliva going, which really enhances that juicy sensation), this was my benchmark for the perfect sausage.

• Pigging Out •

> Pigs with character farmed by people with character will tend to produce pork with character.
>
> Hugh Fearnley-Whittingstall, *The River Cottage Meat Book*

Before I even contemplated something approaching perfection, however, I had to find the meat that best suited a banger. I tasted lots of loins, and the one that fitted that bill came from Graham Head's farm in Northumberland: it had exactly the taste and texture I had in mind. I travelled to Lowick to meet him and talk pork.

The weather was doing its best to dampen my enthusiasm. The sky was a theatre curtain of pale grey. Earlier it had bucketed down but now it had settled into a steady drizzle – fine if it's olive oil over salad leaves, not so great when you're tramping across muddy fields and skirting mini-lakes created by the rain. We hurried towards the pig pens.

With his beret, denim shirt, wire-rimmed glasses and close-cropped silvery beard, Graham looked more like a Left Bank painter than a farmer – but then I guess you could call him an artist of the pig world. He led us into a corrugated-metal shed where large, straw-strewn pens gave the pigs plenty of room to run around in.

It was feeding time and the pigs knew it. They reared up out of their pens and placed supplicatory trotters on top of the railings. Their shrieks of excited anticipation were deafening as Graham tipped out the feed. As he moved from pen to pen, the volume would diminish slightly as a set of pigs ceased squealing and started eating. It was like the end of some cacophonous piece of modernist classical music, the discordant crescendo gradually falling off as each section of the orchestra finished, until suddenly there was silence.

Well, almost. The pigs now grunted continually and contentedly as they hoovered up what Graham had put before them. His pigs were rare-breed Middle Whites, and I was interested to know why he rated them so highly.

'Middle White used to be regarded as *the* pork pig. Between the wars, this is what British housewives would have bought. The Middle White does produce exceptional pork,' he insisted with pride, 'partly because it's been crossed with Chinese pigs. You can tell that from the snub nose. Chinese pigs laze around and don't burn off much energy, much like Vietnamese pot-bellied pigs.'

'So they'll develop plenty of fat to give flavour to the meat.'

'Exactly. The Middle White also produces a lot of piglets, which is why it was crossed

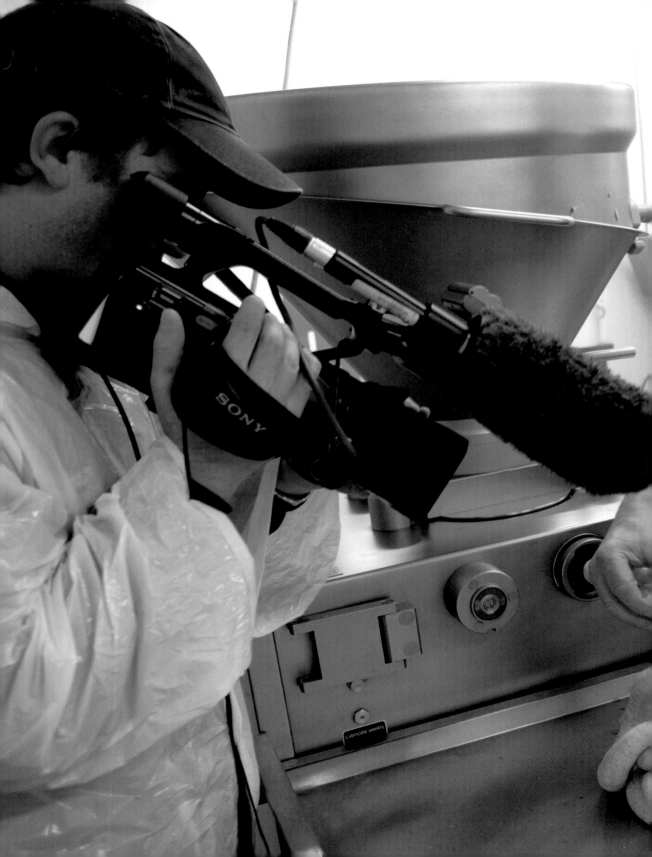

with Chinese pigs back in the mid-nineteenth century. But the problem is that it's a relatively small pig and it didn't grow fast enough – or big enough – for commercial concerns. The Large White is a much bigger pig.'

It was a familiar story. 'Yes, as commercial pork producers grew, they wanted an animal that yielded more meat.'

'They were also looking for a general-purpose pig – one that would provide not just pork but bacon as well. If you look at rare breeds, the Middle White's a pork pig, Tamworth's bacon: it's got a long back that gives good rashers. Middle Whites went out of favour, to the point where, in the 1970s and 80s, they were really threatened.'

'But you're clearly devoted to them.'

'These guys produce a really good pork experience. Their genetics mean there's a lot of fat on the outside, which is good for basting, and also on the inside, to make the meat very succulent.'

'I can vouch for that. It's why I'm here. The loin tasted fantastic.'

'Thanks. Part of the reason for that is Middle Whites are old-fashioned pigs: they go to slaughter at an older age. Most commercial pigs go off at four months, before they're fully mature. Middle Whites go at seven to eight months – you're getting a more mature pig; the flavour's had a chance to develop.'

'In contrast to the commercial approach, where the whole point is to get pigs as big as possible as quickly as possible and then flog them off.'

'True, but it's not the producers' fault, it's because of the reward system that applies in Britain: no account is taken of the quality of the meat, and we need to replace it with a system that does. I know there's one in Australia for beef …'

'Yes, MSA.[*]'

'Well, we need one for pork here.'

'I agree. It's done wonders for the beef industry over there. And pigs like this should be recognised and rewarded for their high quality. What part does diet play in the development of that quality?'

'How the pigs are fed in the last six to eight weeks of their life is extremely important. I give them a mix of wholemeal barley and concentrated protein – soya plus vitamins with lots of lysine in. It finishes them up really well. The pigs are wet-fed, which is a very nice way of doing it: they eat a kind of polenta or porridge. Taking on water and feed at the same time is a very natural way of "growing on" the meat. You can see it: they begin to grow a lot faster and get a lovely sheen of fat on them.'

'And what happens if you speed up the process and feed a pig too quickly?' I wanted to know. 'Do you end up with too much fat?'

'Inside, the intramuscular fat remains pretty much the same. What you will get is a huge piece of fat round the outside. Sometimes this grows so large and fast that it actually depresses the muscles and you get a very thin piece of protein. That's no good. At the same time, people shouldn't be frightened of a bit of fat on the outside. A lot renders off anyway, but it's great while it's cooking: I call it "self-basting". You don't have to eat loads of it.'

'Pigs are one of the most intelligent and sociable farmyard animals. In your experience, Graham, what happens if they get stressed on the way to the abattoir?'

 See 'Making the Grade', pages 162–3

'Stressing an animal's selfish and unforgivable. But even if you discount moral concerns, there are compelling reasons for treating pigs well – and lambs, cattle and poultry, for that matter. Stress affects the taste. You end up with far tougher meat.'

Stress before slaughter can be caused by many things: lack of water or food, bad transportation, exhaustion, overcrowding. Whatever the cause, it results in the animal drawing on its energy source, glycogen (the 'animal starch'). This ruins the quality of the meat because, after death, glycogen converts to lactic acid, which then tenderises the meat. If the glycogen's used up, there'll be no lactic acid to soften it up.

This process goes hand in hand with the hanging of the meat. For a short while after death, an animal's muscles are relaxed. After about one to two-and-a-half hours, however, depending on the type of animal, rigor mortis – a clenching of the muscles – sets in. The muscle fibres run out of energy and the protein filaments contract and lock in place. Hanging goes some way towards preventing this via gravity: the muscles are stretched so the filaments can't contract and bunch up, which produces very tough meat. And eventually protein-digesting enzymes from within the muscle fibres begin to break down the meat, softening its texture.

Graham was so interested in his subject that our roles often switched: he ended up asking me about hanging meat. 'Pork requires a lot less hanging than beef. What do you think is the ideal hanging time?'

'For cured products like sausages, fresh is best – a day or so after slaughter. There I'd say a lot of the tenderising happens during the mincing. But for a loin, where you need to develop a certain level of tenderness, I've found a week or so to be good. Any longer and the fatty acids in the meat get oxidised, leading to that slightly sweated, rancid note.'

We continued talking as we headed off towards Graham's farmhouse, a beautifully solid brick building with orange tiles and a pointed tower at one end. Large arched windows overlooked a neatly kept garden with flagstone paths, a scatter of small trees and an immaculate lawn glistening in the drizzle.

'Time for breakfast, I think,' he said. 'Fancy a bacon sandwich …?'

• Back to the Grind •

I was in a white room with a blood-red floor. A man approached wearing a lab coat and black and white chequered hat, as though he'd donned a Formula One flag. Below beetle brows, his eyes twinkled with mischievous humour. He advanced towards me, knife in hand. The tinny, scraping sound of the metal blade scything the sharpener rang out – zing, zing, zing – faster and louder with each step. 'Halloo Hairrston. It's rrreally grrrreat to meet yoo …'

No, I wasn't having a nightmare brought on by the toxic combination of adrenaline and sleep deprivation that is the chef's lot. The resonant Scottish brogue belonged to Sandy Crombie, owner of Crombie's butcher shop in Edinburgh. I'd eaten sausages in the street and in the lab. Now I'd come to Scotland to see what went into those sausages.

Sandy lifted a slab of meat on to the table. 'We use shoulder and belly of pork. That makes the nicest sausage because it has the right amount of fat to lean – enough fat to give it flavour and a special taste.'

'Yes, you've got to have fat and lean, and in the right amounts. Do you have an ideal fat percentage?' I wanted to know.

'What we really want is a 70/30 split. We make a lot of sausages with a higher lean content, but for me 70/30 is the most flavoursome. There's an old-fashioned way of rearing that makes the pigs incredibly fat, but then you've got to make sure you use all the pig in your sausages so the meat is properly leaned-up.'

I was thinking hard about the number of different processes I'd need to master to make a great sausage. The grind seemed particularly important. 'Do you play around with grind sizes?' I asked Sandy.

'Aye, we do, depending on the kind of sausage. A Toulouse needs a 12.5 millimetre disc and a single grind, but for these traditional sausages I'll use an 8 millimetre disc and the double-mince method – grinding it once, putting it in the mixer, then grinding it again.'

'That'll make for a more even distribution of lean meat and fat.'

'Absolutely,' affirmed Sandy. 'But the main thing to remember while making sausages is that you need to release the proteins inside the meat. Until that happens it won't all stick together.'

Meat contains muscle fibres, which are largely made up of two proteins: myosin and actin. The chopping, grinding and mixing of sausage meat draws these proteins out of the fibres (especially once salt is added) and on to the meat surfaces, where they act as a glue (or emulsifier), binding meat, fat and water together – much as the protein in egg yolk can be used to bind a fish cake.

Mincing was the start of this transformative process. The machine emitted a dull, insistent rumble as Sandy fed in the meat, which soon tumbled out of a long, solid-looking pipe in thick strands. 'The size of the mincer is extremely important,' he explained. 'The bigger it is, and the faster the meat goes through, the less heat is going to be generated. And that's vital because a warm environment encourages the growth of microbes – something you definitely want to avoid.'

Once the white plastic tub was full, Sandy cut the rumble from the mincer and hefted the tub over to the mixer. 'Mixing will help the protein release. But before we do that, we need to add the secret ingredients.'

Fortunately for me, these weren't so secret they couldn't be divulged. Sandy ripped the lids off several storage boxes and showed me the contents.

'We start by adding the seasonings because, as you'll know yourself, Heston, they should always be added directly to the meat.'

I felt a little like a school pupil being tested. I resisted the urge to put my hand up. 'You'll get a better mix that way,' I offered, 'and the seasoning is absorbed into the meat directly.'

'Absolutely. A lot of our seasonings are just spices, so we add salt separately. As well as tenderising and flavouring the meat and drawing out its proteins, salt will prevent microbial growth.'

'Yes. Just as it draws out proteins, so it'll draw water out of the microbes' cell walls and replace it with salt. The microbes die or slow down to the point of being ineffective.' I was beginning to sound like the class swot. 'How much salt do you add?'

'We usually work to 1.5 grams per kilo,' Sandy said as he weighed and added it. 'Now, here's the rusk. It doesn't really matter what type you use. This is what we normally choose.' He held out a plastic tub containing a coarse yellow powder for me to try. It tasted like dried, hard-baked bread. 'And the final and perhaps most important ingredient is iced water. As I've said, it's vital that you keep down the heat while making sausages. Iced water helps ensure this.'

I saw this in action when the mixing got under way. Sandy periodically stopped the machine to add more of the ingredients, along with iced water to keep everything cool. By now the meat was a lump of pink and ochre, dotted with specks of seasoning. It looked a little like mulched sesame-seed toast. Sandy hauled the tub back to the grinder and ran it through again. Now it emerged looking like tinned spaghetti – fat strands, pale and pink-flecked. 'You can see the mix is more homogeneous. The fat and lean are more integrated,' he said. 'It's ready for filling.'

Once again the tub was carried over to a heavy, silvery machine, this time a square metal tank with a hopper attached. 'After the double-mince, as the meat strands clump together, a lot of air is trapped between them,' Sandy told me. 'One of the things the filling machine does is take out some of that air. You need to get rid of as much as possible, otherwise the sausage will burst during cooking. Obviously people at home wouldn't have a machine so they'd have to work the mix – as you might a dough – to get the same effect.' At this point the mix did indeed have the appearance of a sluggish, sticky dough, and Sandy kneaded it like a baker to show me what he meant.

I realised I could probably achieve something similar to the filling machine's air expulsion with the vac-packer at the Fat Duck: put the sausages in it, shut the lid and – *schlooop* – all the air would be drawn out. Nifty – a nice piece of insider's knowledge from Sandy that I definitely wanted to try out sometime, even if it was outside the scope of the domestic kitchen.

'It'll make a better end product,' he agreed. 'But perhaps we're getting too fussy …?'

'No, no,' I contradicted. 'It's impossible to get too fussy. Not if it results in a better end product.'

And I stand by that. Sometimes people have suggested to me that life's too short for the kind of lengths to which I go to create a recipe. But if it results in something delicious, stimulating and surprising, if it turns a meal into an event, a piece of real pleasure, then surely it's worth it? (Julia Child put it another way: 'Non-cooks think it's silly to invest two hours' work in two minutes' enjoyment; but if cooking is evanescent, well, so is the ballet.')

Away from the soapbox and back at the filling machine, I watched Sandy feed in the sausage meat. 'If you're doing this by hand,' he advised, 'you've got to get the right amount of meat in the casing. Too much and it'll burst. Too little and you get a flabby sausage – and you don't want that.'

Out of a nozzle at the side spooled an endless pale snake, like the mother of all Cumberland sausages, now sheathed in its casing and twisting into coils on the stainless steel surface. For the benefit of the cameras, it was being done at quarter the usual speed, but there was still an anaconda's worth in seconds. At full throttle it must be an unnerving sight – like a scene from some viperous horror movie.

'Right,' said Sandy with a certain finality. I felt a lesson coming on. 'Basically we lay one part of the sausage over the other' – he lifted up one end of the snake and turned it back on itself in a loop – 'to roughly the size of sausage we want. Then press and roll with the fingers, using the weight of the sausage to help us. Twist up and through for the next sausage in the link. You've got to be careful not to burst the skin as you're doing it. I use the underhand method …' He paused. 'Nothing is implied by that, of course.'

Sandy gyrated his hands with skill and assurance and soon enough he had a bunch of linked sausages dangling from one hand. He reminded me of the magician at kids' parties who effortlessly twists balloons into poodles or aeroplanes. I knew what was coming next.

'Would you like to try?'

I'd never done this before and, as you might imagine, it's the kind of thing that looks

easy in the hands of a master but actually turns out to be fiendishly complicated. Perhaps the hardest part was remembering which way to twist and feed the sausage through to get to the next on the link, especially when I already had several hanging from one hand. Sandy ended up calling out, 'That way; the other way', like a driving instructor. Eventually, however, by following his traffic directions, I managed to make a string of sausages that any dog would be proud to steal and run off down the street with, links flying behind him.

'Yeah, they're coming on. That's quite good,' was Sandy's opinion, so I guess the pupil passed.

● The Fickle Finger of Phosphate ●

There were so many variables involved in sausage-making that it was difficult to narrow down the options. In the development kitchen my team and I weighed up the merits of different casings, of hand-mincing versus machine-mincing, of fresh meat versus aged, of packing methods, of types and amounts of filler, of spicings, seasonings and flavourings. Each change to the recipe seemed to require a re-evaluation of all the other ingredients, as though this were the culinary equivalent of a Rubik's Cube.

Eventually, though, we'd got something that worked. It required a little tweaking, but it was taking shape. Then we hit a bigger problem, which eclipsed all the others we'd had before.

Phosphates.

In animals (including humans), adenosine triphosphate (ATP) is an essential part of the body's energy pack: among other things, it triggers the protein group actomysin to separate into the proteins actin and myosin. This is what allows muscles to flex and move.

After slaughter, ATP soon gets used up. The muscle proteins stay bound as actomysin and, because there's no ATP left to reverse the process, remain in that form (the stiffened-up condition called rigor mortis).

For butchers, actomysin is undesirable: unlike actin and myosin, it's difficult to dissolve it into the meat and it doesn't hold water well. It's not a good banger-binder. On the Continent they get round this by turning meat into sausages before rigor mortis sets in, but in Britain the slaughter set-up means this isn't possible. Instead, commercial producers add polyphosphates to the meat to cause the actomysin to revert to actin and myosin, which can then glue together the meat, fat and water.

However, I was reluctant to use polyphosphates for two reasons. First, because they're an E-number – E452 – and there are understandable concerns about such food additives. For many people, the perfect sausage would have to be E-free. Second, polyphosphates are almost impossible to get hold of in Britain (we had to order them online from America). If I was going to create a recipe that people could prepare at home, I had to find a way of preparing a sausage without phosphates.

It was a worthwhile aim, but I came to appreciate how far we were falling short of the target when Chris prepared the current recipe with and without phosphates.

It was an unusually domestic scene for the development kitchen – the frying pan on the hob, the rich meaty aromas rising as two sausages steadily and stickily darkened – marred only by the fact that Chris, with his chef's asbestos fingers, was nudging the bangers round the pan with his hand rather than a spatula. He cut thick slices of each and placed them on separate plates for me to try.

In the first, the phosphates had done their job, integrating the meat and fat to give a lovely, juicy sausage. It had a nice dense texture and a full flavour – still a little too salty perhaps, even though we'd cut the salt content right back, but none the less this was the best so far, a really encouraging result after all the months of work.

And the phosphate-free sausage? The cameras zoomed in as I took a bite.

'Yeuch! That felt like half a gallon of fat flooding my mouth! The fat hasn't integrated with the meat at all.'

You could see it wasn't working. A sheen of fat filmed the cut surface of the sausage and, if you squeezed it, fat ran out on to the plate – and my hopes along with it.

It seemed as though 'phate was against us.

This was doubly problematic because during testing I had come to realise that, for me at least, a proper banger had to have a bready note. We'd worked hard to add that to the sausage, eventually soaking heavily toasted bread in water to give a kind of stock that would then be incorporated in the mix. It worked spectacularly well – except for the fact that bread is far less effective than rusk at holding in moisture and fat, which simply compounded the problems we were having with phosphate. Each route we took seemed to lessen our chances of successfully binding our sausage.

• Spuds-I-Like 2 •

Sausages weren't the only thing offering complications. At MBM's Norfolk distribution centre, Tom Dixon and I had discussed some of the difficulties involved in roasting potatoes. Now we turned our attention to mash. My own experiments had convinced me that choosing the right variety for mashing was only one of many important considerations. Tom agreed.

'The characteristics of a particular variety will give you a guideline as to how it's going to behave in the pot. But dry-matter content's probably more relevant than variety. And how it's been handled, how it's been stored, how it's been managed and grown – all of these also affect what you get on the table.'

'So what happens after a potato is picked is just as influential as the make-up of a particular variety?'

'That's exactly right,' said Tom. 'As always, you have to be very careful about the temperature at which you store potatoes for mashing. You've got a little more leeway than you have with potatoes destined for roasting or chipping because you don't have to worry about fry colour. So instead of 7–8°C, we store potatoes for mashing at about 3°C, which is the best temperature for preventing sprouting and dehydration.'

'So, the million-dollar question is: what would you look for in a perfect potato for mashing?'

'I'd seek out a variety with about 19 per cent dry matter. You can go higher with chips and roast because the fried crust will help the potato keep its shape. But with mash a high dry matter means you run the risk of the potato disintegrating on you during cooking. At the same time, if you choose something with a lower dry-matter content, it's likely to end up bland: a potato with a high water content is going to give a more watery end result.'

'Well, I'd like to pick your brains, Tom. I'm going to try mashing a standard variety such as Maris Piper to set a standard for comparison. But I'd also like to try some new types, preferably exhibiting a wide range of dry-matter content so I can explore how best to manage it and get the

most flavourful mash I can. Are there any you can recommend?'

He suggested some varieties that were entirely new to me. I felt excitement rising – I was like a scientist who has been given pieces of moon rock to experiment on – and looked forward to taking them back to my development kitchen.

• Monster Mash •

We'd cooked the potatoes for a long time at a low temperature, then cooled and re-simmered them for another hour before gently crushing them with a masher. Now generous dollops of each potato were laid out before us in eight white china bowls. Chris and I tried the results, looking for the one that best suited bangers.

You could tell from its appearance that Lady Olympia wasn't right: it looked 'wet' and that's just how it tasted. Lady Claire had the same problems – maybe not as wet as Olympia but still pasty. Claire had a nice chunky texture, but both Chris and I agreed that we expected something drier and fluffier in a mash. We had high hopes for the next on the list, Yukon Gold.

Prospectors might have ended up disappointed during the Klondike gold rush, but with Yukon Gold we hit the jackpot. It had exactly the kind of light texture we were hoping for, and allied this to a fantastic earthy flavour.

Maris Piper got the silver, maintaining its reputation as a great all-rounder, but it just couldn't match Yukon Gold's airiness and lightness of structure.

	% dry matter
Lady Olympia	22.8
Lady Claire	21.8
Yukon Gold	20.3
Maris Piper	21.9
Desiree	20.8
Lady Rosetta	23.4
Melody	18.7
Juliette	18.2

Despite its name, Desiree had become particularly undesirable: the potato had failed to hold the butter, which now pooled, swamp-like, round the edges of the bowl. This only happened to the Desiree and suggested that something other than dry matter had an effect on mash (since Desiree's dry-matter proportion was almost identical to Yukon Gold's). Testing often throws up as many questions as it answers: although I'd found a great potato for my mash, at some point in the future I'd have to look further into the composition of the starch molecules in a variety of potatoes, and how this might affect their behaviour when cooked.[*]

Lady Rosetta, meanwhile, demonstrated that there's a limit to how much dry matter you can put in a mash. It was visibly drier than any of the rest and far too chewy in the mouth. It was altogether the wrong potato. As were Melody and Juliette, but for different reasons. I'd included them as examples of potatoes with a dry-matter content lower than Tom's recommendation of 19 per cent, just

[*] Starch granules are made up of two types of molecule: amylose and amylopectin. Amylose molecules consist of about a thousand glucose sugars organised in a long chain. Amylopectin molecules, on the other hand, have anywhere between five thousand and twenty thousand sugars in hundreds of short branches. The structural differences influence how each behaves during cooking: the more orderly amylose molecules need a higher temperature, more water and more cooking before they break up, and they re-form far more easily upon cooling. The differences are perhaps best appreciated in rice: short-grain has about 15 per cent amylose; 'sticky' is almost all amylopectin. Starch's response to cooking depends heavily on the amount and interplay of these two molecules.

in case they produced an interesting result. But in the end they both had the wrong texture – a silkiness that was perfect for a real French-style *pommes purée* but hardly right for mash.

It had proved harder than expected to get the right proportion of dry matter for a mash that was neither too wet nor too dry. So it was very satisfying to have one potato really stand out as the winner. We were going for Gold. It had the fluffiness and flavour that would provide the gutsy comfort food to complement our sausages.

I'd learned something else during the tasting, the kind of thing that only falls into place when you're actually physically doing it, rather than just thinking about it, which is why testing like this is always worthwhile, even when it seems unnecessarily finicky.

I've always had a great affection for *pommes purées* and in the back of my mind I'd wondered whether it might turn out to be a better accompaniment for sausages than mashed potato, even though many people had insisted to me that you couldn't possibly have bangers without good old British mash.

Tucking into mash in the development kitchen, I had to admit that the gainsayers were correct. Mash just felt right – I could imagine digging into a mountain of the stuff while chewing on some sticky, succulent bangers. The two went together. Purée, on the other hand, suddenly seemed too refined. There were plenty of sausages it'd be perfect for, but not this one, not a proper, old-fashioned banger.

BANGERS
& MASH

Serves 4

Toasted-bread stock really turned a sausage into a banger, especially once I'd come up with the idea of smoking the back fat to get that chargrilled, campfire note. (I could have achieved a similar effect by putting the finished sausages on the barbecue, but the aggressive heat might have burst them, losing all those precious juices.) By using pork leg I was able to boost juiciness because the muscle structure there is better at retaining moisture than other parts of the animal. And putting golden syrup in the mix added a colour and sweetness that balanced the spices really well, and helped develop those all-important browning flavours.

However, the key to sausage success is keeping the meat cold as you prepare it. If it warms up too much (the rapidly spinning food-processor blade soon heats up to 65ºC – hot enough to begin cooking the meat!) the heat causes the fat to split, which wrecks emulsification (just as heating butter causes it to melt and split, losing the emulsion of fat and water). So work in batches, probing continually, and whenever it seems as though the meat is getting too warm, put it in the fridge or freezer to let it chill back down.

There can't be many things as stylish as serving up a batch of handmade sausages, but if you don't want to wrestle with hog casings and a stuffer, you can still prepare the sausage meat and use it in sausage rolls and pork pies, or form it into patties or skinless sausages (roll the meat in clingfilm and form into a tight sausage shape, then leave in the fridge to firm up). You don't even have to smoke the back fat: the sausages will still taste great, especially if fried in smoked oil. But it won't be the classic banger experience. I say get out the barbie and get hold of some casings – go the whole hog!

That campfire note also took the mash in a particular direction. A wood fire and a baked potato go together so well, there's something so right about them, that, in the end, nostalgia pushed science aside: these bangers had to have a mash with the flavours and fluffiness of a baked potato. So that's what you've got here.

Special equipment: oak chips (approx. 500g), barbecue, charcoal, firelighters, safety or barbecue gloves, large tongs, food processor, digital probe, sausage stuffer, pressure cooker, stick blender and beaker (optional)

Timing: With practice, making sausage meat becomes straightforward – a matter of getting the ingredients to hand and gradually processing them together while keeping an eye on the temperature. And since sausages can be stored in the freezer for three months, there's a lot of freedom as to how far in advance they're prepared, leaving plenty of time on the day to cook the gravy. The mash, meanwhile, is simplicity itself: no prep, just put the potatoes in the oven and forget about them for an hour so.

For the sausages (and for the base of the gravy; if you're not making gravy, halve the quantities):

1 x 800g loaf of medium-sliced white bread
500g pork back fat (a single piece rather than slices), rind removed
50g rusk
1 tsp ground black pepper (it's best to grind all of these spices yourself, just before using)
1 tsp ground white pepper
$^1/_2$ tsp ground nutmeg
1 tsp ground mace
$^1/_2$ tsp ground ginger
20g (2 tbsps) golden syrup
1kg minced pork (preferably from the thigh), chilled
2 tsps table salt
2.5m of hog casings (32–45mm in diameter)
groundnut oil

For the onion gravy:

6 large onions (about 1.2kg), finely sliced*
2 star anise
75ml light olive oil
250g pork leg or shoulder, roughly chopped
400g sausage meat (from the recipe above)
100–150g pork skin (it should be possible to obtain this from a good local butcher), chopped
3 fresh sage leaves
sherry vinegar, to taste

For the mash:

6 large Yukon Gold or Maris Piper potatoes (about 1.5kg)
150ml whole milk (or to taste)
150g unsalted butter (or to taste)
table salt and freshly ground black pepper

For the gelled butter:

125g butter (I'd use Anchor for the full nostalgia trip)
60g water
2g (approx. $^1/_2$ tsp) powdered agar agar

MAKING AND COOKING THE SAUSAGES

1. Preheat the oven to 180ºC/350ºF/Gas 4. Leave the oak chips to soak in a bucket of water. Light the barbecue and leave for 20–30 minutes, until the coals are white flecked with glowing red spots.

2. Meanwhile, lay 16 slices of bread on baking sheets. Place them in the oven and leave for 30–40 minutes, until the bread is an even dark brown colour throughout. Break up the bread and put it into a large bowl. Fill the bowl with cold water and set aside for at least 1 hour.

 These onions are to be caramelised: the process can be sped up by removing water from the onions beforehand. Place them in a sieve over a bowl, and toss with a tablespoon of table salt, then leave for 20 minutes.

3. Drain the oak chips and throw them on the barbecue. Once these begin to smoke, place the back fat in the centre of the grill and barbecue until it is blistered and charred on the outside and giving off that flame-cooked sausage smell. (The fat will catch fire: that's what reinforces the charred, smoked flavour. It's dramatic and needs to be handled with care. Wear safety gloves and use a large pair of tongs.)

4. Remove the fat from the barbecue, allow to cool and then chill in the fridge. Once chilled, cut it into small cubes. Blitz the cubes, in 2–3 batches, in a food processor until smooth and paste-like. (It will have an ashen grey appearance.) Scrape the fat into a bowl and set aside (not in the fridge) until required. Wash the food processor's blade and mixing bowl, ready for the next step.

5. Tip the rusk into the clean mixing bowl of the food processor and blitz until it is as fine as possible. Pass it through a fine sieve into a large measuring jug. (The rusk should now resemble fine flour.) Rinse the blade and bowl of the food processor and place them in the freezer to chill.

6. Pass the spices through a fine sieve into the measuring jug containing the rusk. Add the golden syrup. Drain the oven-baked bread pieces into a colander set over a bowl, then squeeze the bread to extract as much water as possible. Pour 400ml of the toast-flavoured water into the jug containing the spice mix, stir and place in the fridge to chill.

7. Remove the food-processor bowl and blade from the freezer, along with the chilled minced pork. Put batches of the pork and salt in the food processor and blitz until smooth and paste-like. Blitz no more than 200g of meat at a time, to help prevent it overheating. Use a digital probe to check the temperature of the meat every 30 seconds or so, to make sure it doesn't exceed 10°C/50°F. If it is in danger of doing so, put the meat, bowl and blade in the freezer. Once all the pork is ready, put the meat, bowl and blade in the freezer once more.

8. Once the pork has chilled back down to near freezing, add the fat, the chilled spice mix and 1 slice of white bread. Blitz in the food processor until the bread has broken down and the mix is a smooth emulsion. (Again, this needs to be done in small batches to ensure the temperature of the mixture does not exceed 10°C/50°F.) Scrape this mix into a large bowl, cover and store in the fridge while preparing the hog casings.

9. Untangle the casings, put them in a bowl and soak in warm water for a few minutes. Flush the salt out of the interior by holding the casings up to the tap and letting warm water flow through. (The water usually collects in the form of a bubble at the top of the casing, which can then be eased down the length of the casing with finger and thumb.) Leave the casings to soak in a bowl of warm water for 15 minutes, or until soft and pliable. (If the casings aren't soaked enough, there is a risk of them bursting during stuffing.)

10. Set aside 400g of the sausage mix for the onion gravy. Scrape the rest into the barrel of the sausage stuffer, packing it as firmly as possible and knocking out air pockets as you go. Push the casing on to the nozzle of the stuffer so that it bunches up, concertina-style. Extrude a little of the sausage meat and tie a knot in the casing as close up to this meat as possible, leaving at least 10cm of casing dangling.

11. Feed the sausage meat into the casing, applying uniform pressure. (Be careful: too fast and the skin will rupture; too slow and air pockets will form, causing the sausages to explode when cooked.) When finished, tie a knot in the other end of the casing.

12. To form the sausages into a chain, pinch and twist the stuffed casings at 12–15cm intervals. (Turn the first clockwise, the second anti-clockwise, and so on, to prevent them unravelling.) Store the sausages until you're ready to cook them. They will keep in the fridge for up to 3 days, and in the freezer for up to 3 months.

13. To cook the sausages, heat a large pan of water to 65°C/149°F. Add the sausages and poach for 20 minutes. (This gentle cooking helps keep in the meat's juices.) Lift the sausages from the water and pat dry with kitchen towel.

14. Put a splash of oil in a large frying pan, add the sausages and fry them until brown all over. (This needs a medium heat: if it's done too quickly, the sausages will split. Too slowly and the outside will overcook.) Remove the sausages from the pan. Serve with onion gravy and baked-potato mash.

MAKING THE ONION GRAVY

1. Place a small pressure cooker over a medium heat for 5 minutes. Crush the star anise and bag it up in a square of muslin. Add this to the pressure cooker, along with 45ml olive oil and the sliced onions. Cook for 20 minutes, or until the onions are soft and nicely browned, stirring occasionally.

2. Meanwhile, place a large, heavy-bottomed frying pan over a high heat for 10 minutes. Add the remaining oil and, when it starts smoking, the chopped pork skin, chopped pork and reserved sausage meat. Stir occasionally until browned all over. (To brown properly, all the meat has to be in contact with the surface of the pan. If need be, fry it in batches.)

3. Remove half the caramelised onions and set aside. Tip the browned meat into the pressure cooker containing the rest of the onions. Return the frying pan to a high heat and deglaze it by adding 100ml water and bringing it to the boil, then scraping the base of the pan to collect the bits stuck to the bottom. When the liquid has reduced by half, pour it into the pressure cooker.

4. Add enough cold water to cover, attach the lid, bring up to a high pressure and then cook for 45 minutes.

5. Remove the pressure cooker from the heat and let the pressure reduce slowly. Leave to cool then take off the lid and strain the mixture into a clean pan. Discard the onions, meat and skin.

6. Tip the reserved caramelised onions into the pan. Place over a high heat and reduce the liquid by half. Remove from the heat. Rub the sage leaves between your palms then add them to the pan. Taste the gravy and add a drop or two of sherry vinegar to cut through the richness.

MAKING THE MASH

1. Preheat the oven to 180°C/350°F/Gas 4. Place the potatoes on a baking tray and bake for $1-1^{1}/_{2}$ hours, depending on their size.

2. Cut the potatoes in half and scoop the flesh into a bowl. Gently warm the milk, then pour on to the potatoes. Add the butter and mash with the potatoes until well combined. Season with salt and plenty of pepper. Serve with gelled butter.

MAKING THE GELLED BUTTER

1. Melt the butter and water in a small pan, then whisk until combined. Add the agar agar, then boil for 1 minute, whisking continuously until the agar has dissolved. Pour through a fine sieve into a small container and leave to set in the freezer. (It needs to chill as fast as possible so that the emulsion doesn't split.) To serve, remove from the container, cut into cubes and dot over the mash.

STEAK

My favourite animal is steak.

Fran Lebowitz

INTRODUCTION

As a child, as far as I was concerned, steak was for grown-ups. Steak was what you graduated to from burgers.

Partly this was due to economics. Meat was very expensive in Britain in the 1970s, and so the kind of top-quality cut you need for steak became the province of the restaurant business, part of a big night out. So my first memories are of the event rather than the food. We'd go as a family to a Berni Inn, with its plush maroon banquettes and flock wallpaper. Everybody would feel awkward in their 'best' clothes (I don't remember if I had to wear a tie), and the food, too, had a slightly self-conscious formality that didn't encourage a relaxed evening: duck à l'orange served on oval willow-patterned plates, steak daintily garnished with a grilled tomato. Though I can laugh at it now as 'mock posh', at the time it seemed like the height of sophistication.

Things changed in my teens. I had a Portuguese friend, Carlos, whose mum cooked for a family in Hyde Park Gardens in London. It seemed as if, whenever I visited him there, a deliciously savoury smell of fried steak would be curling its way out of the kitchen, like the aroma wafts in the Bisto ads, only better. Even now, that smell is what gets me going. It's what makes steak special.

Later, my dad took us on holidays to South Africa, where meat was cheaper and a big steak culture existed. I began to appreciate how sublime a good steak can be: the dark chargrilled surface with its butch, browned flavours giving way to the red velvety centre; the rich, meaty juices providing the perfect sauce for it. More primal than posh – and all the better for it.

HISTORY

That's my steak, Valance. Pick it up.

John Wayne in *The Man Who Shot Liberty Valance*

All domestic cattle breeds descend from a single ancestor, the aurochs, a large long-horned beast that once roamed Europe, south-west Asia and Africa, and can be seen depicted in many cave paintings. Its domestication occurred early: in Turkey remains of domesticated cattle have been found that date from 6500 BC. By 55 BC Romans had recorded the existence of red cattle in south-western England – almost certainly the Red Devon cattle that can still be found in the region and are considered one of the oldest breeds in existence.

Steak itself has a similarly lengthy provenance. The word derives from the Old Norse term *steikjo* – 'to roast on a spit' – a method of cooking that has been around as long as there has been fire to perform it, and that has been a favourite with the English for centuries. The Harleian Manuscripts in the British Library contain a recipe from around 1430 for broiled venison or beefsteaks that wouldn't look particularly out of place on the modern table. By 1748 the Swedish traveller Pehr Kalm could declare: 'Englishmen understand almost better than any other people the art of properly roasting a large cut of meat.' (Though he undercut his praise by pointing out that this was 'because the art of cooking as practised by most Englishmen does not extend much beyond roast beef and plum pudding'!)

The English were noted for their taste for plain food: even in the eighteenth century the preference of most people (even royalty) was for roasted and boiled meat, puddings and pies. Plain food seems to have encouraged plain speaking: our steak cuts are still named after the part of the animal from which they come – fillet, sirloin and rump. France, not surprisingly, has made a more elaborate affair of it, dividing the fillet (a long muscle below the bones of the sirloin) into chateaubriand, tournedos and filet mignon, cutting between the ribs for entrecôte, and removing muscles from the carcass to give other tender cuts.

However, it is in the US that steak cookery has acquired true cult status (in *The Oxford Companion to Food*, Alan Davidson laconically observes that the American tradition of eating large steaks has 'associations of virility'). Basic cuts include filet, club, rib, shell or strip, sirloin, T-bone and tenderloin, but the need for mythology and romance has given rise to a panoply of more exotic names, often for the same cut. Most of us are probably familiar with the porterhouse steak and the carpetbag steak, stuffed with oysters, but there are also the ambassador steak, Kansas City steak and NY strip steak, not to mention the Delmonico and country club steaks, the Flatiron steak, plus of course names associated with styles of cooking: planked and Swiss, steak Sinatra and steak Jack Daniels, among others.

Given this vivid steak lore, it's surprising to discover that beef was a relatively late addition to the American diet. Before the Civil War it rarely appeared on the table. Part of the reason for this was that cattle are not indigenous to the Americas; they were brought to the New World by the Spanish in 1540. Even then, the sheer size of the country and its harsh winters prevented cattle-raising from becoming widespread. The railways made the difference. In the 1860s trains made transport feasible, and within fifteen years refrigerated trucks meant the slaughterhouses of the Midwest could send beef east, where a taste for it was developing.

THE QUEST FOR THE BEST

*Average American's simplest and commonest form of
breakfast consists of coffee and beefsteak.*

Mark Twain, *A Tramp Abroad*

• Up the Empire •

Given its veneration for steak, America seemed the best place to go in search of the perfect one.
I flew to New York.

Although the restaurant scene in New York is one of the most varied, energetic and inventive in the world, and several of its food writers have championed the idea that science plays an important part in cooking, I had never been to the city. So, before we started filming in earnest, I begged the TV crew's indulgence.

I wanted to start my visit with a trip up the Empire State Building.

From the observation platform, the surrounding buildings were all stark light and shadows, reinforcing the impression that I was looking down on an architect's model rather than the real thing. It was in any case a rather unreal experience – so many of the buildings before me had a visual history, and a thousand movie moments crowded inside my head. Above me I could imagine the planes circling an enraged King Kong. To the north-east I could see the silvery geometric patterns of the tip of the Chrysler Building – home to the Kingpin in *Spiderman* cartoons, and highlighted as the pinnacle of architectural perfection in *Hannah and Her Sisters* and *Kramer vs. Kramer*. Further east were the News Building – where the helicopter crashed in *Superman*, leaving Lois Lane dangling in mid-air – and the square bulk of the United Nations, scene of the stabbing in *North by Northwest*. Due north was the green expanse of Central Park, home to hundreds of angsty conversations between New York couples, from Alvy Singer and Annie Hall to Harry and Sally. Downtown there was the impossible thinness of the Flatiron, sharply bisecting Broadway and Fifth like the prow of a ship and, beyond it, the sad absence of the Twin Towers, prey to a destruction that outstripped even the most apocalyptic scenarios thought up by superhero comic-book illustrators.

Even up here you got a sense of the energy and determination in the city, the headstrong craziness, the whole broadway boogie-woogie of it all. And, though I didn't know it at the time, before I left I'd sample some of that: stumbling across one of my best friends and biggest rivals unexpectedly in a restaurant on the Lower East Side, and ending up in a strip joint near the Hudson …

But that lay in the future. Downtown, to the south-east, I could see the castle-like towers and cat's cradle of suspension wires that marked out the Brooklyn Bridge, reminding me that we had an appointment at the most famous steak-house in New York.

Short/ribs (5) $260.65
10/7 - 11/18

• Porterhouse Brown •

Peter Luger at 178 Broadway in Brooklyn is a phenomenon. It has been going since 1887 and Zagat's, the most influential restaurant guide in New York, has voted it the number-one steak-house fifteen years in a row. Framed certificates attesting to this fact line the wall opposite the bar, along with a photo of Johnny Carson on which is inscribed: 'The best meal of my entire life was at Peter Luger's.'

At first glance, the restaurant seems an unlikely place for such adulation. It is brown throughout – the two dining rooms have heavy wooden panelling and timber beams, dark bent-wood chairs, and battered square wooden tables. The décor is German bierkeller: stamped brass plates and ceramic beer mugs adorn the walls. It is resolutely unfashionable and has a macho, no-frills ambience about it that suits the clientele: in one corner several bulky men in silk suits were talking animatedly in Italian, as though auditioning for a mobster movie. The sidewalk outside was littered with fat cigar butts.

It suits what's on the menu, too: porterhouse steak, pure and simple – a gargantuan piece of meat cut from the wing-rib end of the sirloin or the tail end of the foreribs, giving you some of the sirloin and some of the filet. It's named after the drinking houses in which it was first served.

Given the macho decoration, I half expected to be greeted by a red-faced man with weightlifter's forearms and mutton-chop sideburns, but Jody Storch was elegantly dressed in blue suede loafers and a light grey suit, and had a fund of tongue-in-cheek stories. As we walked down-stairs to the meat-drying room, she told me how she got into this business.

'My grandfather, Sol Forsman, loved this place. He worked across the street and ate here with clients twice a day. So when he heard that Peter Luger was selling up, what else could he do? He bought it, even though he was this simple guy with little education and certainly no experience in the restaurant business.'

It has been in the family ever since. Quality control is one key to their success. Jody's grandfather was determined that all the meat should be dealt with personally. During Jody's child-hood, while the other kids were playing, she would be taken by her mother to the meat market, to learn the tricks of the trade.

'You need to look for beef that's a rosy pink colour rather than dark purple. It should feel silky to the touch, not gummy. And there's a part of the meat that's known as "the button" – if you look at a steak, it's that thumb-sized chunk of meat out on its own, surrounded by fat. My mom used to tell me to check that bit. She said that if the fat marbling had reached the button, then you knew it had spread well through the animal. And that fat is important. Even though the recent trend for lean meat has hit us hard, in the world of Peter Luger, fat is good. It gives the meat its flavour, makes it much tastier.'

Now Jody, her mother or one of her aunts goes to the meat market. 'They take down the dirty calendars when we're doing the buying.' Each of them has their own stamp, with which they mark the cuts they've chosen. Jody's is 4F4. 'It makes sure there are no switcheroos. Though I've had a guy actually cut off the slice of

fat with the stamp on and then melt it on to a different flank.' They keep up the rigorous standards of quality control first introduced by Jody's grandfather. 'The US Department of Agriculture grades beef according to quality, from "Prime" and "Choice" at the top end to "Cutter" and "Canner" at the bottom. "Prime" beef accounts for only 2 per cent of the meat available, but I usually still reject about half of that. There's a lot of Prime that should really be called Choice – my grandmother used to call that "Prime Crime". You have to have the best beef. Get second-best and your customers will know. You can't mask low-quality product.'

Jody told me that they generally buy Hereford or Black Angus (the American name for black Aberdeen Angus cattle). At first they graze, but for the last 180 days they're fed mostly on a diet of corn. Although young beef carcasses are more tender, Jody prefers to go for thirty-month-old animals, which give a more complex flavour.

As we talked Jody led me to the basement of Peter Luger, a warren of interconnecting cellars and alcoves, occasionally interrupted by a staircase or trapdoor leading to the street. We threaded our way past steel tables upon which slabs of steak were piled high, ready for trimming, and came to the drying room.

Dry-ageing gives beef a wonderfully chewy, buttery, nutty taste. As the meat is hung, its natural enzymes (proteins that act as catalysts, building, altering or taking apart other protein molecules) begin their work: generating flavours as a by-product of the catalysis; breaking down largely flavourless proteins, fats and sugars into smaller units that do have flavour; and weakening connective tissue to make the meat more tender and succulent. During ageing the temperature, humidity and air movement must be carefully controlled to avoid bacteria, drying out and spoilage.

This time and effort comes at a price. Only prime cuts can be used because they have sufficient marbling to protect the outer layers while the beef ages. And a large percentage of the meat's original weight is lost due to water evaporation and the necessary trimming of the meat's dried surface. (Jody described this as 'a diamond in the rough: get rid of the outside, and inside is this great solitaire'.) As a result, in the last thirty years dry-ageing has fallen out of popularity to the point where almost no one does it. Peter Luger's is one of the few places that do.

The steak-house buys ten tons of meat each week, so I shouldn't have been surprised at the size of the dry-ageing room, but I was. Jody swung back the huge metal door of a room twenty feet long. Inside, on four-tier wheeled steel shelving, cuts lay humped in rows as though on bunk beds in a dormitory.

'The drying time's not set in stone,' Jody explained. 'We adapt to the quality of the cut. Beef with fine-flecked marbling takes less time.'

I asked Jody what she thought of wet-ageing, where the meat is vacuum-sealed and stored in a fridge for three weeks. The enzymes still do their job but the result is a wetter product with a less developed flavour. The process was pioneered in the 1970s and quickly became attractive to restaurants ruled by economics rather than taste: wet-aged meat is ready quicker and retains its water so there's far less wastage; and the vac-pac prevents spoilage and most bacteria, making it easier and cheaper to oversee.

'Meat in a bag sitting in its own juices decomposing? No thanks!' she replied. 'It's soft, sure, but it has little flavour. The only good thing about wet-ageing is it's cheap, and that's not good enough for Peter Luger. We've always done dry-ageing and our customers like it that way.'

They certainly do. The restaurant has a devoted following: it has its own credit card (it accepts no other) and they presented me with one numbered around the 85,000 mark. That's a lot of committed returning customers. Jody pointed out a group on one table that come in every

Monday for steak and a $250 bottle of wine. By resisting change and pursuing an ideal of porter-house perfection, Peter Luger has carved a unique niche for itself. It's a formula for success they're fiercely proud and protective of. When I asked about minimum and maximum drying times for the meat, Jody replied, 'I'll be fired if I tell you that!'

Although they have their secrets, I was allowed into the inner sanctum of the kitchen, where the broilermen can have as many as a hundred steaks on the go at the same time. Depending on the thickness of the steak, they shoved it in the hotter grill for seven or eight minutes, then removed and sliced it, basting the thick slices with melted butter before putting them under the second grill for three or four minutes, after which a pronged plastic model cow was stuck on top (colour-coded according to doneness: blood-red is of course rare) and the grill-hot plate ferried out to the restaurant.

I was surprised that they didn't rest the meat, and I wasn't sure why the slices were cut up for the second grilling. There was no doubt that it was a great piece of theatre – the meat arrived at the table still sizzling. And it *was* a great steak … but was it the best steak of my entire life? I didn't want to go *mano a mano* with Johnny Carson, but I wasn't convinced it was the last word in steak cookery. I figured I'd hold my judgement until I'd finished the trip.

• Getting a Flavour of New York •

Because location work is expensive, TV companies try to cram as much filming as they can into the shortest possible time. Most days we'd be up at first light and spend the next fifteen hours filming or barrelling down a motorway to the next location. So it was ironic that, in the city that never sleeps, I suddenly found I had a day off. (Well, almost – I still had cameras tracking my every move.) It was Sunday: the steak-houses and meat markets were either closed or unavailable. I decided to do some sightseeing, but with a culinary bias. Let's call it a cook's tour of New York.

THE BIG BREAKFAST

The diner is such a classic slice of Americana there's even a film named after it: Barry Levinson's 1982 masterpiece, where the diner is the social hub for a bunch of disaffected young men and women in 1950s Baltimore. In midtown New York there's a diner with brass strips on the booths bearing the names of famous people who have eaten there: you can eat at the favourite table of director Busby Berkeley or actor Ed Harris. A few blocks away is another diner where the waitresses belt out show tunes as you chow down on English muffins or eggs over easy. A diner seemed the only way to start the day. I headed for the Empire Diner on 22nd and Tenth, which is so much a part of New York's visual history that it featured in Woody Allen's parade of landmarks in the opening of *Manhattan*.

The Empire Diner is sleek and beautiful. Built during the same wave of industrial optimism that gave rise to the Empire State Building, it's a symphony of chrome and glossy black. We perched on stools by the counter and waited for the waitress to take our order.

Cash-strapped friends of mine who'd come to New York had made a science out of finding the best breakfast deal: for a few dollars you could get the equivalent of a full English several times over, plus unlimited coffee, and then not need to spend a penny on food for the rest of the day. Eggs any style with bacon/ham/sausage; omelette with any of six cheeses or peppers, salsa, apple, walnut; French fries, home fries, sweet potato fries; pigs in a blanket;

Belgian waffles the size of dinner plates with a jug of maple syrup and whipped butter on the side – the range and variety were spectacular. Sure, this was in part a hangover from a time when food was an indication of wealth, but what struck me was the harvest-festival abundance of it all. In their own way, Americans celebrate food as much as the Italians, turning it into folklore and surrounding it with a sense of drama. And sitting here, in a lovingly constructed imitation of a railcar, I felt the perfect expression of that.

DELI BELLY

In *When Harry Met Sally*, Sally memorably fakes an orgasm in a restaurant to persuade Harry that, when it comes to sex, he doesn't know what he's talking about. The film then cuts to an old lady who has observed all this and says to the waiter, 'I'll have what she's having.'

Well, I was going to have what she was having too: the next stop on the cook's tour had to be Katz's Deli on East Houston Street.

Katz's has been going almost as long as Peter Luger's, and is just as much of a New York institution. Its huge L-shaped room – which resembles a school refectory – is covered with photos of the owner, Fred Austin, standing Zelig-like with a number of famous people: Dan Aykroyd, Elliott Gould, Jerry Lewis, the celebrity lawyer Alan Dershowitz. As in Naples, I found myself face to face with a framed picture of a grinning Bill Clinton, who apparently once held up the traffic on Houston for hours when he spontaneously stopped his motorcade and nipped into Katz's for a bite.

The phrase 'the joint is jumping' could have been invented for this deli: every table was full and many more expectant customers milled around the counter and filled the aisles, so that it was only by shouting out 'Hot soup!' or – waggishly – 'Hot soda!' that the ancient, unimpressed waiters in their sky-blue jackets could carve a way through the crowd and get their trays to the tables. The queue for the till was almost as long as the queue for the counter. I joined the latter and tried to decide what to have.

Chicken noodle soup, chilli dog on a bun, matzo ball or split pea soup, chopped liver sandwich – it was all so evocative, so American. But in the end I chose a true classic: hot pastrami on rye. My server, Eddie Romero, speared a vast steaming slab of pastrami on a carving fork and cut it into thin slices at top speed. 'You want pickle widdat? Some guys say it's the best part of the sandwich.' I did.

It wasn't so much a sandwich as a geological cross-section: a three-inch-high stratum of pastrami between two slices of bread. Even the pickle was the size of a large pebble. And the texture and flavour were genuinely fantastic – without question this was one of the most memorable sandwiches I had ever had. What impressed me most was the sheer quality of the meat, something I encountered time and again in New York. It didn't matter whether the establishment was highbrow or high-turnover: the meat was better than almost anything you get in the UK. And at Katz's it was cut to order; it didn't sit there, drying out under hot lamps. There was an attitude to meat here, a set of values and expectations, that we could really learn from in Britain.

HOT-DOGGIN'

'How can you tell a real New Yorker?' demanded *Gourmet* magazine, before answering its own question: 'By his addiction to Gray's Papaya.' The hot dog is an enduring emblem of New York, sold on street corners from one end of the city to the other. No trip would be complete without consuming at least one, and everybody agreed that Gray's was the place to go.

The biggest bargain in Manhattan! blares a placard in the window, quoting the *New York Times*. Gray's likes placards: its mustard-yellow tiled interior has several to entertain you as you work your way through a foil-wrapped dog. *Nobody but nobody deserves a better frankfurter*, they insist, or, *The best damn frankfurter you ever ate*. Another simply claimed *Snappy Service!*, which tempted me to go to the counter and order a crocodile sandwich, but I played it safe and asked for a hot dog.

Gray's takes the trouble to keep the bun warm and they serve up a good frankfurter, though probably what I liked best was the way they encourage you to have a fruit juice with your dog. It's an odd combination that works – papaya and pineapple really aid digestion. (Both contain protein-digesting enzymes that will help break down food.)[*] It's a neat and thoughtful touch that shows the kind of care, even when it's street food, that often typifies American cooking.

What I also liked was the sheer buzz surrounding the place. Gray's has been going for twenty years (another placard behind the till tells you this and punningly finishes: *Franks for your business*) and there's a constant stream of customers – kids, businessmen, even a guy in cowboy hat, waistcoat and bootlace tie – through its simple stand-up premises. They grab a dog and go outside to eat and watch the Greenwich Village bustle. Food is fun here, a piece of street theatre, and the placards and puns are part of that. It gives American food a vitality and identity that is somehow missing from our native dishes – and they are all the poorer for it.

WD-50

Although it's home to what has become known as 'Restaurant Row', the Lower East Side is still a surprising place to find a Michelin-starred restaurant. But there it is, at 50 Clinton Street (him again!), amid psychedelic supermarkets and boho bars: Wylie Dufresne's WD-50.

Wylie is one of the most creative chefs in the States, combining technical skill, an enthusiasm for science and technology in the kitchen, and a real sense of fun. I'd wanted to eat at his restaurant for a long time, and I found myself trotting ahead of the film crew towards the kitchen, barely able to contain myself. I knew I'd be stimulated and surprised by his dishes.

'Hey, Heston,' he greeted me. 'There's someone you know here.'

'Who?'

'Guess,' he teased, but I could see him looking over my shoulder and spun round to catch sight of Ferrán Adrià, the chef at El Bulli, standing in the kitchen's entrance with a big smile on his face, flanked by another of America's greatest chefs, José Andrés.

 Bromelain is the major protein-digesting enzyme in pineapples; papain is the equivalent in papayas. Both are used as meat tenderisers, and bromelain is so powerful that plantation and cannery workers have to wear rubber gloves to avoid their hands being eaten away. (One hundred years ago, a group of sailors who got shipwrecked on an island off the coast of Indonesia ended up losing their teeth after living on a diet of pineapples for several weeks.)

Scientists are still undecided as to why various fruits (melon, fig and kiwi are other examples) 'eat' meat. One theory is that the enzymes discourage animals from eating too much of the fruit. So take nature's hint and eat in moderation. In any case, bromelain is destroyed by heating, so cooked and canned pineapple is harmless.

In many ways, Ferrán has revolutionised modern gastronomy and opened the eyes of young chefs all over the world to new culinary possibilities. He and his brother, Albert, had become good friends of mine. So it was a huge pleasure to meet him in New York, but how unlikely a scenario! Four chefs, from three different countries, all coming together on the same day at the same time. Once again, New York had performed its movie magic. It was as though we were in the hands of some unseen director, shooting to a script of which we were unaware.

Like starstruck kids, we posed for group photos and had a drink together. I'd have loved to talk longer with Ferran but it was late and I knew Wylie was keen to show me his cooking. I didn't want to miss the moment so I said goodbye and sank into one of WD-50's generous booths.

There's an ocean-liner elegance to the place, with its geometric lines and sumptuous caramel leather banquettes, its orange and blue walls, its artful abstracts. The whole experience is really harmonious and provides the right setting for the menu: modern, minimalist, subtle but not too stuffy, and exuding a certain jazzy excitement. I looked at the menu to see where Wylie's improvisation would take us.

Shrimp cannelloni with chorizo and Thai basil, mussel–olive oil soup, toast ice cream, butternut sorbet – we were treated to lots of marvellous, inventive dishes. At one point we were all given bowls of steaming brown broth accompanied by a small tube marked 'Hair Applicator', the kind of thing you might find in a fancy retro barber's. The soup turned out to be a form of dashi. Squeeze the applicator into it and instant noodles instantly formed. The courses were served up by Dewey, a solidly built man in a denim shirt, with a hangdog expression and a sense of humour so deadpan it was hard to tell whether he was joking or not. Although Dewey's business card drily identifies him as 'chef Wylie's dad', he's a key part of the restaurant's personality, responsible for both the décor and the wine list, which he guided us through with unostentatious expertise.

By the end I had eaten and laughed way too much. It was seriously late and I had to get up early to check out some American pizza joints and see how they compared to Neapolitan pizzerias. I flagged a cab uptown and settled back into my seat. New York cuisine, it seemed to me, was in great shape. From simple steaks to Wylie's innovative creations, I had encountered a spectacular diversity and superb quality. Clearly the New World could hold its own against the Old World, and the future of creative American cuisine looked very good indeed.

For a day off, it had been a long one. In the Paramount Hotel, I plodded to my stark white cube of a room and quickly fell asleep, watched over by Vermeer's *Girl with a Pearl Earring*, a huge reproduction of which served as headboard to my bed.

• Strip Steak •

The next evening, as we drove up Eleventh Avenue, past truck and repair shops and lumber merchants, a vast hoarding caught my eye:

Penthouse Executive Club
New York City's newest and most upscale
Gentlemen's Club
FEATURING PENTHOUSE PETS

'This is the place,' I told the driver, and he pulled up alongside its floodlit façade.

At this point, you might be forgiven for thinking that I'd stepped out of character – that time on the road had finally had an effect, propelling me towards some rock 'n' roll-style bad behaviour. Whatever next? Maybe when I'd finished here I'd go back to the Paramount, trash the room, turf the TV out of the window and put my boot through the canvas of *Girl with a Pearl Earring* …

But you'd be wrong. I was here because the club is home to Robert's Steakhouse, which, according to *Vogue*'s Jeffrey Steingarten, offers 'the best steak dinner in town – the meat could not have been more flavourful, tender or juicy, and grilled to that precise point of perfection between rare and medium-rare – while a beautiful young dancer just eight feet away moved with energy and originality.'

Jeffrey has plenty of energy and originality himself. He is one of the best and most fastidious food writers in the world (he's been known to carry his own salt around with him in a walnut box), so his views are to be taken seriously. He's also one of the funniest, and as such is a bit of a wind-up merchant. Was a strip joint *really* the best place for steak in the city? The only

way to find out was to go there and try it.

Robert's Steakhouse is on the mezzanine level of the Penthouse Executive Club and could easily feature in the pages of a design magazine – it is a very contemporary mix of louche lite and borderline kitsch. An enormous glitterball hangs from the ceiling, which seems to be moulded from undulating, coppery-coloured reflective plastic. The lighting is low, the walls mirrored, the colour scheme predominantly red and purple. Down two sides of the room are formally arranged tables for the diners; on the third side is a scattering of high-backed velvet armchairs for barflies. In the corners are small podia for a couple of go-go girls (the main stage is on the floor below), and on the back wall a series of lightboxes illuminate soft-core erotic images: bronzed bare backs silhouetted on the seashore; close-ups of sculpted curves or parted lips. Here was another example of how blurred the line between reality and cinema is in New York: the place looked exactly how you would expect a set designer to style a strip club for a movie.

Robert's head chef, Adam Perry Lang, brought me back to reality by taking me into the subterranean world of kitchen storage. We clattered downstairs to the basement, past industrial-sized mixers and vast stainless steel Ice-O-Matics, and opened the door of his meat ager.

The room wasn't as generously proportioned as the one at Peter Luger's, but gave the same impression of humped figures in bunks. Meat slabs the size of small coal-sacks lay along the shelves, named and dated, and varying in colour from faded red to almost black. The unusual hues and still-life formality made it look like some kind of weird art installation, but it was the smell that made the biggest impression. The air in the room was suffused with a fantastically rich, savoury odour – nutty and grassy, with a strong blue-cheese note, as though someone had just opened a packet of Roquefort.

'That wonderful smell's a sign of the ageing process,' said Adam. 'Meat that has been in here only a week doesn't have that: like a good wine it takes time to mature and develop its characteristic aroma.' He handed me a week-old cut and he was right: it had none of the richness and complexity of smell I'd just been experiencing. 'The oldest we have here at the moment are twelve weeks, but we can age for up to eighteen; we're not afraid to do that. The results are really interesting. As you can imagine, the process gives meat an extraordinary taste and texture. Ageing is nature's flavour enhancer. That's why we do it.'

'Eighteen weeks – that's over a third of a year. It must cost a lot to keep it that long, and it'll shrink a lot.'

'Oh yeah. You can expect 70 per cent loss at a three- to four-week range.'

'What about feeding? Do you prefer grass or grain?'

'The grass-fed in the US – and I'll go on record with this – doesn't have a good flavour because of the moisture in the grass. That has a huge impact on flavour. We choose animals that have been grain-fed for the first twenty-six months, followed by four months on a 99 per cent protein feed.'

The result is meat with incredible marbling, which is crucial to the taste of that steak on your plate. 'You need that fat,' insisted Adam. 'Dry-ageing gets rid of the meat's juices. Fat provides the moisture instead, keeping the steak juicy and giving it lots of flavour as well.'

I've done a lot of work on meat-ageing, so I was eager to see the effects of Adam's ageing process. We decided to take cuts that had been aged for one, four and ten weeks, cook them and taste the results. Adam hauled out three huge chunks, wrapped them in greaseproof paper, and we set off for the cutting room.

The saw kicked into action. Adam snapped on a pair of surgical gloves and ran meat of

each age through the machine. The differences between one, four and ten weeks' ageing were clear in the thick slices he laid out on a tray. At one week the meat was still livid red: the colour of a knee graze. 'Beautiful,' said Adam. 'Look at the even distribution of fat. There are no chunks of solid white fat. That's a sign of an animal that's been properly fed. If you rush it, and try to force feed the animal just before market, there's no time for the fat to get into the muscles. It simply collects in large clumps, which is no good for your steak: the fat just falls out when you cook it and does nothing to flavour and moisten the meat.'

At four weeks, the meat had developed to a cigar brown. It now looked like a rock, and a pretty scuffed, beach-weathered one at that. 'You notice how it's already got a musky smell,' Adam pointed out. By ten weeks the meat was vermilion rather than red and looked more like biltong, the sun-dried beef you get in South Africa. It's an extraordinary transformation, changing the whole character of the meat.

Back in the kitchen, Adam outlined his cooking technique while he seasoned the steaks and rubbed them with oil. 'I like to char the crust – beyond even caramelisation. It cuts into the dryish flavour and the gaminess of the fat,' he said as he flipped my trio on to the grill. They were a good four inches thick and about a foot long. Each fizzed angrily in the heat.

'To get that charredness they go first on the top grill, which is super-hot – up to 500°C. After ten minutes or so they'll be moved down to the lower grill and a lesser heat for a while.'

'Do you turn them just the once?'

'Nah, I jockey them around a little bit. Look at them now – the meat's already beautifully striped from the grill. They'll be ready soon. You'd better go get your table.'

By now the club was open for the evening. The glitterball revolved, spangling the walls with starlight. On the podia, two girls in white fringed bikinis, knee-high white boots and lots of diamanté were dancing to a heavily discofied version of 'Silly Love Songs'. It was a bizarre experience. Adam and I sat down together to discuss one kind of flesh in the most intimate detail – its firmness and taste; its muscle tone and fat – and all the while another kind of flesh was on intimate display behind our heads, writhing to the music. Out of the corner of my eye I would occasionally catch a glimpse of movement – the white blur of a slow pirouette; the haughty toss of dark hair – as though the twists and turns of our conversation were mirrored by the sinuous moves of the girls on stage.

Quarter-turn, knee bend, hip sway …

'OK,' said Adam, 'we'll start with the unaged beef. You'll notice it's very juicy and clean-tasting. No funk to it.'

'That's amazing. Even without the ageing, this is fantastic steak with a superb roast-beef quality to it but still exceptionally tender. You simply don't get this kind of meat back in Britain.'

Arm stretch, side-step, booty shake …

Adam signalled for the next plate to be brought. 'Here's the four-week-old. It's very mild to me but very good. It sets the standard.'

'Yes. There's a slight livery note. And it's got that Stilton-like quality that I really prize.'

'Particularly on the outside,' Adam agreed.

'Though I wonder whether some people back home would find it just too rich …'

Shoulder twist, back arch, high kick …

'Right, this is the ten-week steak. What do you think, Heston?'

'Technically, this is more tender, though now I think you've got a kind of livery texture as well. All three are wonderful. This is how beef should taste. Even with all my experience, this is

a revelation for me – above all just how good the meat here is even before you work your ageing magic on it.'

    'I know you've done some work on ageing, too. What have you come up with?' Adam wanted to know.

    Hip twist, pelvic grind, pirouette …

    'At the moment, the consensus is that dry-ageing makes no difference to the tenderness of meat after about twenty-one days, but I wonder if it still makes a difference to the flavour. The way I see it, you've got moisture evaporating from the meat as it dries. Eventually this'll mean that there's a disparity between the density of the air and the density of the meat's moisture content. Osmosis will try to balance that disparity, and as it does so, it might transfer some of the flavours on the outside of the meat to the inside.'

    Side shuffle, half-squat, two-step …

that transfer of flavour wouldn't reach the centre of the meat, only the outer parts. Osmotic pressure would probably take it as far as the deco, the strip of meat that lies under the fat of the rib. And it turns out that that's one of the tastiest bits of the meat. I know there has to be a lot more going on than that, and it's a bit of a long shot, but it's an idea I'm pursuing.'

'Oh yeah? Tell me more …'

We talked long into the night, exchanging theories and ideas, going into the kind of detail that it would be impossible to describe here. I recognised a fellow obsessive when I met one. It was as much of a pleasure talking to Adam as it was tasting his food. And his level of devotion had paid off: his steaks were incredible. It was a great starting point for the steak I'd have to prepare back in the research kitchen.

• Against the Grain •

Inspired by my experiences in the States, I decided to track down a British steak that could rival New York's finest, and to use the porterhouse cut in my recipe: the combination of ribeye and filet gave an interesting variation in texture that really appealed to me.

I researched breeds and came up with a shortlist of six: Orkney, Aberdeen Angus, Red Poll, Hereford, South Devon and Longhorn.[*] Then I sought out the best supplier of each. Although American cattle are grain-fed, which leads to superb marbling and gives the meat a particular richness, I mainly opted for grass-fed animals because I was increasingly convinced that grain-fed meat would actually be too rich for British tastes. (I reckoned in any case that I could get still get that wonderful Roquefort character in my steak with a blue-cheese butter, as long as I could get the consistency right, avoiding that gooeyness and mouth-puckering acid note …)

I suffered a setback when the steaks were delivered for tasting, however. Three were porterhouse cuts; the rest had got it wrong. It brought home to me just how unfamiliar a cut the porterhouse is in this country. And if the best butchers in Britain had trouble identifying the cut, it seemed to me vain to try to structure a recipe around it. I portered the porterhouse out of my imagination and decided there and then to opt for a simpler, more familiar cut.

The tasting, then, was no longer like-for-like, but I felt it could still go ahead. Chris and I sniffed around the raw steaks like a couple of stray dogs. The Hereford and Aberdeen Angus (the breeds used by Robert's and Peter Luger) looked and smelled very different from how they had in New York, less characterful somehow, and only the Red Poll gave off an enticing aroma that held some promise.

I cooked and tasted each of them, looking at juiciness, tenderness and flavour. None of the first four – Orkney, Aberdeen Angus, Red Poll and Hereford – had the right balance of the things I was looking for. Even the South Devon, which was the only grain-fed cattle we'd included, lacked the richness and depth of its American counterparts.

So it was a real surprise to find a clear winner right at the end. The Longhorn had it all for me – the nutty, grassy, blue-cheese note I'd hoped to find, plus a marvellous moisture and juiciness alongside a firm but giving texture. The oldest pure breed of cattle in England had come up with the goods.

[*] A different breed from the American (or Texas) Longhorn.

MAKING THE GRADE:

HOW BRITISH BEEF COULD BE BETTER

As I've said before, the single most striking aspect of my trip to America was probably the quality of the meat. Even without ageing, the steak served up by Adam Perry Lang was extraordinary – tender and flavourful to an extent I've rarely found in Britain. And everywhere I went the story was the same. Katz's pastrami and corned beef were equally delicious. It seemed to back up what I'd been told: in terms of eating quality, American and Australian beef is ten to fifteen years ahead of ours.

This shouldn't be the case. Scotch beef is a world-renowned brand name, and we have both abundant supplies of grass and a discerning consumer base. The conditions are perfect, so what's holding us back?

The grading system.

In the UK, carcasses are graded and paid for on yield (the EUROP grid). Only amount counts: there are no controls to ensure that a cut doesn't taste like leather. Nothing is done to ensure the consistency of the product, even though breed alone is no guarantee of quality.

By contrast, both America and Australia have grading systems (the USDA and MSA, respectively) that are consumer-driven: they objectively sort carcasses according to the kind of eating satisfaction they will provide.

In America, the US Department of Agriculture's system has a seventy-year history and its shield of approval is recognised and respected. It assesses the yield grade of a carcass but allies this to a quality grade, which takes into account the marbling in the ribeye and the physiological maturity of the animal – two of the most effective objective indicators of meat quality. Carcasses are sorted into one of eight grades: Prime, Choice, Select, Standard, Commercial, Utility, Cutter and Canner. In the top grade, Prime, carcasses must have at least 8 per cent intramuscular fat (slightly abundant marbling) and levels of rib ossification that correlate to an animal under thirty months old. Only 2–3 per cent of carcasses meet this specification, and almost all are bought by restaurants such as Robert's and Peter Luger. They buy in the knowledge that they're getting meat that will give their customers exactly what they want: tender, tasty beef. Guaranteed.

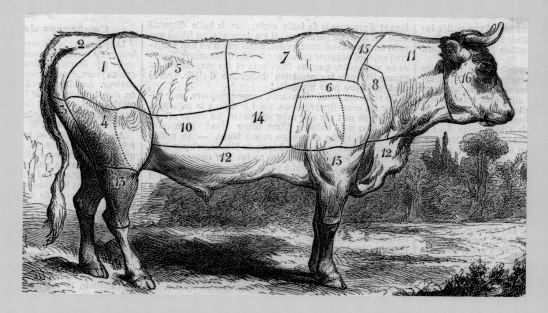

In the US, of course, the consumer is king. Americans spend half their food dollars on eating out, and they consume 90 million beefburgers a day. That huge demand no doubt allows consumers to influence how the system is organised. You might think it's a specific set of circumstances – American can-do attitudes backed up by the USDA's long history – which couldn't be reproduced elsewhere. But the situation in Australia contradicts that view.

Australian beef is now widely considered the best in the world, yet twenty years ago consumption and quality had fallen to an all-time low. Meat Standards Australia (MSA) was set up in 1997 and its system promises 'this beef, cooked as labelled, will eat as described, every time'. To do this, taste panels were set up that tested meat for tenderness, juiciness and flavour, and cross-referenced these against production factors such as storage, maturity and marbling to produce overall scores for each muscle. Cuts are then categorised as: Ungraded, 3-star (Tenderness Guaranteed), 4-star (Premium Tenderness) or 5-star (Supreme Tenderness).

Such careful selection has resulted in world-class beef. In Britain, selection generally seems to stop at the breed, which is not enough to ensure consistency. That's probably why many chains here source their striploins from Australia.

We've done so much in the last decade to overturn Britain's bad food reputation that it's disappointing to find we lag so far behind in terms of meat quality. However, there are signs that the situation is changing. The English Beef & Lamb Executive (EBLEX) has set up a Quality Standard scheme to improve product integrity. The approach differs from the American and Australian systems (for example, its criteria don't include marbling content, which is a central part of USDA and MSA grading), so it remains to be seen whether it will have the same influence on standards. None the less, it's a step in the right direction and is the first scheme in the UK to take eating quality into account.

If you want to know more, consult www.beefyandlamby.co.uk or www.eblex.org.uk.

STEAK

Serves 2–4

Blue-cheese butter captures something of the spectacularly nutty, cheesy character of aged beef. Iceberg lettuce – all too often overlooked in favour of more 'fashionable' salad leaves – provides a crispness that goes perfectly with steak. A marvellous mushroom ketchup adapted from an eighteenth-century recipe boosts all the meaty notes in the recipe, and smoked sea salt accentuates the chargrilled flavours. But, if you've sourced a good breed that has been handled properly, the star of the show will be the meat – blowtorched until browned on the outside, then cooked long and slow for a truly tender inside.

Browning doesn't seal in the juices of the steak (searing at a high heat inevitably leads to the evaporation of water); it kickstarts a complicated process known as the Maillard reactions, which add fantastic depth and complexity to the flavours of meat. To get those flavours without drying out the steak, you need to brown the surface quickly and then take the heat right down.

At the lower temperature muscle proteins contract and squeeze out water far more slowly, which is crucial to keeping the meat moist. But it also needs to be tenderised, which at this temperature is done by enzymes, particularly calpains and cathepsins that weaken or break down collagen and other proteins. Calpains stop working at 40ºC/105ºF, cathepsins at 50ºC/120ºF, but below these cut-off points, the higher the temperature, the faster they work. Heating the meat slowly means these enzymes can perform their magic for several hours before denaturing, effectively ageing the meat during cooking. The result is the tenderest, tastiest meat imaginable.

Special equipment: food processor (optional), oven thermometer, blowtorch (the heavy-duty kind from a DIY store: a *crème brûlée* special won't do the job quickly enough), digital probe

Timing: On the day, a meal for four will take under half an hour, including getting the pan hot enough to fry the steaks. The background prep needs to be staggered over a couple of days: at least 48 hours ahead of time, the cheese and butter should be sliced and left in the fridge to infuse. About 30 hours in advance, the meat has to go in the oven for a long slow cook on its own. The mushrooms for the ketchup have to sit in the fridge for 24 hours, and then cook for about half an hour. But since the ketchup will keep for a month in the fridge, you can easily prepare this ahead of time – it's a versatile condiment that goes with lots of other stuff anyway.

For the blue-cheese-infused butter:
250g unsalted butter
250g Stilton

For the mushroom juice:
1.5kg button mushrooms
75g table salt

For the pickled mushrooms:
200g baby button mushrooms
100g unrefined caster sugar
300ml red wine vinegar

For the mushroom ketchup:
mushroom juices and pickled mushrooms, prepared as above, plus (per 600ml of mushroom juice):
120ml red wine
60ml red wine vinegar
$1/4$ tsp ground mace
$1/2$ tsp whole black peppercorns
2 whole cloves
1 shallot, roughly chopped
cornflour (to thicken)

For the steak:
1 well-aged two-bone forerib of beef (on the bone)
black peppercorns
sea salt
smoked sea salt
groundnut oil

For the salad:
1 iceberg lettuce
16 vine-ripened cherry tomatoes
2 tbsps white wine vinegar
6 tbsps groundnut or light olive oil
table salt and freshly ground black pepper

INFUSING THE BUTTER WITH BLUE CHEESE

1. Slice both the butter and the cheese lengthways into slabs about half a centimetre thick.

2. Tear off a large sheet of parchment paper. Place a slice of butter in the centre and top with a slice of cheese. Continue stacking alternate slices of butter and blue cheese until all have been used. Wrap tightly and place in the fridge for at least 2 days. (The flavour will improve the longer you leave it.)

PREPARING THE MUSHROOM JUICE

1. Wipe the mushrooms clean with damp kitchen paper then chop them finely or blitz briefly in a food processor.

2. Tip the mushrooms into a fine sieve, over a bowl, and stir in the salt. Store in the fridge for 24 hours or until the salt has drawn the juices from the mushrooms.

PICKLING THE MUSHROOMS

1. Wipe the mushrooms clean using damp kitchen paper. Remove the stalks, cut the mushrooms into quarters and place them in a bowl.

2. Tip the sugar and vinegar into a small pan and boil until the sugar has dissolved.

3. Pour the hot pickling liquor over the mushrooms, let it cool, then place in the fridge for 24 hours.

MAKING THE MUSHROOM KETCHUP

1. Weigh the mushroom juice that has collected, and calculate the quantities of wine, vinegar, shallot and spices you will need.

2. Tip the mushroom juice, wine, vinegar, shallot and spices into a pan and bring to the boil. When the liquid has reduced by half, remove it from the heat and strain through a sieve, discarding the spices and shallot.

3. Pour the strained liquid back into the pan. Thicken this by adding cornflour. (To thicken 300ml liquid, mix 20g – approx. 4 tsps – cornflour with 45ml/3 tbsps cold water. Whisk this into the hot liquid. Return the pan to the heat and continue to whisk until the ketchup thickens.) Remove the thickened ketchup base from the heat and set aside.

4. Strain the pickled mushrooms through a sieve, discarding the liquor. To add piquancy to the ketchup, stir pickled mushrooms into the base, to taste.* (Leftover pickled mushrooms are a great accompaniment to cheese and cold meats.) Spoon the ketchup into a clean jar or container, cover and store in the fridge. It will keep for up to 1 month.

COOKING THE STEAK

1. Using an oven thermometer, preheat the oven to 50°C/120°F.

2. Place the forerib in a roasting tin. Brown the outside as quickly as possible using a blowtorch (It needs to be powerful: if it's not hot enough it will start to cook the flesh. If your blowtorch isn't up to the job, use a very hot pan to brown instead.) Once the meat is browned, place it in the oven. Use a digital probe to establish when the internal temperature of the meat has reached 50°C/120°F (this should take 4–8 hours, depending on the animal; don't let it go higher than 50°C/120°F – a few extra degrees will ruin the recipe), then let it cook at this temperature for a minimum of 18 hours. Remove from the oven, cover and leave to rest at room temperature for a minimum of 2 hours – 4 hours would be better – it's important that the meat cools down before being subjected to the fierce heat of the pan.)

3. To prepare the steaks, hold the forerib upright with the rib bones side on. Run a sharp knife between the meat and the bones and free what should be an L-shaped piece of meat. Trim off any overly charcoaled exterior. Slice the meat in half vertically to give 2 steaks, each about 5cm thick.

4. Place a large cast-iron pan over a high heat for at least 10 minutes. Meanwhile, take the blue-cheese-infused butter out of the fridge and remove the slices of cheese. Crush peppercorns in a pestle and mortar, mix in table salt and a little smoked sea salt and put this seasoning mixture on a plate. Dip both sides of the steaks in the seasoning.

5. Add a film of groundnut oil to the pan and, when it's smoking, add the steaks. (The whole surface of each steak needs to be in contact with the pan, otherwise they won't cook properly. If they overlap, fry the steaks one at a time.) Fry for 4 minutes, flipping the steaks every 30 seconds. They should develop a nice 1mm brown crust while the interior should be uniformly pink.

5. Let the steaks rest. Allow the frying pan to cool slightly, then add the flavoured butter and stir to melt it and collect any bits of meat that remain. Pour into a jug.

7. Cut the steaks into diagonal slices. Add a few grindings of black pepper and a sprinkling of sea salt and smoked sea salt, then drizzle over the butter. Serve with a dollop of mushroom ketchup.

 The ketchup becomes saltier with age, but the pickled mushrooms temper it. So if you're preparing it advance, it's best to store the base and the pickled mushrooms seperately, and put them together just before serving.

PREPARING THE SALAD

1. Fill a large bowl with cold water. Remove the outer leaves from the lettuce and discard. Pull off the remaining leaves, cut into bite-sized squares (make sure the knife is sharp, otherwise you will bruise the leaves) and place in the bowl of water for 10–15 minutes so that they will rejuvenate.

2. Drain the lettuce and leave to dry for 5 minutes. Meanwhile, cut the tomatoes into quarters and place in a serving bowl. Add the lettuce and dress the salad – first with the vinegar, then with the oil. (The oil will gradually seep into the leaves' interior, displacing air and collapsing the structure of the leaves, so it's best to dress the salad at the last minute.) Season, toss gently and serve.

SPAGHETTI
BOLOGNESE

Those who forget the pasta are condemned to reheat it.

Anon

INTRODUCTION

Was there ever a dish more misunderstood than spaghetti Bolognese? Even now, many people see it as a quick and easy option that takes care of itself. My wife and I once went to dinner with friends who announced, 'We're having spaghetti Bolognese. It's great! You just put the sauce and the pasta on at the same time, and leave it for a while.' Beneath the slurry of meat and tomato, the spaghetti had swollen to gargantuan proportions and begun to break up.

But this is nothing compared to misguided attempts to cook it in the 1970s, in the hopes of turning out something 'continental'. Like some culinary version of Chinese whispers, the dish's original principles and techniques had become confused, unrecognisable. Some vague folk memory of the *soffritto* (the sautéed mix of onion, parsley and carrots or celery that forms the base of almost every Italian pasta sauce) dictated that carrots were usually present, but usually accompanied by all sorts of surprising vegetable additions. In my mother's version, mushrooms or even peas would surface from the sauce, as though spag bol were interchangeable with shepherd's pie. (And a one-size-fits-all attitude did seem to prevail where Bolognese sauce was concerned. The leftovers might well be topped with potato for a shepherd's pie, or turned into chilli con carne by the addition of a couple of chillies and a tin of kidney beans.)

Of course, it wasn't easy to get the right ingredients in Britain at that time. Most people had to make do with those impractically long blue paper packets of spaghetti and cardboard tubes of foul-smelling pre-grated Parmesan. Fortunately, that has changed, and even the most basic corner shop now offers more than just tinned ravioli and macaroni cheese. But spag bol is still stuck with a reputation as a student stand-by when in fact it should be seen as something far more artful and impressive – the meat simmered for hours to a rich, silky sweetness and melt-in-the-mouth texture, interleaved with strands of pasta for contrast and bite; the wine and tomatoes making it moist, juicy and full-flavoured.

HISTORY

In his book *Everything on the Table*, Colman Andrews complains that food nomenclature has degenerated into 'a hash of misnomer, a stew of garbled terminology'. The focus of his frustration was fettuccine Alfredo but he might just as easily have been talking about spaghetti Bolognese.

In Italy, spaghetti Bolognese doesn't exist. If you see it on a menu there, keep walking and keep your eyes open for a restaurant offering *ragù*, which is the Italian word for a meat-based pasta sauce. It won't necessarily be a *ragù alla Bolognese* either, especially if you're not in Bologna: each region has its own version of the dish – in Abruzzo the meat will be lamb, in Sardinia wild boar. And it won't be served with spaghetti because meat tends to fall off the thin strands and stay on the plate. The bigger surface area of a ribbon pasta such as pappardelle or fettuccine holds the sauce much better. The people of Bologna traditionally use tagliatelle.

• Tagliatelle •

'Tagliatelle is a type of Italian noodle,' the hook-handed man explained …
Lemony Snicket, *The Carnivorous Carnival*

Although 'mullet' can refer to a fish or a fourth-division footballer's haircut, food and hair don't generally share a long-standing, intertwined tradition. None the less, tradition has it that tagliatelle was created in 1487 by a cook called Zafirano, on the occasion of the marriage of Lucrezia d'Este to Annibale Bentivoglio, son of Giovanni II, Lord of Bologna, inspired by the beautiful blonde hair of the bride.

However, just as the myth that Marco Polo discovered pasta in China and brought it back to Italy in 1295 turns out to be untrue (there's a reference to pasta in Genoa as early as 1279), so records suggest that tagliatelle pre-dates Lucrezia's locks. In the 1300s there are illustrations of tagliatelle in a health manual, and in the same century there is a list of local Emilian produce that has an entry for fermentini, which sounds a lot like what we now call tagliatelle.

• *Ragù* •

The word *ragù* comes from the French *ragoût*, meaning stew. It began life as the filling for lasagne and only later became more commonly thought of as a pasta sauce. This was the first of several metamorphoses. The original *ragù* was roughly chopped rather than minced, and contained no tomato. The addition of tomato is, once again, an example of the curious culinary exchange between Italy and America. And even now, the true *ragù alla Bolognese* is sparing with the tomato.

Spag Bol

Spag bol is, of course, about as far from a traditional *ragù alla Bolognese* as you can get. The name alone suggests something unappetising, and in some areas it's even referred to as 'spag bog', which captures exactly the stodgy, blob-like character of the British version. So how did the dish get so misinterpreted and messed about with? One theory is that when the first Neapolitan immigrants reached America they would often serve meat with pasta as a sign of their newfound prosperity. As their standard of living grew, meat became a commonplace part of many dishes (not least because meat in the States was far less expensive than in Italy); it might well have been added to spaghetti (by far the most popular and readily available pasta abroad) with tomatoes, and given the name of the most famous such sauce: Bolognese.

THE QUEST FOR THE BEST

Pasta Testa

It's easy to dismiss pasta as bulk, a carb-fest that simply provides the base to some tasty sauce, when in fact it's an integral part of the dish and one of the key tastes that will determine its character.

In short, pasta should have flavour. I was determined to track down something suitably delicious for my *ragù*. I also needed to refine my ideas about which shape was the best accompaniment for it. I decided to taste as many types as I could in order to find a top-quality producer, and then go to Italy to talk to them.

Martelli, De Cecco, Barilla, Delverde, Rummo, Pasta dello Scugnizzo, La Molisana, Rustichella d'Abruzzo, Agnesi, Cipriani, Sapori di Casa, Ivana Maroni … I contacted a number of shops and websites and came away with pasta from many producers in all shapes and sizes: papardelle, spaghettini, bucatini, bavette, spaghetti, tagliatelle. I'd bought some fresh pasta for comparison, but I was expecting to use dried pasta in the *ragù*: it keeps its *al dente* texture better, giving the kind of body and 'bite' you need in a meat dish. (At the Fat Duck we make fresh pasta for a lobster lasagne dish, but then dry it to capture that bite.)

Back in the lab I put two large saucepans on hobs and added to each 1 litre of boiling water, 10 grams of salt and 100 grams of pasta. 1:10:100 – the golden ratio of pasta cookery, providing enough water to rehydrate the pasta and dilute the starch that escapes from it, and enough salt to reinforce the 'bite'. Ten or so minutes later, the pasta testing began.

I was almost disappointed that the first two pastas out of the pots were so good. It always makes testing more difficult when the benchmark is set early on. Nevertheless, I felt already that these were the ones to beat. I'd had a hunch before we started that an egg pasta might capture what I had in mind, and these had an eggy note that I really liked (though Chris complained that it reminded him more of a Chinese stir-fry, which just goes to show that one man's perfection is another man's poison). The texture, too, was excellent: firm and chewy but not too dense.

None of the next four were likely to knock these off the top spot. The texture was all right, but there was no taste. I could happily have eaten a bowlful of one of the first two on its

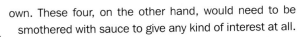

own. These four, on the other hand, would need to be smothered with sauce to give any kind of interest at all.

The next two were from smaller producers La Pasta di Aldo and Rustichella di Abruzzo. They looked right and, more importantly, they *felt* right.

I mean this literally. Some mass-market producers put out a reasonably tasty pasta, especially given their high levels of output, but they none the less have to cut corners – and that shows in the finished product. Using soft flour instead of semi-milled 'semolina'; adding hot water to it rather than cold; quick-drying the strands with hot air – all of these practices bulk profit margins but reduce quality. Originally pasta was dried in the open air and then extruded through bronze dies, which gave it a special texture that held the sauce perfectly. Now major producers tend to use nylon or Teflon dies that create a surface too smooth for sauce. The two pastas I had in front of me had a roughness, a glass-paper texture that suggested care had been taken in their preparation. I expected something special, and I got it: cooking produced pasta with a richness and a big mouthfeel.

Though we sampled many more pastas throughout the afternoon, none approached the quality of these two. La Pasta di Aldo, in particular, captured the opposites that characterise great pasta – good body but with a lightness; a rich flavour that doesn't overpower; substance twinned with a delicacy – and the colour was fantastic: a vivid yolk-yellow that signalled a high egg content and the use of durum wheat semolina, the hard flour that is vital to good pasta. It was clear that my next trip to Italy would have to include a visit to Monte San Giusto to see if Luigi Donnari would let me in on how he created it.

• History and *Osterie* •

Even though spaghetti Bolognese doesn't exist in Italy, and forms of *ragù* can be found throughout the country, Bologna still seemed the best place to start my search for the perfect recipe. Besides, according to Claudia Roden, the people of the region 'eat more, care more and talk more about food than anyone else in Italy'. So much so that Bologna has become known as '*la grassa e la dotta*' (the fat and the learned) and earned a reputation as the food capital of the country. I was going to the source for my sauce.

Appropriately enough, in the land of the *Rinascimento*, my trip took shape around the kind of dualities you might find in Renaissance art: old and new; conservative and modern; private and public; traditional and iconoclastic. The journey proved to be a real inspiration – a glimpse into Italy's preservation of its culinary past, and how that might play a part in its future.

That journey began among the medieval and Renaissance splendours of Bologna's expansive main squares, Piazza Maggiore and Piazza del Nettuno, dominated by the imposing bulk of the Palazzo Re Enzo. The palace is a fantasy of battlements and buttresses, galleries and crenellations, as though it has sprung straight out of a fairy tale (though perhaps one by the Brothers Grimm: it is named after a king who was imprisoned there for the last thirty-five years of his life). Each town I visited in Italy had a *centro storico* of similarly breathtaking beauty: it's easy to believe

this has an effect on the outlook of the inhabitants, and it's easy to see how the gravitational tug of tradition might be strong in a place where you could take your morning coffee – as Bolognese all around me were doing amid the vaulted roofs and stone porticoes that lined the piazzas – surrounded by some of mankind's finest achievements.

The porticoes seemed to invite a slower pace. Here there was none of the hurried chaos of Naples; instead, well-heeled people strolled, hunched into their overcoats. It felt relaxed and ordered, tranquil. I'd swapped dingy, impossibly narrow alleyways shrouded by washing for open piazzas with fountains and wide vistas; I'd forsaken the south for the north – and with the drop in heat a different outlook prevailed: somehow less Mediterranean, more European. It would be interesting to see how this dramatic contrast expressed itself in their cuisine.

• Trad *Ragù* •

The Antica Trattoria della Gigina doesn't nestle among the elegant stone columns of Bologna. It's on a busy intersection on the road to Ferrara and is situated among the usual businesses of suburbs everywhere: sofa showrooms, brightly lit hair salons and anonymous-looking banks. Step inside, however, and you return to old-style grandeur. In the front room there is a framed set of witty and faintly carnal tarot illustrations. Along the pale orange walls are elaborately carved mahogany dressers, upon which I noticed bottles of Ardoino extra virgin olive oil (a good sign: it's used by many of the best chefs in Italy). Beneath extravagant, cascading chandeliers, waiters in ankle-length white aprons and natty grey pinstripe waistcoats hurried between tables. Downstairs, the wine cellar looked more like the library of a well-to-do bibliophile: hundreds of bottles sat in ordered rows in floor-to-ceiling dark wooden glass-fronted cabinets, with placards to indicate their provenance: *Sardegna*, *Campania*, *Sicilia*, *Calabria*. I could see the labels of some of the great wines of Italy: Barbaresco from Gaja, Ornellaia, Sassicaia, among others.

At the entrance to the restaurant was a heavy marble-topped counter with an ancient, fantastically ornate brass cash register. Above this were two photographs of stocky, serious-faced, dark-haired women in striped shirts and white aprons. One was stirring a large saucepan; the other looked impassively at a big plate of pasta. They were Gigina Bargelesi and her daughter-in-law, Arduina, the founding deities of the trattoria over fifty years ago, and it's their recipe for *ragù* that chef Carlo Cortesi cooks to this day.

In the kitchen one section was devoted to pasta-making. On an L-shaped wooden work surface a woman smoothed and stretched pasta dough with a four-foot-long rolling pin before hanging it on the slatted bars of a drying rack. She worked with a speed and confidence born of experience, and soon several large, bright yellow ovals of dough hung above her head, looking more like washing hung out to dry than the basis of many of Carlo's dishes. When I asked him what pasta he'd be serving in the restaurant he told me that the choice was dictated by who was at work in the pasta section. 'Some varieties aren't on the menu today because the woman who makes them isn't here.' This shows how seriously pasta is treated in Italy, and how specialised a job it is. Only an expert will do.

As if to confirm this, there was a little window set into one wall of the kitchen, through which customers in the restaurant could see the pasta-maker, hard at work in her blue overall and white apron (she could have stepped out of one of the photographs behind the cash till), and appraise the sheets of pasta drying above her. It is as though the pasta is so important, the

diners need the reassurance of seeing it with their own eyes: if the pasta is OK, then the rest of the meal will be too.

That Carlo's *ragù* is traditional is beyond doubt: here was a recipe genuinely handed down the generations. Yet his version contained as many surprises as any other I encountered. It brought home to me again that authenticity and perfection are elusive: even a dish of long provenance, with a city of origin attached to its name, tended to evolve into as many variations as there were imaginative chefs to make them. Carlo made a *soffritto*, as I expected, sautéing onion, celery and carrot to flavour the sauce; then he put beef and cured pork in the pan. But, unlike most Italian recipes I had come across, he added no stock or milk, only a little wine and some tomato purée. The *ragù* was allowed to fry for a couple of hours, by which time the oil was flavoured by the *soffritto*. That was the keynote of Carlo's approach: a long, slow shallow fry rather than a liquid simmer. When the *ragù* was ready, he spooned a small amount on to the tagliatelle but left it unmixed. I'd expected to see the two tossed together, so the pasta could absorb some of the sauce's flavour. I asked him why he kept the two separate, and the reply was: 'That's how it's done.'

I guess there are some parts of tradition that remain sacrosanct.

As Carlo brought the *ragù* to the table, I could see that he had regained his customary ebullience. There had been a period during the afternoon when this had deserted him. I could understand this. Cooking and filming make awkward bedfellows: as a chef you want your creations

to be seen at their best. All too often what sits on a plate looking perfect has sagged into some-thing unrecognisable by the time the cameras are trained upon it. The rhythms and energy of the kitchen falter before the demands of the lens – the shots repeated ad infinitum, the slow-paced chess game of manipulating everybody into position. Throughout this series of trips I was amazed at the willingness of people to give up their time for relatively little reward, and at their generosity, even when their patience was stretched to the limit.

'This is going to be my first taste of genuine Italian *ragù*,' I said to camera before digging in. It looked very appetising – the deep yellow of the pasta perfectly offset the rich red of the *ragù* – an almost shameful reminder of how insipid and unappealing the classic Brit Bolognese is, with its wan spaghetti and faded brown mince. The fried approach made for quite a dry sauce, taking it in an unusual direction (I'd have to weigh up whether I preferred a wet or dry sauce, and which one would genuinely tap into most people's notion of the essential character of *ragù*), but the oil gave it a deliciously nutty flavour that I really appreciated.

• Nu *Ragù* •

We arrived at Osteria Francescana in Modena four hours late, but Massimo Bottura was waiting and ready to go.

Massimo is one of the cleverest and most inventive chefs in Italy. One strand of his cooking might be called 'deconstruction': reducing a dish to the most minimal form of its essential elements. (Later, we'd be treated to an extraordinary example of this.) His cuisine is witty, allusive and playful, demonstrating an iconoclasm that is sometimes ill-received: the flipside of Italy's stalwart adherence to tradition in cooking (which gives it strength and character) is a deep-rooted resistance to radical change. There are times when Massimo's restaurant has been almost empty (fortunately his well-deserved two-star status has changed that), and there have been fist fights between customers over some of his creations and their provocativeness. If anyone could offer me some eye-popping ideas about *ragù*, Massimo could.

Bouncing along with a barely restrained energy, he led us away from the restaurant through a courtyard, up wide stone steps and across a gallery to his test kitchen. Here, instead of photographs of venerable female chefs hard at work, the walls were covered in modern art. A vast canvas with trowelled smears of oil paint vied for attention with an equally monumental picture of what looked like an apartment block drawn in a kind of crazed pencil scribble. Beyond the Persian rugs and a 1950s Coca-Cola dispenser was an enigmatic photograph of grassland at night, illuminated only by a faint and slightly sinister blue glow.

Art was obviously a central source of inspiration for Massimo: his conversation was peppered with analogies from artists and their ideas or the movements they established. (A first edition of the futurist Marinetti's *La Cucina Futurista* lay on the table next to the eggs and flour for our session.) Perhaps coming at food from an artistic angle is what fuels his idiosyncratic approach. 'I was born here in Modena. It can be a very blinkered town, thinking only along straight lines,' he said. 'The people are often quite conservative. They just come in and ask for pasta, tortellini. That's why I want to shake it up a little. Do crazy things.' Above Massimo's head an old neon sign flashed out 'Rock 'n' Roll', as though underlining what he was saying.

It seems to me that, in some ways, it's easier to explore culinary innovation in Britain precisely because we have no strong food tradition to enchain us. Massimo agreed: 'In Italy, every-body is a football coach – and a food critic!' At the same time, Massimo knows that to break the

rules you first have to understand them. 'Before his blue period and cubism, Picasso learned how to draw and paint like an angel. To arrive at the point where you can change things, you first have to know the tradition. Otherwise you're just a silly boy,' he said. 'But I can show you this better by cooking than talking. Let's get in the kitchen.'

Like any chef with a restless imagination, Massimo is constantly changing and evolving his dishes. Before showing me the *ragù alla Bolognese* that he serves now, he showed me his version from three years ago – a version so deconstructed that any innocent customer who ordered it expecting a plateful of tagliatelle and meat sauce would have been seriously nonplussed.

He began by rubbing the surface of a frying pan with fat from a pig's cheek, then popped in two small squares of pasta that he'd pressed together. 'This is just a suggestion of pasta. When I was a kid I used to steal pasta from my grandmother and cook it like this. It's a big memory for me.' He took a hen embryo and blanched it in a mixture of chicken and beef broth before sucking out the yolk with a syringe and replacing it with concentrated essence of *ragù*. 'And that's it! Bolognese,' Massimo finished with a flourish as he placed the embryo on the pasta.

It was a brilliant piece of theatre – the finished dish looked like a child's toy or an architectural model: a flat square plane with a sphere on top – but it was more than that; it had all the elements we associate with Bolognese but in a different form. It's the sort of food that makes you think about what you're eating, how it is constructed, how it works, how it might be made different – and that's fascinating. True food for thought. I could see how Massimo's passion for art might have informed this dish, because in some ways you had to decode it like you would a painting, thinking about its possibilities and intentions until you'd 'got' it. Of course, you could enjoy the dish without thinking about it at all – it was unquestionably delicious – but if you did think, it could add an extra dimension to the pleasure of the meal (especially if you were an Italian who had maybe pinched pasta and fried it in this way, making the food a kind of keyhole through which to glimpse old memories; food often has such powers of allusion).

Massimo, however, was already moving on. 'That was my *ragù* in 2002, but now I've gone more back to the roots. Sometimes you have to go one step back to go three forwards.' He was still using the hen embryos, this time to make tagliatelle. 'In the Emilia Romagna region people expect a strong-tasting pasta. It has to be rich and crunchy, so you need these.' As he pierced one the liquid pooled a rich red colour, like cream of tomato soup. I tasted it and the flavour was incredible. Massimo added five embryos and two egg yolks to 500 grams of '00' flour and started to knead 'as my grandmother taught me. Memory is one of the major parts of my cooking. People say I'm an experimentalist when in fact I'm just a romantic. Nostalgia plays a great part in this *ragù*.'

Making pasta requires patience. Massimo worked the dough until smooth then let it sit for forty-five minutes before flattening it out with a long pasta pin. 'The pasta needs to be rough so that it absorbs the flavour. When I'm eating *ragù* I like to feel the rough edges on my tongue. It shows that the food comes from the heart, that love and care have gone into making it,' he said. The pasta was left again, this time to dry, after which he rolled it into a long loose tubular shape, so that it looked like an oversized enchilada, and made thin slices across it, then unfurled these immediately to make sure the cut strips didn't stick. For cooking, it's best if the tagliatelle is a little bit dry. By the time we'd finished preparing the sauce, it would be ready.

'For me,' said Massimo, 'the most important thing in cooking is the idea. Then pick the ingredients and think about the best way to use them as a route to the idea. And then think about the architecture – the colours, the aesthetic. So, the ingredients ...'

He made a *soffritto* with finely chopped celery, onions and garlic. Garlic had turned out to be a source of controversy on this trip. Several chefs, including Carlo at Gigina's, had declared it had no place in a true *ragù*, though they generally couldn't tell me why, or resorted to an adamant, 'That's not how it's done.' For Massimo garlic was 'something nice to smell and taste. So why not?' Why not indeed? Once again I was confronted with how personal the idea of perfection is – and how crazy it was to try to pin it down, even though I was picking up lots of ideas in the process. 'The *soffritto* is the major flavour of the *ragù*,' Massimo continued. He added wine to it for a touch of acidity and then combined it with the meat.

'I always look for the best ingredients. The meat is 36-month-old, free-range, grass-fed Chianina, the white Tuscan cow that you see in a lot of Renaissance paintings. I use the *braghetta*, the "skirt" from the belly, which is very, very tasty. I used to use veal but now I've found the Chianina I've switched.'

The meat was mixed in a bowl then put in a vacuum bag along with bay leaves, marrowbone, tomatoes, pork ribs, beef stock and *fleur de sel* before going in the oven. 'I want the *ragù* to be really strong so I use no milk or cream.'

The choice of a vac bag was encouraging because I'd been contemplating using one myself (it's one of the ways we braise meat at the Hind's Head), but I had wondered whether using shredded rather than minced meat would take a Bolognese too far in the wrong direction, giving it an unfamiliar texture that altered appreciation of it.

The bag went in the oven for a long, slow cook. Fortunately, like a *Blue Peter* presenter, Massimo produced one he'd prepared earlier. He removed the bones and chopped it up before putting it in a pan and adding some cooked tagliatelle. There was a pause while the pasta absorbed the sauce, and then it was ready.

You could see how good the tagliatelle was even before eating it. There was almost no juice left in the pan – it had all been absorbed by the pasta. If you held up a strand the meat clung to it, promising a particularly delicious union of the ingredients. It was a promise that was kept: the meat was an enticing, light brown colour and had a grainy, chunky texture. You could still see the bits of tomato in it – there was a roughness that added interest. There was also a richness, a real mixture of flavours that developed and grew as you chewed. As for the tagliatelle, it was silky smooth from the liquid it had absorbed, and it had a taste that stood up to the meat and genuinely complemented it. Though this was in many ways a more traditional *ragù alla Bolognese* than Massimo's 2002 version, it was equally fine. He really had taken one step back to go three steps forwards.

Massimo's *ragù* had given me a lot to think about, but I was equally taken with his insistence on the role memory and nostalgia played in food, because it reflected something of what I was trying to explore at the Fat Duck, and something that I already felt needed to be incorporated into the eight dishes I was going to cook for this project. All eight tapped into a deep well of nostalgia and memory. Most of them were comfort foods, the food of childhood, and everyone's view of them was overlaid by a sense of personal history – perhaps eating pizza for the first time as a kid on a holiday abroad, or digging into a plate of steaming mash and succulent sausages while winter raged outside the windows. I needed not only to cook these as well as I possibly could, but also to capture that nostalgia, to bring to each dish the kind of trigger that would transport people back to their cherished memories of that food.

How to achieve that? I guess you could say I had a lot on my plate ...

• Tag Team •

Travelling south, towards Rome, the landscape began to change. The director was playing DJ and, as *Funk & Drive* scudded out of the car's speakers, we whizzed down wide plains, past hills crowned with crumbling *palazzi*. Eventually we left the motorway and began to climb the winding road to Monte San Giusto, home to La Pasta di Aldo – the pasta that had outstripped all the others in our testing.

We pulled in by a nondescript block of flats, in front of what looked like a bungalow. This was an area where people worked hard for a living. Small plots of vines and olive trees dotted the valley amid the usual farm paraphernalia: rusting tractors, jagged sheets of corrugated metal. Each property had its guard dog, and barks and birdsong filled the air.

Luigi Donnari was waiting for us on the gravel in front of the bungalow, which turned out to be where he created his extraordinary pasta – a real cottage industry! With his sober shirt and rimless glasses Luigi had the air of a university professor, but his enthusiasm for pasta was anything but academic. Get him talking on his favourite subject and the words tumbled out.

'This is not something I do for money. During the day I work for a shoemaking company so that I have the funds for my passion – the making of pasta. Come and see.'

It's true that Luigi's not in it for the money. He could have expanded his operation but he's determined not to compromise on quality. He has scoured the country for machines that will make perfect pasta. More often than not this means tracking down older models geared towards excellence rather than speed. A bigger output would require more such machinery, and that

requires a long-term commitment on the part of the wholesale buyers of his pasta.

We stepped through the row of plastic strips dangling across the doorway and entered Luigi's 'factory'. It was on a completely different scale from anything else I had encountered during my travels: four small rooms contained the entire process, from mixing to boxing-up. It was the workplace of a real artisan. As sun slanted into the preparation room, picking out the vibrant yellow-orange glow of strips of tagliatelle hung up to dry, Luigi explained his methods.

'You need egg whites to help the texture of the dough, egg yolks for the taste and colour.' As we talked, Luigi's wife Maria poured these into a mixer not much larger than a domestic version. 'For every 100 grams of whole eggs, 25 grams of yolks. Then add semolina – 100 per cent durum wheat semolina, not the "00" flour you often use in Britain. One kilogram for every 500 grams of eggs. The semolina helps to give the pasta its golden colour.'

In the mixer, the churning dough had taken on a wonderful bright yellow hue. And the durum wheat would give the pasta that coarser, almost sandy texture that confers character and helps bind the sauce. I had a hunch that the size of the semolina was important, that if it were too small the starch granules would be damaged and lead to an unresponsive dough. Luigi agreed that the mix of grain was crucial.

'Each type of pasta needs a different mixture of durum wheat to hold its shape. Take the wide flat strips of pappardelle. Their size means they need a longer cooking time, and so they have to be strong. For pappardelle I use only 80 per cent Italian durum wheat. The rest comes from abroad, from wheat with a higher gluten content. I read somewhere that the Chinese call gluten "the muscle of flour". Add it to water and the gluten proteins bond together and make a tensile elastic mass.'

By now the dough was ready. It had started off in the mixer looking like a clump of yellow rags, but by the time it was taken out it looked and felt more like a giant lump of Play-Doh. Maria took a big chunk and cut it into squares using a two-handled blade.

'So far we have been trying to keep the pasta light,' Luigi explained. 'We try to do this until it reaches the plate. It should retain an "emptiness" so that it takes up the sauce.' He held up the dough. It had little holes, dents and craters in it. 'If we press out these holes, the pasta won't have that lightness. As we shape and roll it we have to be extremely careful to keep the air pockets in the dough – just as you would if making puff pastry.'

Maria took a square of dough larger and thicker than a phone directory and fed it repeatedly into the rollers. Each time it emerged longer and more compact than the last. She began to fold the dough between each roll, as though folding a sheet. There was a confident rhythm to her movements – *fold over, feed through, fold over, feed through* – and she narrowed the gap between the rollers as she went, until eventually the dough had transformed from directory to table runner.

Maria folded this in a sort of concertina – over and back on itself, dusting semolina on each time – until she had a fat square once more; she then halved it, flattened out the two pieces and spliced them together. Finally it was judged to be the right thickness, with enough air trapped in the folds. The dough was ready to be cut into its shape.

The cutting machine was automated but not much bigger than the hand-cranked stainless steel models people have at home. The long thin sheet of dough was fed into the top and came out of the bottom in a row of flat strips, like the fringes on a cowboy's jacket. Maria put a thin metal rod under the dangling fringe and lifted it up and over to a wheeled, double-rowed, four-tiered metal rack. The rod fitted niftily into grooves in the rack. When the rack was full Maria

simply trundled it next door and into the drying chamber, heaved shut the doors, flicked a few switches, and a vigorous turbine hum kicked in.

I wanted to know how much importance Luigi attached to the drying process. 'It's a fundamental part,' he replied. 'If the drying goes wrong, you ruin all the care you've put into making the pasta in the first place.'

The drying process removes moisture from the pasta. I wondered how far this governed its ability to suck up a sauce. Luigi explained that, rather than laying the pasta flat to dry – as others do – he hangs it up. 'This is the most important thing. It keeps it porous. My pasta is so porous that, if you leave it near cheese, it'll absorb the smell!'

'Why is hanging the pasta to dry better than laying it flat?'

'The crucial factor is the air that circulates around the pasta, which allows the moisture to be released *gradually*. It must be not too quick, not too slow. It's a delicate balance.'

'I've heard some people say you should start the drying with a high temperature, to fix the colour and the proteins, and then reduce the heat.'

'Hmm, I'm still experimenting.' Luigi peered at me, a little owlishly, through his spectacles. 'But so far for me the long time, low temp works well.'

It worked well for me too. Luigi made the most textured pasta I'd ever felt: it was speckled with semolina and almost like bark to the touch. That and its superb colour made it really enticing, something you'd want to cook and eat as soon as you caught sight of it, which is surely one benchmark of perfect food.

It was already late afternoon. The road – and the director's headsplitting collection of CDs – awaited. But Luigi was determined that we have lunch with him. It was an offer I couldn't refuse. I knew that, this being Italy, the meal would be turned into an event; and, given Luigi's sympathy and flair, he would make this something special. I wasn't wrong. We sat down with all his family – sons and daughters, aunts and grandmother – to a banquet: prosciutto, olives stuffed with meat, refreshing local white wine and a syrupy warmed red, and of course his unbelievable pasta, simply dressed with lemon and parsley – all prepared by a young chef from the nearby catering school who wore a tall white chef's hat. The cuts of meat came from Luigi's own animals; the olive oil was home-made. It was hard to believe that he found the time to do all this, and work for a shoemaker, and produce perhaps the finest pasta in Italy. Perfection requires this kind of dedication and devotion, and Luigi was a real inspiration.

• Dun Roamin •

A couple more appointments and then we pushed south to our final destination. We got hopelessly lost on the Rome ring road and drove up and down the darkened boulevards as *Deep Dish Remix* segued into *Trippin' on Sunshine* by Pizzaman. 'You and me are looking for the key that will open the door to the world of love,' cried the singer.

Frankly, right then, I'd have settled for the key to my hotel room.

Eventually we found our hotel, the Mach I. Like Concorde, it had seen better days. The lobby was shrouded in plastic dust sheets and paint spots covered the carpet. We had a last supper in the kind of restaurant found on airport outskirts everywhere: over-lit and with over-fancy dishes that didn't really work. After the marvellous culinary experiences of the last few days it was a sobering and useful reminder of another world, where food is merely functional and fails to live up to expectations. A reminder that it's worth taking the trouble to get it right.

• A Load of Bologs •

A chef spends a large part of each day in a windowless kitchen surrounded by a bunch of equally enthusiastic obsessives. It's a pressure-cooked environment that's not necessarily the best in which to keep a firm grasp on reality. (Indeed, there were those who'd suggested that, with snail porridge and bacon-and-egg ice cream, I'd already crossed the line.) I'd used what I'd learned in Italy to develop a really vibrant *ragù*, a heady mix of pork skirt, beef and oxtail. I'd tinkered with the taste by adding star anise to accentuate the meat flavours, and with the texture by mincing, hand-chopping and shredding the meat to see what each would bring to the dish. To me, the end results seemed faithful to the Italian tradition while adding a few flavourful twists – but could it still be called spaghetti Bolognese? Was it too far from what the British palate expected? I'd reached a point (let's call it spaghetti junction) where I needed to seek out some honest opinion …

Which is why I found myself standing before Allan and Julia, two customers at the Hind's Head who'd agreed to interrupt their meal and try out three versions of spaghetti Bolognese.

Mary-Ellen had cooked my new recipe with hand-chopped and with shredded meat, and had tossed each with spaghetti. She'd also prepared a magnificently faithful bog-standard spag bol: supermarket minced beef cooked with a shop-bought jar of sauce and plopped bang in the middle of a tangle of spaghetti. For a final touch of 1970s authenticity, we even had a cardboard tub of pre-grated Parmesan. As I placed three small white bowls on the table, I felt a bit like an Oxford Street card-sharp about to perform 'Chase the Ace'. Through his spectacles, Allan blinked at me, suggesting perhaps that he thought so too.

I trotted out my patter: 'Hi. Thanks for participating in this. I'm working on a spaghetti Bolognese recipe for a TV series, and I'm trying to see how far I can push it. I'd like you to taste these three versions and tell me what you think of them …'

Julia eyed up the spag bol. 'It looks like the sort of thing my daughter used to cook at university. Mmm, it's nice though. You try it, Allan.' She passed over the bowl and tried the second. I have to admit my heart was in my mouth at this point. All my research and recipe development would look pretty ridiculous if people's preferred pasta topping came out of a jar. 'Oh, that's even nicer. It's got a slight spicing, almost oriental.'

'That's the star anise.'

Allan, meanwhile, had moved on to the version with shredded meat. 'This is good, too. It's meatier. I like the way the sauce coats the pasta. I don't know whether you could call it spaghetti Bolognese, though. It looks – and feels – different.'

It was beginning to look as though I had some freedom to play around with ingredients as long as the first impression of the dish – both to the eyes and the mouth – retained something of its traditional British character. I left Julia worrying about whether she'd been caught on camera with *ragù* all round her mouth and collected three new bowls of bol from the kitchen, moved on to Gudrun and Hilary's table, and delivered my spiel once more.

The spag bol took Gudrun on a nostalgia trip, just as it had Julia. 'This looks the most like spaghetti Bolognese. It reminds me of home and childhood.' (Since Gudrun was from Austria, this showed that calling spag bol a classic British dish was a misnomer: it had squeezed out its Italian rival on a truly international scale.) 'This is the kind of stuff kids will eat,' she continued. 'Even now we make it like this at home. Whereas this' – she waved a fork at the shredded meat – 'is not what I would normally associate with the dish. That said, it's got a lovely taste. I like the carrots, the big pieces of meat. Yes, it's good.'

Hilary admitted that Gudrun was the foodie of the two, and had railroaded her into taking part. She was formally dressed in a pinstriped brown shirt, and her comments were equally reserved as she tried the hand-chopped version. 'To me this is also quite unconventional. It's nice. The tomatoes are nice.'

'It's a compote,' I offered.

'But …' She was obviously reluctant to be forthright. It's not easy to pass judgement when you've got not just the chef standing next to you but a camera crew inches from your face. It's maybe a little too sweet …'

'That's good to know. That's exactly why I'm doing this – to find out whether it matches expectations. Would all of these be accepted as spaghetti Bolognese, do you think? Or are some too far beyond the boundaries?'

'The shredded meat might be a step too far, yes.' Hilary seemed almost relieved to have admitted it.

So far, both tables had chosen hand-chopped *ragù* over traditional spag bol. (Phew! Both had baulked at shredded meat. Would Chris and Lisa (who were having a drink in the Hind's Head before dining at the Fat Duck in honour of their wedding anniversary) confirm the trend? With practice, my spiel was getting slicker: I'd started to sound like some dodgy fairground barker. 'Spaghetti Bolognese is such a part of our culture,' I announced, 'it's bound up in memories – and there's nothing wrong with that. But how far can I play around with people's expectations?'

Chris and Lisa went at all three bowls with enthusiasm and curiosity. They were determined to identify the key ingredients that gave each version its particular personality, as though this were some kind of forensic test. I found myself morphing from fairground barker to game show host. Perhaps I could call it 'Spot the Bol'.

'There's game of some kind in this hand-chopped version,' Chris declared.

'Good guess. There's oxtail in there giving a gamey note.'

'And something spicy. Aniseed? Fennel?'

'Yes. Good spot.'

'I'm not sure about the fennel,' added Lisa. 'It kind of dominates.'

'And what about the third bowl?' I asked.

'Eating it is like being a schoolboy again,' Chris said. 'The white ring of pasta with the blob of meat at the centre. At home we had that every Monday night, with grated Parmesan that smelled like sweaty feet.'

'You think that's bad,' said Lisa. 'We had spaghetti out of a tin, so anything's going to be better than that! I've probably just undermined any credibility my comments might have, but my favourite's the shredded one, even if it is less traditional than the others.'

'I'm very glad you said that,' I told her. 'What about the pasta to go with it? Does it have to be spaghetti? What about tagliatelle?'

'*Tagliatelle?!*'

I tried several other tables that simply confirmed what I'd learned: I could experiment with the taste of a *ragù* – boosting the flavours; adding new subtleties with unusual ingredients – but the texture had to have a certain homogeneity, a relative smoothness. And, even if it wasn't authentic, even if it held the sauce less well, spaghetti had to be a part of my dish. It might not be an Italian's idea of perfection, but in Britain people's affection for spaghetti with their Bolognese

SPAGHETTI
BOLOGNESE

Serves 4-6

As you might expect from a classic of the Italian kitchen, this involves no special equipment, just a long, slow simmer to allow the flavours to combine. However, I've added in a few things to boost those flavours. Caramelising onions with star anise produces vibrant flavour compounds that really enhance the meaty notes of the sauce, and the oaky quality of the chardonnay complements the sherry vinegar in the tomato compote. Finishing the compote on a high heat captures something of the fried character I enjoyed at Trattoria della Gigina. The use of milk might seem strange but it's a standard part of many Italian *ragù* recipes: as it cooks, the proteins and sugars in milk react to give extra flavour and body.

Timing: Once the meat is browned and the caramelised onions are ready (an hour's work at most) the sauce is virtually left to simmer unattended for 8 hours. Do the prep first thing in the morning and then the day's your own until it's time to serve up dinner (especially if you prepare the tomato compote in advance, though even this involves a fairly simple preparation, followed by a slow, carefree simmer). You can even do all the cooking of the Bolognese in advance, then simply warm it through and add the tarragon bouquet garni on the day.

For the sauce base:

125ml extra virgin olive oil
250g oxtail, boned and minced
250g pork shoulder, cut into 1cm cubes
375ml oaked chardonnay
1 star anise
2 large onions (about 450g), finely sliced*
2 large cloves of garlic
2 large onions (about 450g), finely diced
3 large carrots (about 400g), finely diced
3 celery stalks (about 125g), finely diced
250ml whole milk

For the tomato compote:

1.1kg vine-ripened tomatoes
1 tsp table salt
200ml extra virgin olive oil
3 large cloves of garlic
1 large onion (about 225g), finely diced
1 heaped tsp coriander seeds
1 star anise
3 cloves
4-5 drops Tabasco
4-5 drops Thai fish sauce
2 tsps Worcestershire sauce
1 heaped tbsp tomato ketchup
30ml sherry vinegar

1 bouquet garni (consisting of 7 sprigs of fresh thyme and 1 fresh bay leaf)

For the finished spaghetti Bolognese:

1 batch of tomato compote
100g good quality spaghetti per person
sherry vinegar, to taste
Parmesan cheese (Parmigiano Reggiano)
1 bouquet garni (in a sheet of leek, wrap 6 tarragon leaves, 4 sprigs of parsley and the leaves from the top of a bunch of celery)
unsalted butter
extra virgin olive oil
table salt and freshly ground black pepper

PREPARING THE SAUCE BASE

1. Place a large, heavy-bottomed frying pan over a medium heat for 5 minutes. Crush the star anise and bag it up in a square of muslin. Add this to the pan, along with 25ml oil and the sliced onions. Cook for 20 minutes, or until the onions are soft and caramelised, stirring occasionally. Set aside.

2. Meanwhile, preheat another large, heavy-bottomed frying pan over a low heat for 5 minutes. Mince the garlic. Pour 50ml oil into the pan, then tip in the garlic, onions, carrots and celery and cook this *soffritto* over a medium-low heat for about 20 minutes, or until the raw onion smell has gone. Transfer the *soffritto* to a bowl and wipe clean the pan.

3. Place the pan over a high heat for 10 minutes. Pour in 50ml olive oil and wait until it starts smoking: it must be hot enough so the meat browns rather than stews. Add the cubed pork and the minced oxtail. Stir until browned all over. (To brown properly, all the meat has to

 These onions are to be caramelised: the process can be sped up by removing water from the onions beforehand. Place them in a sieve over a bowl, and toss with a heaped teaspoon of table salt, then leave for 20 minutes.

touch the surface of the pan. If it doesn't, do it in batches.) Tip the browned meat into a sieve over a bowl (to allow the fat to drain off), then transfer the meat to a large pot or casserole. Deglaze the pan by adding a splash of wine, bringing it to the boil, and then scraping the base of the pan to collect all the tasty bits stuck to the bottom. Once the liquid has reduced by half, pour it into the large pot containing the meat.

4. Remove the bag of star anise from the caramelised onions and then tip the onions into the large pot containing the meat. Add the remaining wine and deglaze the frying pan (as in step 3). When the wine has reduced by half, pour it into the large pot. Add the *soffritto* to the pot as well.

5. Place the pot of Bolognese over a very low heat. Pour in the milk and enough water to cover entirely, and simmer very gently without a lid for 6 hours, stirring occasionally. At all times the ingredients should be covered by the liquid, so be prepared to add more water. (Don't worry if the milk becomes slightly granular: it won't affect the end result.)

PREPARING THE TOMATO COMPOTE

1. Bring a large pan of water to the boil. Fill a large bowl with ice-cold water. Remove the cores from the tomatoes with a paring knife. Blanch the tomatoes by dropping them into the boiling water for 10 seconds and then carefully removing them to the bowl of ice-cold water. Take them out of the water immediately and peel off the split skins. (If the tomatoes are not ripe enough, make a cross with a sharp knife in the underside of each, to encourage the skins to come away. They can be left in the hot water for an extra 10 seconds or so, but it's important that they don't overheat and begin to cook.)

2. Cut the tomatoes in half vertically. Scoop out the seeds and the membrane with a tea-spoon, over a chopping board. Roughly chop the seeds and membrane, then tip them into a sieve over a bowl. Sprinkle over the salt and leave for 20 minutes to extract their juice, after which you can discard the seeds and membrane, reserving only the juice.

3. Roughly chop the tomato flesh and set aside.

4. Meanwhile, place a large, heavy-bottomed pan over a low heat. Add 100ml of the olive oil. Mince the garlic, then put it into the pan along with the onion. Cook for 10–15 minutes, until soft but not coloured.

5. Crush the coriander and put it in a muslin bag, along with the star anise and the cloves. Add it to the softened onions and garlic.

6. Take the juice drawn from the tomato seeds and membrane and add it to the onions and garlic along with the tomato flesh.

7. Add the Tabasco, fish sauce, Worcestershire sauce, tomato ketchup and sherry vinegar. Drop in the bouquet garni and cook over a low heat for 2 hours.

8. To add a roasted note to the compote, add the remaining oil and turn up the heat to high. Fry the compote for 15–20 minutes, stirring regularly to make sure it doesn't catch, then pour off any olive oil not absorbed by the compote. Set aside a little to coat the cooked pasta. (The rest can be stored in a jar and makes a great base for a salad dressing. The compote itself will keep in the fridge for a week.)

COOKING THE SPAGHETTI BOLOGNESE

1. Stir the tomato compote (including the bag of spices) into the Bolognese sauce and cook over a very low heat for a final 2 hours, stirring occasionally.

2. Bring a large pot of salted water to the boil for the pasta. For every 100g of pasta, you'll need 1 litre of water and 10g salt. (If you don't have a large enough pan it's essential to use two pans rather than overcrowd one.)

3. Put the spaghetti into the pan, give it a stir, then bring back to the boil and cook until the pasta is just tender but with a bite. Check the cooking time on the packet and use that as a guideline, but taste it every few minutes as this is the only way to judge when the pasta is ready.

4. Before taking the Bolognese sauce off the heat, check the seasoning and then add some sherry vinegar (tasting as you go) to balance the richness of the sauce. Add a generous grating of Parmesan (but not too much, as it can make the sauce overly salty) and remove the sauce from the heat. Take out the original thyme and bay bouquet garni and the bag of spices. Replace these with the parsley and tarragon bouquet garni, stir in 100g unsalted butter and let the sauce stand for 5 minutes.

5. Once the pasta is cooked, drain and rinse it thoroughly. Return to the pot to warm through. (Since the *ragù* is not going to be mixed with the pasta, it needs to be rinsed to prevent it becoming starchy and sticking together.) Add a generous knob of butter (about 50g per 400g of pasta) and coat with olive oil and the reserved oil from the final frying of the compote. To serve, wind portions of pasta around a carving fork and lay them horizontally in wide, shallow bowls. Top with the Bolognese sauce and finish with a grating of Parmesan.

FISH &
CHIPS

... fried fish and chips served by
S. Gamgee. You couldn't say no to that.

J. R. R. Tolkien, *The Lord of the Rings: The Two Towers*

INTRODUCTION

After 'a roast', fish and chips is the nation's most popular dish. And more than any other it shows how subjective perfection is. Fish and chips makes foodies of us all. Everyone has preferences that brook no argument. It *has* to be cod, or haddock, or plaice (unless you're in Scotland or Northern Ireland, in which case it's whiting). Chunky soggy chips the size of your fingers, or thinner, crispier ones? Does it taste better from newspaper, speared on to one of those lovely but impractical little wooden forks? The debate doesn't stop there. Whether it's accompanied by ketchup, mayonnaise, gravy or curry sauce probably depends on where you grew up. For me, fish and chips have to be doused in Sarson's malt vinegar. The smell alone really takes me back.

For some people, fish and chips is a coastal memory – gulls squawking as they hover, hoping to snatch the leftovers; the sea's briny tang mixing with the salt of the chips – but I grew up in London so I've a more urban take. On the way home from work, Dad would pick up fish and chips from Micky's Fish Bar in Norfolk Place. On my birthday one year, I was given the money and allowed to get them myself. I felt like a real adult and can still vividly remember the scene: the brisk fizzing noise of the fryer, the wonky menu board, the yellow glow emanating from the glass-fronted warmers on the counter, the hushed babble from a radio in the background.

I took them home and we ate them from the paper. I always loved digging down to the bottom for the smaller bits that had gradually settled there, the chunky shards of batter that had broken off the fish. That marvellous mix of textures has stayed with me ever since: crisp batter giving way to fat, smooth, moist flakes of fish; the chip's crunchy exterior contrasting with a light fluffy centre.

HISTORY

• Fish •

Confined as the limits of Field Lane are, it has its barber, it coffee-shop, its beer-shop, and its fried fish warehouse.

Charles Dickens, *Oliver Twist*

For a meal that has virtually become Britain's national dish, fish and chips has a surprisingly short history – barely 150 years. And, despite its recent appearance, its birthplace is unidentifiable. Lancashire, London and Dundee have all put forward a claim. The combination of fresh fish and a working class hungry to consume makes it likely that a tradition developed in the northern ports. In the south, the alliance of fish and potato could well have been forged in the crucible of the East End of London, where the close confines of the tenements meant the fried-fish tradition of Jewish immigrants would have come into contact with the Irish immigrants' diet of potato. Food history is rarely neat and tidy: it's entirely possible that both claims are true.

What we do know is that fish and chips came out of a tradition of street food that was already growing in the nineteenth century: the hot-pie shops of Victorian England satisfied an increasing need for fast food on the go, and showed the way forward. Certainly fried fish was a feature of street life by 1837, when Dickens began publishing instalments of *Oliver Twist*, though it was then sold with a hunk of bread or a baked potato. It's not clear when divorce from

the baked spud and the happy marriage of fish and the chipped potato took place, but it's a union that has prospered.

The rapid growth of industrialisation in Britain provided a market for quick and thrifty meals such as fish and chips. It also provided the means to expand that market. Three factors in particular furthered the dish's popularity: manufactured ice meant fishermen could travel further and catch more, preserving what they caught in ice in the hold; steam trawlers also greatly increased the range of fishing opportunity; and railways meant distribution could reach inland areas. Cod became commonplace, and so too did the fish and chip shop.

• Chips with Everything •

The main reason potatoes are up there among the top crops boils down to one thing: chips. The fast-food industry is in many ways the potato's saviour. Although potato consumption in parts of Europe has declined drastically over the last forty years (as we have switched to a more Mediterranean-type diet with an emphasis on pasta and rice, and gained access to more fruit and vegetables), American production has more than doubled, with most of it turned into crisps and frozen chips.

Although the potato has a long history, the story of chips – or fries – is comparatively short and obscure. Both the French and the Belgians say they invented them in the nineteenth century. Fries were certainly popular in both countries by the 1830s and had reached Britain before the turn of the century. Like pizza, the chip's status as an international food is the result of the cultural shake-up of a world war, in this case the first rather than the second. American soldiers stationed in France (or Belgium) developed a taste for chips and took them back to the States on their return. For the chip, it was then a short skip to world domination.

THE QUEST FOR THE BEST

• Underneath the Arches •

The railway arches off Black Prince Road in Lambeth have a Dickensian air about them. Most have been colonised by car-repair and body-part shops, where every surface is coated in a thick patina of sticky, sooty blackness and the tart tang of engine oil hangs heavy in the air. The street seems almost deserted and dog-legs abruptly into a dark tunnel that stretches off under the tracks.

What was I doing, walking around here at six in the morning?

You might think it all seems a bit fishy – and you'd be right. For somewhere hereabouts, unlikely as it may seem amid the grime and garage grease, are the premises of James Knight of Mayfair, fishmongers by appointment to Her Majesty the Queen. I hurried past the gloomy tunnel and came upon a courtyard of scrubbed yellow brickwork, a sharp contrast to the surrounding premises. I could see men and women in heavy blue plastic aprons carrying polystyrene cartons of fish and sacks of crushed ice. Memories of bad puns on the signs of a thousand chippies filled my mind. *This must be the plaice*, I thought.

I was here to buy some fish from David Blagden, a big cheery man with a nice turn of

phrase – just what you'd want in a fishmonger. He has had many years' experience – first in his own shop on Marylebone High Street and now with James Knight – and he seemed like the ideal person to advise me on how to finesse my fish dish. I had a lot of questions that needed answers.

Cod, haddock and plaice have long been the most popular options for a fish and chip supper. But are they the best? I didn't know whether these three had become the chippie's choice because they were – at least at one time – plentiful, local and cheap, or because they were indeed the top fish for the job. Their mild flavour certainly goes well with frying, and cod and haddock also have firm, large-flaked flesh that seems the perfect contrast to a crunchy textured batter, but I still wondered whether other fish might have these qualities and be able to add something extra to the experience. Might not a fish with a pleasant texture and a fuller flavour produce a more complex and delicious dinner? My own candidate for this role was turbot, followed by John Dory and brill. I wanted to see what David thought of these, and whether he could suggest any other interesting alternatives.

He led me through a curtain of heavy plastic strips into a high arched room: the Goods Out Fridge. Large sinks with hose-taps lined the walls, and a worker was bent over each one of these, briskly gutting and cleaning the deliveries. Down the centre ran a long stainless steel table piled high with polystyrene boxes; a slew of monkfish tails filled one of them, another was stamped 'wild pacific halibut'. David hoisted two cartons on to a worktop and took me through their contents.

We'd decided I would take a cod away with me as the benchmark fish. David also suggested haddock, plaice, lemon sole, red mullet and Dover sole. 'I'm a haddock man myself,' he said, 'but all of these might give you the combination of texture and flavour you're looking for.' He explained that, as with meat, the cut you choose is important. 'Plaice, brill, turbot and sole are flat fish, perfectly adapted to feeding on the bottom of the sea. Their belly keeps its creamy white colour but the back gradually darkens so that, from above, predators can't distinguish it from the ocean floor. It's the back that does all the work – fighting the fish's natural buoyancy to keep it on the bottom – and the back that therefore has most of the muscle. For my money, that makes for a fleshier, tastier fillet.'

The question of muscle appeared to be crucial to the flavour, whether you chose a flat fish, a flaky fish like cod or haddock, or a round fish like red mullet or John Dory. David advised me to use male fish, if possible: they develop more muscle while swimming around trying to impress females, and they don't waste energy on reproduction. And what did he think of my turbot-charged option? 'Ah, turbot. Well, if salmon is the king of fish, then turbot is the queen. It's very expensive, which at least means it's unlikely to be in danger of overfishing. And it's likely to stay expensive because they've had little success with farming it.' He showed me an example of farmed turbot. The skin was unpleasantly waxy and the flesh drumskin taut. 'Turbot's undoubtedly tasty, but I wonder whether it'd be too gelatinous when deep-fried. I prefer my fish a little drier.'

David went on to tell me how much geography affects the look and taste of a fish. 'Most of the lemon sole we sell come from Scotland, but I'd say those from the south coast are better. Lemon sole prefer warmer water. And the southern ones look completely different. Instead of a green colour, they're more pale caramel.'

If I wanted the best, he explained, I needed to consider where exactly in the world I got my fish from. 'Brill like the sandy warm waters of the south-west coast. Turbot like a similar environment but the best generally come from the south coast. Plaice also like a sandy situation but prefer the colder water round Denmark. Dover sole like the fast flow and purity of the waters round

Fastnet, while cod and haddock like it cold. Iceland is a good source (and currently sustainable). For red mullet, on the other hand, it's got to be the Gulf Stream.' The list of compass points was becoming bewilderingly diverse. I was glad to hear that John Dory is equally tasty wherever it's fished.

'Thanks,' I said. 'You've given me a lot to think about. I'll have to mullet over.'

David's expression suggested he might have heard that joke before.

In the end, he loaded me up with six fish: cod, plaice, Dover sole, John Dory, turbot and brill. And I drove back to Bray to batter them.

OVERFISHING

Fish are one of our most ancient food sources. Geologists have found huge piles of oyster and mussel shells – evidence of fish feasts – dating back 300,000 years. This lengthy and relentless plundering of the oceans' abundance has come at a cost. Many once-common fish are now rare. Others suffer a kind of boom–bust economy, appearing on market stalls only to vanish suddenly as stocks deplete. The productivity of our seas and rivers is all but exhausted, and if we don't adopt a responsible attitude and change how we eat, we're going to run out of fish. It's as simple as that. The consequences are unthinkable: it would certainly be a disaster for our diet and health, and a catastrophe for the world's ecosystem and biodiversity.

We're not powerless to prevent this. First, check accreditation. The Marine Stewardship Council (www.msc.org) is an independent charity that inspects fisheries and certifies those that comply with sustainable fishing practices. Find out if what you buy is from MSC-approved sources. And if the fish is farmed rather than caught, make sure it's organic and, preferably, Soil Association-accredited. (Fish farms exact their own damage on the environment so it's important that these too are run in a responsible manner.)

Second, find a good local fishmonger and make friends with him. He should be able to tell you which fish to choose and where they come from. His advice will, in any case, be invaluable. You'll be helping the environment, and you'll learn a lot about fish that will help you in the kitchen. It's certainly worth finding out which fish are abundant in British waters and trying them out as an alternative to fish that have been air-freighted thousands of miles.

There are other sources of information on what to fry and what not to buy. The Marine Conservation Society's *Good Fish Guide* is a great starting point (obtainable from their online shop at www.mcsuk.org), as is the website www.fishonline.org, which has a search facility so you can check instantly whether the fish you're after is on the endangered list.

Frying Tonight!

That fish is a riddle!
It's broke in the middle,
A turbot! a fiddle!
It's only a brill!

Thomas Hood

I deep-fried my top six one at a time at 190°C. The perfect batter would have to wait until I'd found the perfect fish (as the size of that fish would determine how long it would take to cook, and I'd have to prepare a batter that suited that timescale), so for the purposes of testing, I used a fairly standard beer and flour mix. I kept the skin on the fillets because I wanted to explore whether, contrary to what *Star Wars* tells us, the dark side really *is* better.

Even while the fillets rested on plain white plates, waiting their turn in the fryer, great variety could be seen, especially in the dark skin – the wide-weaved pattern of the brill's skin resembled a snake's, whereas the turbot was almost crocodile-like: seaweed-green and knobbled. Plaice and Dover sole were finer patterned, as though cross-hatched. I wondered how far this variety would be reflected in the tasting.

To make this test objective, I'd asked Ashley and Chris to try the fish with me. First up was Dover sole. It had a good taste and texture but what was most noticeable was the difference between the light and dark sides of the fish. And it was the latter that was disappointing: it was denser and drier. In plaice, too, this turned out to be the case. (These were the most exaggerated examples. For the rest there seemed to be little difference between light and dark. I made a note to investigate this some time in the future: it would be interesting to discover what it was about Dover sole and plaice that caused the variation.) And the flavour of plaice was altogether too delicate – less tasty than the sole. Neither was the right fish.

John Dory was much more promising – an altogether heftier chunk with a dense texture and a distinctive rich flavour. But, just as in our mammoth sausage-testing we had tasted superb examples that were none the less too far from the ideal of the British banger, so here John Dory was perhaps too dense in texture and thus too far from what we expect to find inside our batter. JD has a lovely flavour, but it felt all wrong in the mouth. Perhaps we really do need a fish with big flakes of flesh.

As if to bear this out, the turbot was terrific. The combination of large flakes, moist, suc-culent flesh and good flavour instantly made it the front-runner. Texture did indeed seem to be the key, for although brill also had a wonderful flavour, its smaller flakes made it less attractive over-all. So we had a clear winner – unless the chippie's choice could come up with something special.

Our final fillet was a block of cod so encrusted in batter it looked like a ship salvaged from the ocean floor. (Frying oil improves with use; coming last, cod probably had the advantage of the best batter.) It had good texture, and a good flavour, though the turbot's was better. The cod was moist, too, but its juices were far thinner than those of the turbot. Despite David Blagden's fears about it being too gelatinous, the gelatin* in the turbot seemed to be the X factor that worked in its favour, thickening up the fish's juices and really adding to its succulence and flavour. This was clearly going to be an important consideration for my recipe: how to make sure the gelatin didn't leak out during cooking. The batter would help lock it in, of course, but perhaps there were other things I could do to reinforce that.

We fried another piece of turbot to make sure we hadn't somehow got a freak fillet. It was still delicious. We had found our fish. Now all we had to do was marry it to a batter worthy of it, and a plateful of lovely crunchy chips.

• Spuds-I-Like 3 •

Recipes are not set in stone. Occasionally, at home, you get lucky and find a recipe that captures exactly what you had in mind. More often than not, though, a good recipe evolves through trial and error, the product of ideas pinched from several sources and combined to achieve the right effect. Unsurprisingly, professional cooking follows the same process. I'd researched hundreds of varieties of potato and forced them through all kinds of experimentation in order to create a great chip. At

Gelatin is a protein. When three of these proteins are twisted into a helix, they form another protein, collagen, which coats bundles of muscle fibres and is a key component of skin and of the sinews that connect muscles to bones.

Meat collagen is tough because it contains a lot of amino acids that bolster its structure, and it gets reinforced with age. Fish collagen contains fewer such amino acids and, because it provides part of the fish's energy store, is continually built up and broken down. Thus even a low temperature quickly denatures the collagen present in fish muscle-tissue, turning it back into strands of juicy gelatin, which contribute to a fish's moistness. That's why fish with little collagen, such as trout or bass, often seem drier when cooked than those with more, such as shark or halibut.

one point I was even pinpricking chips between stages in the frying, as though acupuncturing them into shape (I was trying to get rid of the excess moisture that would make the crust soggy). The result had garnered many column inches in the papers – sometimes satirising the lengthiness of the process, sometimes focusing on the price, but more often declaring how tasty they were. But a good recipe doesn't stand still, either: that's part of the fascination of cooking. I was forever changing the recipe and looking for ways to make it even better. My trip to MBM offered a valuable opportunity to talk about chips and exchange ideas.

It's hard to convey the overwhelming impression that the storage chambers at MBM make when you first encounter them. When I was a kid and heard talk of EU wine lakes and butter mountains, I imagined them literally: a huge pool of red in some spacious part of France perhaps, or a vast peak made up of brick-shaped butter pats. Here, these childhood misunderstandings seemed suddenly to be made real. In the hangar I was confronted with a ten-foot-high surfers' wave of potatoes. I clambered up a metal ladder on to a gantry and saw that it extended back twenty metres or so, like some phenomenal groundswell. Against this strange backdrop, Claire Harrison and I discussed which potato makes the perfect chip.

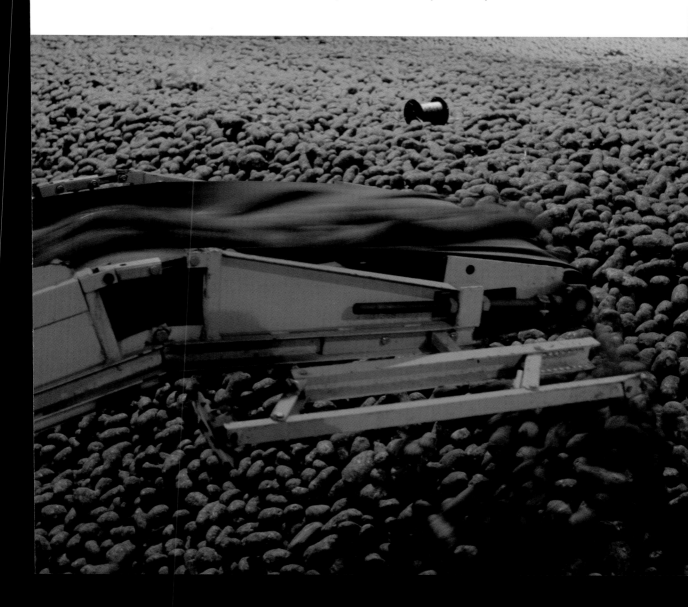

'I'm looking for a potato that, when fried, will be light and fluffy on the inside, with a wonderful glass-like crunch to it. It needs to break up a little on cooking, too, so that those rough edges will absorb some fat.'

'Of course, we all know about Maris Piper,' said Claire, 'but have you tried Lady Rosetta? It's used by a lot of commercial chip companies because it's got the high dry-matter content that's the key to good flavour and texture.'

Already I was getting useful advice. I'd not tried Lady Rosetta before, and dry matter was one area I really wanted to push to the limit – to see whether higher dry matter automatically meant a tastier potato. 'I want to try whatever potato you've got that has the highest dry matter of all.'

'Yes, it'll be fascinating to find out at exactly what point dry matter stops improving a chip. Certainly you'll want to avoid waxy potatoes with low dry matter. They fry too dark and the inside is almost wet. It sticks to your tongue, like eating wallpaper paste … not that I've ever tried it,' Claire added. 'But you also need to consider how well your chipping potatoes are stored. If they're kept badly they'll be ruined, no matter how suitable the dry-matter content. They need to be stored at the same temperature as those for roasting – 7–9°C – and for the same reason: you want to avoid the starch turning to sugar and giving the potato a dark fry-colour.'

'So, in addition to Lady Rosetta, what would make your top three?'

'Daisy will give a crisp outside and a lovely flavour – very different from Maris Piper. And I'd go for Pentland Dell, which is a lovely potato. Are there any others you want to try, Heston?'

Greedily, I seized my chance. 'I'd like some Arran Victory, Bruise and Yukon Gold. I'd like to take a look at another lady – Lady Claire. And I'd also like some Russet Burbank, since that's popular with the American fast-food industry.'

'With the Russet, you can take your pick,' said Claire. 'That's what you're standing on.'

• When the Chips are Down •

Like a gambler finishing a spree at Vegas, I was ready to tally the chips. My haul from MBM looked like this:

	% dry matter
Russet Burbank	22.3
Daisy	21.1
Pentland Dell	21.2
Maris Piper	21.9
Lady Rosetta	23.4
Yukon Gold	20.3
Lady Claire	21.8
Bruise	24.7
Arran Victory	21.8

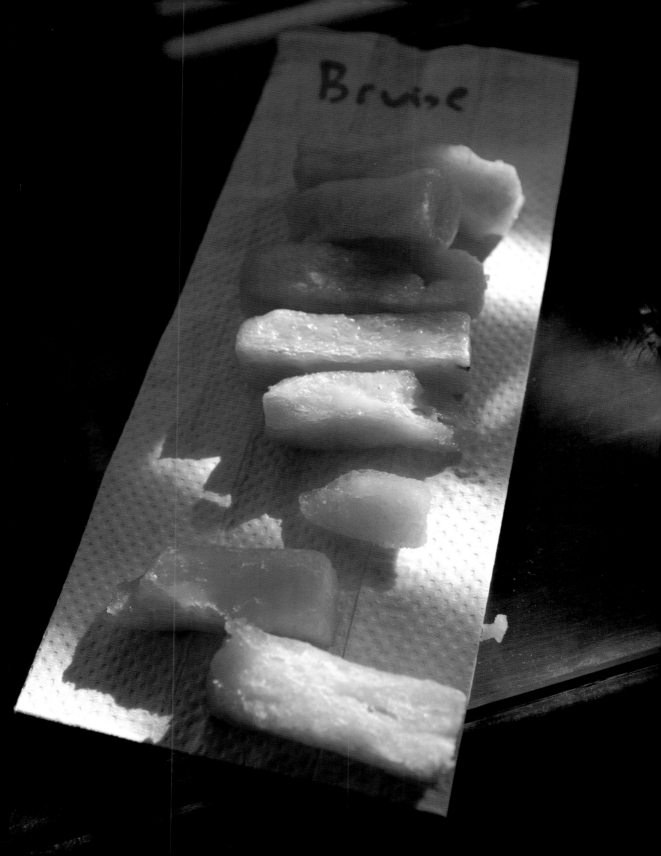

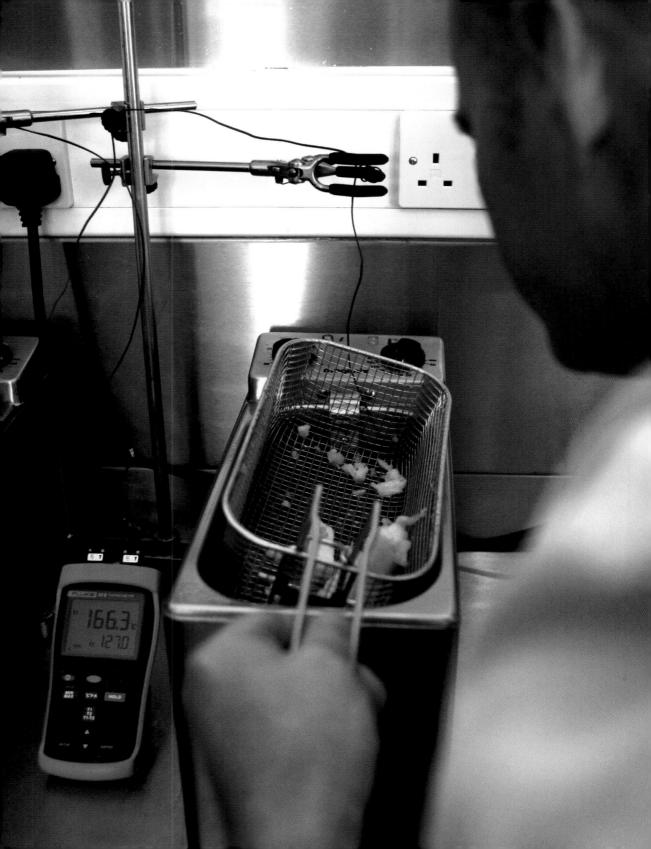

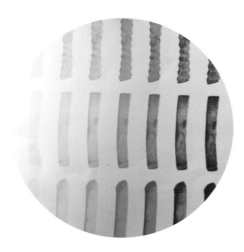

Each was cut into chunky rectangles, like miniature two-by-four planks, and then cooked by the method I'd developed: simmered until barely holding their shape (a tricky business this, requiring constant vigilance as the transition from softened strip to potato soup can be surprisingly swift), then dried and fried twice at different temperatures. This was how chips were prepared at the Hind's Head, using Maris Pipers. It might seem laborious but the end result was delicious. I was very keen to see how my new potatoes would respond to the process.

First out of the pot was Russet Burbank. I'd been curious about this potato for a while because it's so ubiquitous in the States and so difficult to get over here. I had high hopes for it but they didn't pay off: it was tough-crusted, slightly leathery. Not at all what I was after.

Daisy and Pentland Dell also went in the discard pile: they both had a crust and centre that was OK, but that was all you could really say about them.

Maris Piper, of course, turned out to be a much better bet: it had a far more delicate crust, which is one of the key attributes I look for in a chip. This was the one to beat. And neither Lady Rosetta nor Yukon could raise the stakes. With its slightly dry, tough crust, Lady R resembled Russet Burbank. Yukon Gold looked fabulous on the outside – living up to its name by presenting a lovely golden colour – but soon slackened to sogginess.

And Lady Claire didn't fare much better. Dense and chewy on the outside, waxy-looking inside, it too dropped out. Only two potatoes were left to trump Maris Piper. I was gambling on Bruise – with its extra-high dry matter – scoring big-time, but it didn't come up with the goods. The skin was way too tough.

Arran Victory, on the other hand, lived up to its name as much as Yukon Gold had – a clear winner. It had the perfect balance of flavour and texture: the glass-like exterior crunching apart readily, the interior soft and delicately fluffy. It's the contrast of the two that makes a great chip – the mix of two very different textures giving the mouth a sublime surprise – and Arran Victory really delivered that.

It was exciting to find a potato that outplayed Maris Piper. But equally exciting to learn something about the limits of dry matter: all the high-percentage potatoes (Russet Burbank, Lady Rosetta and Bruise) had turned out too tough, and it seemed that as little as 0.5 per cent could make a huge difference to the end result. It was an area that clearly deserved more exploration in the long term.

FISH & CHIPS
A SALT & BATTERY
FISH AND CHIPS
WE HAVE CC CAMERAS AND WE VIDEOTAPE

• Fryer Tuck •

This series had thrown up some odd combinations. I'd had one of the best steaks I'd ever eaten in a strip club, and I was expecting to put French or Italian chocolate on a very German dessert. Now I was visiting a fish and chip shop in New York, of all places.

In part this was – as the mountaineer George Mallory replied when asked why he wanted to climb Mount Everest – because it was there: the TV team and I were in New York researching steak and it seemed too good an opportunity to miss. In part, too, it offered insights into the role memory and nostalgia play in food. The chippie – A Salt and Battery – is part of a little enclave of British shops on the edge of Greenwich Village, a kind of expatriate paradise where you can indulge in a romanticised celebration of British culture. At Tea & Sympathy you can pig out on roast beef and Yorkshire pudding or scones with clotted cream before visiting Carry On Tea & Sympathy to buy Weetabix, tea cosies and, of course, *Carry On* DVDs. As I arrived a stream of kids left the shop clutching brown paper bags filled with butterscotch and sherbet lemons. Parked in front of the store was a pillar-box red Mini Cooper with a Union Jack painted on the roof, as though I'd stumbled on to the set for the next *Austin Powers* movie. (It belonged to Nicky, of course, the owner of all three stores. How else would an expatriate Anglophile get around town?)

A Salt and Battery was almost too perfect: it was as though a magazine stylist had isolated all the elements that give a chippie its character and set about faithfully eproducing them for a shoot. Everything was gratifyingly familiar, everything triggered off fond memories, but you'd never find all of these features in one place in Britain. It was uncanny. The steel and glass partitions where the fish were kept warm were disobligingly high, just as I remembered as a child, when I'd have to stand on tiptoe to see the fabulously crusty, golden brown battered fish. Above these was a row of available drinks: R. White's Lemonade, bitter shandy, Irn-Bru, Newcastle Brown Ale and Dandelion & Burdock. (D&B was proving a disappointment to one American customer, who suggested it was one export we could take back.) In suitably haphazard lettering the menu board offered cod, mushy peas, steak and kidney pie and even deep-fried Mars bars. It was all there, right down to the terrible puns that a good chippie revels in. You could join the Frequent Fryers' Club (ten meals and you got the eleventh free) or show your appreciation for the service in a jar on the counter marked 'Fish 'n' Tips'.

Of course, this could all be a cynical cash-in, a bit of marketing genius to mask an inferior product. After all, the shop has a captive audience of hungry Brits. But I discovered that fryer Matt's attention to detail matched his surroundings. He was as dedicated to his craft as any other artisan I had met in this series, and had encountered difficulties just as great. He showed once again, the lengths you have to go to to achieve perfection.

Matt was tall and skinny, and his head was as close-shaven as mine. I could imagine that New Yorkers had trouble deciphering his northern accent. 'I come from a family of fryers,' he told me. 'My mum and dad have a fish and chip shop in Accrington. But here in America things are different. For a start, potatoes are a problem. I can't get hold of Maris Pipers and have to use Russet Burbanks, which behave differently during cooking. And, unlike Britain, America has only one potato harvest a year, in September. This means that the potatoes I'm cooking the following August are fairly old and tend to scorch because some of the starch has broken down. That said a lot of Americans seem to like their chips really well done – what I'd called burnt. So I guess they've got used to it.'

It was another reminder of how impossible it is to pin down perfection. For me a scorched chip was an inedible one, yet others were clearly devotees. One man's meat really is another man's poison. After all, there are even people who don't like Dandelion & Burdock.

Matt had had problems with oil too. 'I blend my own, using mainly corn oil, but it's taken a long time to get it right. I had to get used to the different starch content in the potatoes here and find a mix that suited it. Plus a lot of our business comes from deliveries so I needed an oil that didn't harden the chips as it cooled.'

Some of Matt's difficulties arose from the fact that no market for fish and chips existed on the east coast: A Salt and Battery was pretty much the first and had to build up its custom. Sourcing the ingredients was a nightmare – probably the hardest part of the whole business. As you might expect, I couldn't easily buy mushy peas or Cumberland sausages. And as for pickled onions … I had to ring up my grandma for a pickling recipe.'

Gradually the determination has paid off. The chippie is *Zagat*-rated and won 'Best Takeout' in the latest AOL CityGuide. 'At first all our customers were expats but now about half our customers are Americans,' Matt told me.

'Don't they expect fries rather than chips with their fish?' I wondered.

He grinned. 'If someone comes in and asks, "Can we get French fries with that?" we tell them, "Here we don't use the F word – only N e C word." '

FISH & CHIPS

Serves 4

No matter how good your fish, it can be ruined by bad batter. Batter has to insulate the fish from the high heat of the fryer, and also turn a crunchy crusty brown in the time it takes for the fish to cook, so for this recipe it was vital to develop a batter that suited the thickness of an average turbot fillet.

A water-based batter takes a long time to go brown because you have to make all the water evaporate before it will cook, and that's a slow process (think how long it takes to boil a pan dry). Vodka, on the other hand, is much more volatile, so it disappears much more quickly. And it has the added benefit of not developing the flour's gluten the way water does, which means you get a crisper crust. The lager and the soda siphon enhance the crispness and crunchiness by introducing lots of bubbles to the batter and giving it a marvellous lightness.

Good chips also depend on the removal of liquid. Allowing the chips to cool right down between each stage of cooking gets rid of much of the moisture that would otherwise escape from the chip as steam during frying, causing a soggy exterior. Instead, you'll have a crisp crust and a fluffy centre – the perfect chip, especially if you use an atomiser to spray it with the juice from a jar of pickled onions. The smell will be a fantastic nostalgia trigger, conjuring up memories of your favourite fish and chip shop and tasty fried suppers.

Special equipment: soda siphon + CO$_2$ charges, digital probe, deep-fat fryer, atomiser (optional)

Timing: Making the batter is easy but it needs to chill for half an hour in the fridge, after which speed is the name of the game in order to keep the bubbles in the batter – a matter of a few minutes' frying. Cooking the chips is a three-stage process; it's not complicated but it takes a little longer because the chips have to cool down before and after the first frying. Preparing the chips to this point and then leaving them overnight in the fridge makes a fish and chip supper a very quick and simple affair.

.For the fish:

200g plain flour
200g white rice flour, plus extra for dusting
1 tsp baking powder
1 tbsp honey
300ml vodka
300ml lager (Kronenbourg 1664 works well)
2-3 litres groundnut oil
4 large turbot fillets, 2–3cm thick (ideally, get 1 whole turbot weighing 2.5kg and either fillet it yourself, or get the fishmonger to do it)
table salt and freshly ground black pepper

For the chips:

1.2kg Arran Victory or Maris Piper potatoes
2-3 litres groundnut oil
table salt and sea salt

To serve:

1 jar of onions pickled in malt or white wine vinegar (whichever is the more evocative)
1 atomiser

PREPARING THE BATTER AND FRYING THE FISH

1. Tip the plain flour, rice flour and baking powder into a bowl. Put the honey and vodka into a jug, stir and then add to the flour to create a batter mix. Open the lager and stir it into the batter until just combined. It doesn't matter if the consistency is a little lumpy. The most important thing is to open the lager just before stirring and transferring to the siphon, to retain as many bubbles as possible.)

2. Transfer the batter to a jug then pour it into a soda siphon. Charge the siphon with three CO$_2$ charges and put it in the fridge for a minimum of 30 minutes to chill.

3. In a large pan or casserole, put enough groundnut oil to cover the fish. Heat it to 220°C/425°F, using a digital probe to check the temperature. (It's best not to use a deep-fat fryer for this because the temperature fluctuates too much, and has trouble reaching 220°C/425°F.)

4. Rinse the turbot fillets and dry them with paper towels. Season well, then dust with rice flour. (This ensures the batter sticks to the fillets.) Shake off any extra flour.

5. Remove the siphon from the fridge. Shake it vigorously, then squirt into a medium-sized bowl enough batter to cover a fillet. (Don't squirt out too much: the batter begins to lose its bubbles as soon as it leaves the siphon.) Dip the fillet into the foamy batter. When it is completely coated, lower the fillet into the hot oil.*

6. As the fish fries, drizzle a little extra batter over it, to give a lovely crusty exterior. When it has turned a light golden brown (which will

 To avoid hot oil splashes as the fillet goes in, hold it by the narrower, tail end and lower it head first into the pan and away from your body, so that the tail is the last part to reach the oil and points towards the outer edge of the pan.

take about 1–2 minutes), turn the fillet over and drizzle more batter on top.

7. Let the fish cook for another minute or so, until it has coloured to a deeper golden brown, then remove it from the oil. Use a digital thermometer to check it is cooked: insert the probe into the thickest part of the fish – once it reads 40°C/105°F the fillet should be set aside so that the residual heat will cook it to a temperature of 45°C/113°F.

8. Repeat the above process with the remaining fillets.

MAKING THE CHIPS

1. Wash and peel the potatoes, then cut them into chips about 1.5cm thick. (Don't worry too much about making them all the same size: the variation will give a greater range of textures.) As soon as the chips are cut, place them in a bowl under cold running water for 2–3 minutes to rinse off some of the starch, then drain.

2. Bring a large pan or casserole of salted water to the boil (10g salt per litre of water), add the chips, bring back to the boil and then simmer until the chips have almost broken up (it's the fissures that form as the potato breaks up that trap the fat, creating a crunchy crust). It is important to make sure the simmer is gentle, so that potatoes don't start to full apart before they have cooked through.

3. Using a slotted spoon, carefully lift the potatoes out of the water and place on a cake rack. Leave to cool and then put in the fridge until cold. (The dry air of the fridge makes a good environment in which to remove excess moisture from the chips via evaporation.)

4. Pour enough groundnut oil to cover the chips in a deep-fat fryer and heat it to

130°C/250°F. Plunge in the chips and allow them to cook until they take on a dry appearance and are slightly coloured.

5. Remove the chips and drain off the excess fat. Place them on a cake rack and allow to cool, then return to the fridge until cold.

6. Reheat the groundnut oil to 190°C/375°F. Plunge in the chips and cook until golden brown. This may take 8–10 minutes.

7. Drain the chips, season well with a mixture of table salt and sea salt, and pile by the fish fillets. Decant the pickling juice from the jar of pickled onions into the atomiser, and squirt it round the room or on the fish and chips.

BLACK FOREST GATEAU

A gin and tonic says a lot about you as a person. It is more than just a drink, it is an attitude of mind. It goes with prawn cocktail, a grilled Dover sole, Melba toast and Black Forest Gateau.

Nico Ladenis, *My Gastronomy*

INTRODUCTION

It should have been fantastic. The basis of Black Forest Gateau is chocolate, cherries and cream – three ingredients that go together so well. It should have been fantastic, but it wasn't. Leaden cream, dry sponge and cheap cooking chocolate conspired to make it cloying and virtually inedible, an utterly ersatz experience. When I was a kid I would try to pick the chocolate off the top, and even that would be disappointing.

I'm not alone in this. I've come across almost nobody who harbours good memories of Black Forest Gateau. So who ordered it and, more to the point, why? Did our parents *really* like it?

Of course, it looked exotic. It offered the promise of luxury and indulgence, which is probably why it became part of a very British idea of the special occasion – an *Abigail's Party* version of posh, with hostess trolleys and Chianti bottles covered in straw, prawn cocktail and gammon and pineapple. 'Blue Nun, sir, or Mateus Rosé? And a sweet sherry for madame?' The Likely Lads would have ordered Black Forest Gateau.

In a way, Black Forest Gateau doesn't belong in this book. It's not a dish the nation has taken to its heart. At least, not any more. It would be a huge challenge, persuading people that it's a perfect dessert – the liquid bitterness of the cherries complementing powerfully dark chocolate; the smooth mousse, rich cream and light sponge giving a lovely variety of textures; the touch of alcohol providing a lively surprise.

But I like a challenge. And besides, I disliked Nico Ladenis's arrogant and sniffy dismissal of Black Forest Gateau as middlebrow, *arriviste*. No food need be beneath contempt: do it right and it becomes something wonderful. At the Fat Duck we serve a reinvention of the sherbet dab that produces exclamations of delight in those who remember it from childhood and, though I say it myself, the flavour is pretty special too.

Food should be fun.

HISTORY

Although the *Schwarzwälderkirschtorte* was created less than a hundred years ago, its history is as impenetrable as parts of the Black Forest. Even the name is open to interpretation: pragmatists say that it's a tribute to the kirsch (cherry distillate) that plays such an important role in the cake's distinctive flavour and is made in some 14,000 distilleries in the region. The more romantically minded suggest that the dark shavings of chocolate on the top remind people of the thickset trees of the forest itself. Those with a historical bent argue that the name is in recognition of its precursor, the *Schwarzwaldtorte*, though this cake is largely Swiss in origin.

The combination of cherries, cream and kirsch was already familiar in the southern part of the Black Forest, though as a dessert rather than a cake. The cherries would be boiled down and then served with cream, sometimes laced with spirits. The addition of chocolate is supposed to have occurred not in the Black Forest but in Bad Godesburg, near Bonn – the work of the pastry chef Josef Keller in his famous Café Agner in 1915. But, like the *Schwarzwaldtorte*, this recipe is more close relative than mother-lode. Keller's confection had only one layer and used *Murbeteig*, a kind of sweet, crumbly pastry, for its base.

In the Black Forest region these stories conflict and coalesce, depending on whom you're talking to. There is also the story – vague enough in its details to feel like yet another myth – of an obscure Dutchman who settled in the forest and developed the cake. The pre-eminence of the Dutch in the cacao trade makes this a possibility, and there is a Dutch cherry cake that has similarities to the *Schwarzwälderkirschtorte*.

Whatever its origins, the first recipe for the cake appeared in 1934 in J. M. Erich Weber's *250 Konditorei – Spezialitäten und wie sie entstehen* ('250 Pastry Shops – their specialities and how they came to be'). From this start, its rise was meteoric. In 1949 Black Forest Gateau was only the thirteenth most popular cake in Germany. Over the next fifty years it beat off the competition to become the best-selling cake in the country, and one of its most famous exports throughout the world.

THE QUEST FOR THE BEST

• Chocs Away •

To research spaghetti Bolognese I had, naturally enough, gone to Bologna. So for Black Forest Gateau I went to ... Pisa.

It was vital that my Black Forest Gateau used the best chocolate possible. (Maybe I simply needed to put to rest all those bad youthful memories, but just for once I wanted to pick chocolate off the top and not be disappointed.) In my development kitchen we had tried out several varieties – Valrhona, Domori, Scharffen Berger, Green & Black's – and one had fitted exactly with my vision of how a Black Forest Gateau ought to be: Chuao by Amedei. It was rich and dark, with a tobacco aroma and a plum or cherry stone note that would complement the dish's other ingredients. Indeed it was so good I was in danger of getting carried away: I almost said on camera that it captured the romance of the Black Forest – and I'd still not been there!

As it turned out, Amedei's chocolate had that effect on most people. At the 2005 World Chocolate Awards in London, it dominated the medals roster, gaining three golds, two silvers and a bronze. I had already made my choice, and was in fact at their factory near Pisa when I heard this news, but it was still gratifying to have my tastebuds vindicated in this instance.

And I was extremely pleased for the founders of Amedei – Alessio and Cecilia Tessieri – because they truly deserved it. They set up the company a mere fifteen years ago with the intention of producing the best chocolate in the world. To do so they worked on a different and, to my mind, fairer approach to the manufacture of their product.

Instead of employing a broker to buy the cocoa and sell it to them (which would keep down Amedei's costs and avoid burdensome commitments to particular plantations), Alessio and Cecilia wanted to set up a relationship with their cocoa farmers and invest in their plantations: a partnership. For the Tessieris this increases quality control and gives them exclusive access to

some of the best beans in the world (for which they pay above the market price). For their farmers it provides a much-needed economic stability. The chocolate market is exceptionally volatile: cocoa trees are highly susceptible to disease and weather damage, and market speculation further exacerbates price fluctuations. If cocoa farmers are to have an existence beyond precarious subsistence, it is absolutely crucial that they have some form of ongoing support from their buyers. Valrhona was the first to eschew wholesalers and foster relationships with the producing countries. So far, however, Amedei is the only company to own its own plantations.*

In the early stages of Amedei's operations, wholesalers had refused to take Alessio's negotiations seriously, and then dismissed them as presumptuous. Valrhona was resistant, too. When Alessio tried to buy some of their chocolate for processing, he was kept waiting at the Lyon offices and eventually turned down because it was considered that the Italian market couldn't appreciate high-quality dark chocolate. Such humiliations only strengthened the Tessieris' resolve to take matters into their own hands and negotiate directly with the Chuao Impresa Campesina, the local farmers' co-operative organisation. It wasn't an easy process: the Venezuelan government was understandably protective of the Chuao plantation, which is considered a national treasure (there are moves by Unesco to make its hacienda a Heritage of Humanity because of its cultural value), but on 3 November 2000 a contract was signed with the Campesina.

Venezuelan cocoa farms seemed a long way away, however, as I drove from Pisa to the small village of La Rotta, amid rolling hills across which cypress trees marched, like straight-backed soldiers: a classic Tuscan scene. The Amedei factory fitted perfectly into this landscape: on its front was a painted mural; against a terracotta-pink background was a riot of deep green foliage and clusters of bright yellow fruits. It took a moment to realise these were not lemons but cocoa pods, a gentle reminder perhaps that, although South America is far away, it's an important part of the Tessieris' venture.

I was met by Cecilia Tessieri (her brother Alessio was in London, receiving their clutch of medals), who managed to look glamorous even in a white lab coat and funny regulation hat. Like many of the experts I'd met on these trips, she was extremely shy, but came alive when the subject turned to her passion for chocolate. Her hands fluttered as she talked, and I'd be gently mocked whenever my questions seemed too obvious to her.

'Three steps are essential to good chocolate: the selection and fermentation of the beans, the roasting, and the recipe,' she told me. 'Only *I* do the roasting,' she added, with that mixture of pride and determination I've often seen in chefs and artisans who want to get to the top.

The Tessieris' 'integralist' philosophy highlights an issue that runs through this book. The best products cost a lot of money. All of Amedei's chocolate is expensive (the Porcelana variety is, in fact, the most expensive in the world). Chefs – including me – will often exhort you to buy the best you can afford, as though our only aim is to empty your pockets. Certainly there's an aesthetic consideration at work here – generally, with a reliable artisan, you get what you pay for – but there's also a moral dimension. A cheap chicken has been treated badly: it's an almost inevitable by-product of cost-cutting. It may be that you're relatively unconcerned by the fate of dumb animals, but it's worth considering where the savings are made on cheap chocolate (or, for that matter, on affordable vegetables and fruit that have been flown halfway round the world). While the multinationals' hold over processing and the supermarkets' control of retail allows them to artificially inflate prices, the cocoa farmer gets only a tiny percentage of this – often as little as 0.5 per cent. (The situation has been described as 'a contest of unequals, with the end buyer and seller barely even aware of each other's existence'.) In a market as unstable as chocolate's, this means a hugely insecure working environment and widespread poverty for the producers. It means farmers' kids working in the plantations rather than going to school, limiting prospects for the next generation. It's better than the fate of battery chickens, but it's still far from equitable or humane.

The fermentation takes place at the plantations. Although it's an essential step in the development of chocolate flavour and a highly unpredictable one, it's often poorly overseen, which is why Cecilia and Alessio were keen to become involved in the plantations they bought from. The cocoa pods are broken open after harvesting and the beans and pulp piled together in wooden tubs covered with banana leaves for several days while microbes work on the pulp. In the beginning, yeasts take precedence, converting sugars to alcohol and altering some of the pulp acids. They are succeeded by lactic-acid bacteria and then acetic-acid bacteria that consume the yeasts' alcohol and convert it to acetic acid.

The acetic acid is important because it eats away at the beans, boring into cells and causing the contents to mix together and react, forming molecules that are much less astringent. This process is complemented by the beans' own digestive enzymes, which break down proteins and sucrose sugar into amino acids and simple sugars – substances that are far more reactive and will play a major part in the development of aromas during the roasting process.

The perforation of the beans also allows a kind of flavour exchange between pulp and bean: flavour molecules from the fermenting pulp travel to the bean, adding sugars, acids, and fruit, flower and wine notes. Thus fermentation turns the sharp, bland beans into something already tastier, and creates some of the chemicals essential to the browning reactions that occur during roasting.

On the plantations, the fermentation process can be scented on the air, as smells of toast, tobacco and spices waft through the village. Once ready, the beans are dried and shipped to Amedei's factory. 'The dried bean has taste, but it's still unbalanced and underdeveloped. It has a distinctly vinegary flavour from the acetic acid. Roasting helps to change that,' explained Cecilia. 'It fixes the flavours that are already there, and develops new ones through the browning of the beans, just as browning sugar gives it that caramelised effect. The process is a delicate one: the right balance of time and temperature is essential to great chocolate. A bad roast will give you bad chocolate, no matter what you do to it afterwards.'

As we talked, Cecilia led me down a white corridor towards the roasting department. A mild chocolate odour, a smell of red berries and leather, hung in the air; and a rhythmic, gloopy ker*plunk* rang out from machines somewhere in the factory. The sound seemed to follow us down each passageway, unearthly and insistent, until eventually I found myself unwittingly trying to keep in step with the tempo. We'd escape each time Cecilia opened the double doors to a different department in the factory. But it would be waiting for us when we re-entered the corridors, and each time it was a little louder.

Cecilia opened a set of double doors now. In front of me was a large spherical hopper. Peering over the rim, I could see thousands of beans crowded together, looking above all like a mulch of wood chips. A turning arm ploughed a furrow through them, keeping the beans moving so that they roasted evenly.

'I taste throughout the roasting, and it is only when I say the beans are right that they are released into the collection bin.'

'What temperature are they roasted at?' I asked tentatively. Most of the places I visited were among the best, if not *the* best, in their field and so had rivals. Often they kept their edge by keeping certain things secret. It was hard to know when I was straying into such territory.

Cecilia's secrets obviously lay elsewhere. 'The temperature varies, depending on the quality of the bean and the region it comes from. It's about 120°C. Try tasting one … It's good, yes?' she said, cocking her head and looking at me, tentative in her turn.

She needn't have worried. I'd chewed roasted cocoa beans before but none of this quality. It was still very unlike chocolate – very acidic and bitter – but it had lots of flavour. Cecilia's vigilance during roasting really paid off. Already you could taste the bean's potential, ready to be brought out further by the next stage in the process.

'We refrigerate the beans, after which they are put through a grinder to crack open and remove the shells, leaving the nib. We also take out the germ – the bean's embryo – which few other manufacturers bother to do because it's difficult and expensive. The law allows for up to 50 per cent of the chocolate to consist of the skins. But we get rid of the lot.'

In the roasted bean, the cocoa butter is locked inside a structure of carbohydrates and protein. Grinding begins the process of breaking down these rigid structures so the cocoa butter can escape. Removing the germ hugely improves the quality of chocolate, but it's an unbelievably labour-intensive process. The fact that Cecilia and Alessio undertook to do it was a sign of their commitment and dedication to the task of producing the perfect chocolate.

Cecilia drew up in front of the grinding machine where flat metal funnels channelled brown powder into large plastic tubs. She stooped and cupped her hands under one brown stream, as though at a fountain. There was a kind of reverence to her actions. She raised both hands and lowered her head to take in the bouquet before holding them out to me.

The smell was incredible. 'It's the aroma of plum ...' she suggested, 'of marmalade ...'

'Yeah, plums,' I agreed, 'but ripe ones, even slightly fermented. And there's something of the plum stone too.' I recognised the aroma: these had to be nibs of Chuao, the chocolate that had captured my imagination in our taste test and brought me to Italy in the first place.

'OK,' said Cecilia, interrupting my reverie, 'now we go to another department where the nibs are turned into cocoa liquor.'

Another white corridor. Ker*plunk*, ker*plunk*, ker*plunk* – the machine noise followed us down it. Another set of double doors.

Inside was a knobbly, bolted-metal column with a cream-coloured conical hopper attached to it. Using a saucepan as a scoop, Cecilia poured nibs in at the top. They ground rapidly, reducing to a fine powder and releasing their stores of cocoa butter. From the bottom of the machine a slow and sludgy flow advanced, like lava. 'That's 100 per cent cocoa liquor,' she told me.

I dipped in a finger. 'That's 100 per cent bitterness.'

'Yes. It's not chocolate,' Cecilia said.

No, it wasn't chocolate. Not yet. But I guess it was close to what the Maya and Aztecs would have drunk. They ground the cocoa beans and added water and flavourings – maize, chilli, pepper – presumably to cut the bitterness. That's the drink Cortés would have come across when he invaded the Yucatán in the early sixteenth century. So far, my tour of the factory had shown me a mechanised version of ancient Central American practices. The rest would show what Europeans did to turn chocolate from bitter drink to addictive bar.

'Next we add sugar and vanilla and mix it well,' explained Cecilia. 'But it's still grainy – you can feel the particles of nib and sugar on your tongue – so it has to be blended and refined, which also helps to release the chocolate aromas. We pass the mixture through big rollers until the particles are microscopic in size. Most producers grind to about 24 microns but we go down to 12. To give you an idea what this means: water is 0 microns, so reducing to 12 gives the chocolate a smoother, more liquid feel in the mouth.'

At the blender a man was scooping the liquor–sugar–vanilla mix out of a plastic vat and pasting it across a metal grid with a hand trowel until it dropped through to the machine's innards. Walking to the other end of the blender, I could see the paste emerging in thick soft twisted braids. It was paler in colour and far less sludgy. Already it looked a lot more like chocolate. (In fact, it looked like Cadbury's Flake.)

It also tasted more like chocolate. 'It's now smooth.'

'Yes,' said Cecilia. 'But it still has some of the acids that developed during fermentation. So the work is not finished yet. It must go to the conching room.'

Conching would heighten and mellow the chocolate's flavour. The machine was invented in 1879 by Rodolphe Lindt, and named after its shell-like shape. Conches roll and smear the mixture while submitting it to a stream of warm air. The friction-heat and air-blast carry away up to 80 per cent of the volatile aromatic compounds developed during processing (including many of the acids and aldehydes that had previously made the chocolate bitter and astringent: acidity declines significantly during conching). At the same time, the friction grinds and separates the solid particles, allowing a proper blending with the cocoa butter; and the heat increases the roasted, caramel and malt aromas we associate with top-quality chocolate.

The conching room at Amedei was the one that most reminded me of Willy Wonka's chocolate factory. Like the pasta-maker Luigi Donnari, Cecilia and Alessio had searched the disused factories of Europe for old machines that would process chocolate in the way they wanted, machines that reacted with the product in a particular fashion and handled things at a slower speed. Their conching machines took seventy-two hours to perform their task (modern large-scale concerns do the same job in eight to thirty-six hours) and had a Dan Dare quality to them. Instead of gleaming stainless steel and sleek, angular simplicity, these machines were oversized and heavily riveted, their cream paintwork scuffed and striated from use. The surreal, sci-fi element was reinforced by the fact that the workers padded around in blue plastic overshoes and white lab coats. Their actions were accompanied by that steady, inexorable ker*plunk*. This was its source. It was the sound of conches slopping chocolate.

In a blocky, rectangular tank, what at first looked like a huge vacuum-cleaner attachment clawed back and forth. As I got closer a better analogy, from a different area of homecare, came to mind: DIY. By now the chocolate had the runny, glossy appearance of paint, and I could see that the clawing arm was in fact a roller, which rubbed and spread the chocolate exactly as you would emulsion in a tray.

Cecilia had a different frame of reference: pampering rather than painting. 'The longitudinal movement gives the chocolate a kind of long massage,' she said.

'The smell is absolutely out of this world. It's like pipe tobacco. Can I taste it?'

Although I'd been to chocolate factories before, it was only here at Amedei that I got the opportunity to try chocolate at each stage in the process, from bean to roast to nib to liquor to blended and refined. It was a real education, and I wanted to see it through to completion. Cecilia dipped a long wooden spoon into the tank and passed it to me, twisting as she did so to prevent it dripping. The only way to avoid a mess was to stand holding the spoon high above my mouth – as though posing for a Soviet propaganda poster – and let the chocolate run off it.

Cecilia glanced quizzically at me. It wasn't clear whether this was because I looked ridiculous or because she was concerned at what I thought of her chocolate. When I chewed and then shook my head, though, she misunderstood and began to look worried.

'No, no,' I assured her, 'I could only shake my head at how good it now is. I love the tobacco note on it. It's deep, rich, complex. Does it stay like this when it's cooled down and turned

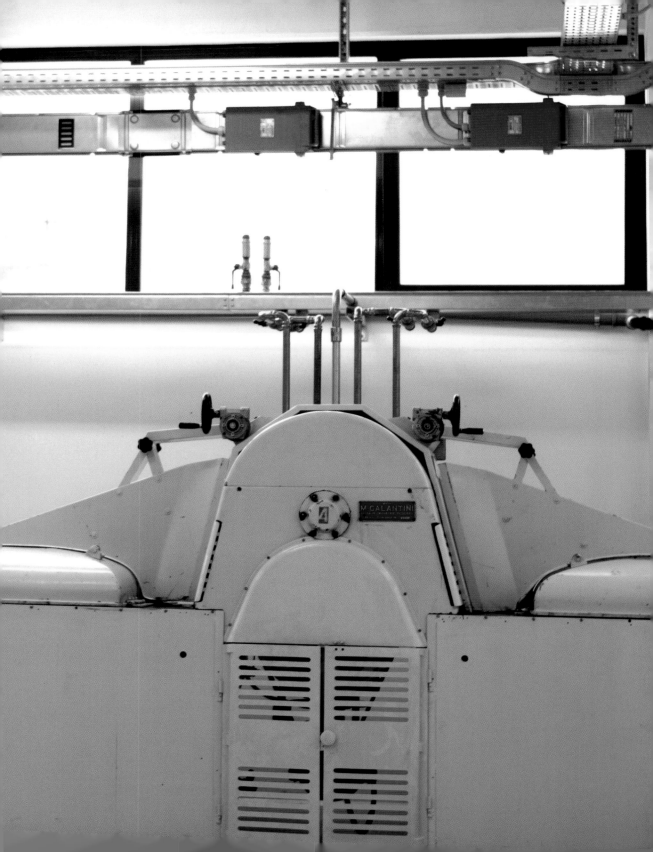

into a bar? Does it retain this complex mix of flavours?'

'Yes, of course. If you liquefied one of our chocolate bars, it would be just like this.'

The final part of the process is all about controlling that kind of liquefaction. The chocolate has to undergo the tricky process of 'tempering' or 'pre-crystallisation': cooling and rewarming to particular temperatures until the cocoa-butter crystals form in a type that stays solid at room temperature – that really does melt in your mouth, not your hand.[*] After which it's ready for wrapping, boxing, shipping and selling. Cecilia took me to taste the finished products and see which best suited Black Forest Gateau.

In the last room on our tour, the finishing touches were being added to various chocolates. A woman placed chocolate balls called *deliziosi* on a conveyor belt that ferried them through a curtain of dripping chocolate, after which another woman hand-piped a zigzag of fine chocolate lines on top, like a miniature Jackson Pollock. It was highly manual labour that resulted in each chocolate being different. Here was food that came from the heart, that had been made with love and care, like the rough-edged pasta in Massimo Bottura's *ragù*. This ethos was evident throughout the factory: everyone I met took pride in their work – they were enthusiastic to show me the machines and how the chocolate tasted.

Cecilia placed on the work surface four slabs of chocolate wrapped in waxy black paper: two versions of Toscano Black, one containing 63 per cent cocoa, the other 70; the renowned Chuao (another 70 percenter); and Number 9, a blend from nine plantations with 75 per cent cocoa, the highest Amedei has ever marketed. She unwrapped them and effortfully cut off brittle chunks with a knife. 'You want to taste?'

I did, and it was an extraordinary quartet: the Number 9 smelled of molasses and had earthy, coffee flavours; the Toscano Black 70 was equally uncompromising, with an almost woody scent and cherry and almond notes in it. I recognised Chuao's red-fruit aromas and creamy smoothness, and appreciated its long finish: the flavours really stayed and developed in the mouth. The Toscano Black 63 was a milder experience but no less pleasurable for that. It was almost fragrant, with notes of lemon and dried fruit, a touch of toffee. I felt as though I were at a wine tasting (and I was beginning to sound like that, too): all four had a flavour complexity that really stimulated the tastebuds. I could see virtues in each one that would add something special to a Black Forest Gateau. Was that what made it difficult to choose between them? Or was it the fact that it's not often you go into a sweetshop to be told, 'Have as much as you like.'

I took the lot.

 Untempered chocolate will melt at 18°C, a low room temperature. Pick it up in your hand and within a few seconds you'll have sticky, chocolatey fingers. What's melting are crystals of cocoa butter.

Fortunately for chefs and chocoholics, cocoa butter can form into six types of crystal, all of which have a different melting temperature, and a different hardness. One of these types – known as Beta 2 or Form V – has the right combination for chocolate: strong yet breakable, with a high melting point (32–34°C). Tempering makes the cocoa butter form into stable Form V crystals rather than other unstable types.

It's a process in three stages. First, the chocolate is heated to 50°C (if it's dark chocolate; milk and white chocolate have slightly different temperature ranges) to melt all the cocoa-butter crystals.

Second, it's cooled to 27°C, a temperature low enough to allow Form V crystals to form quickly, but high enough to prevent most of the other crystal types from forming (because their melting point is 16–26°C). At this stage the chocolate is stirred to break up and increase the number of crystals, which ensures that the final product is smooth and glossy rather than gritty. But you still need careful control over crystal formation: too many of even the right crystals will result in too solid a matrix, so the third stage is a reheating, to 31°C, which slows down the formation of Form V crystals while at the same time getting rid of any unstable crystals that have developed during cooling, leaving the stable crystals to grow into a network of the right density and hardness.

● Gateau Life ●

So I had four types of chocolate to test. Now it was time to discover how a *Torte* oughta taste. Time to visit the Black Forest.

Like many spa towns, Baden-Baden is a magnet for retirees. It is reputed to have the country's highest concentration of millionaires. Drive through the outskirts and the steeply winding streets are lined with vast mansions, each with its complement of marble statues and security cameras. The town centre is full of fur shops and classy art galleries, and elderly couples walk at the slow pace of people with time – and money – on their hands. Forget the ladies who lunch, here are the ladies (and gentlemen) who *indulge*.

What better place to have a *Konditorei*, that excellent German combination of cake shop and café? The Café König opened in Baden-Baden some 250 years ago and is still going strong. As I stood beneath its grey and pink striped awning, gazing in through the window, I felt like a small boy with his pocket money hotly clasped in his hand, trying in vain to decide what to choose. Laid out in inviting rows were pastries, petits fours and cellophane-wrapped chocolate geese and hedgehogs with orange bows. I could have *Kirschtorte*, *Zuger Kirschtorte*, *Pralinentorte*, *Baumkuchentorte*, *Sacher Torte*, *Malakoff Torte* or *Sonnentorte*. If any place was going to come up with a worthwhile *Schwarzwälderkirschtorte*, surely this was it.

Although it was a mild autumn with a weak sun filtering down, it was still too cold to sit outdoors for long. I walked past the small courtyard with its white marble-topped tables and curlicued chairs and took a seat inside. The café had a genteel, mock-Regency feel to it. Cream and white colours predominated, with decorative plates and paintings of flowers in oils or pastels on the walls. A couple of aspidistra stood in pots, and there was the faintest undercurrent of piped classical music. Well-groomed people sat at small round tables on cane-backed chairs. Opposite me were two silver-haired gentlemen in tweed jackets with silk handkerchiefs deftly tucked into their top pockets. One even wore a cravat. In the corner a single woman with an immaculate chignon earnestly studied the newspaper through a magnifying glass. I gave my order and pushed a silver sugar pot the size of a sporting trophy to one side, in anticipation of the delicacy about to come my way.

In truth, I was slightly nervous about what I was going to eat. What if it was as disappointing as I remembered? What if the idea of a good Black Forest Gateau turned out to be an illusion, a vain fancy that had never really existed, turning my journey into a fool's errand? As it turned out, I needn't have worried. What arrived at my table bore little resemblance to the ersatz versions of my youth.

The König's gateau was a tall sharp wedge crowned with chocolate flakes and a rounded hillock of cream topped with a cherry half. Beneath this at least six layers of light and dark alternated. It wasn't a cake so much as an architectural creation, inviting me to explore its construction, to taste each part separately. The cream was rich, the mousse powerful but delicate; the kirsch had the sweet sharpness of a well-balanced spirit rather than the mule kick of a cheap one. The frozen cherries had an abundance of malic acid (an acid found in many fruits, especially apples: think of biting into a Granny Smith) which provided a perfect counterbalance to the fat of the cream. The chocolate had a cherry note that went well with the other flavours. All of it rested on a classic biscuit base.

I was surprised and pleased by what I'd found. Although the true *Schwarzwälder-kirschtorte* was very different from the Great British gateau, I could see how one had gradually been transformed (and traduced) into the other. I was looking forward to fooling around with the *Torte*'s complex architecture, and I could see ways in which I might still be able to summon up – in a pleasant form – some of the nostalgia surrounding the humble, misconstrued gateau. Combining the two would make a cake that was really special.

• Getting Romantik •

The fine arts are five in number, namely: painting, sculpture, poetry,
music and architecture, the principal branch of the latter being pastry.

Antonin Carême

I had said to camera that I wanted to soak up the atmosphere of the Black Forest and somehow put it into my recipe. My overnight stay in Oberkirch gave me a taste of what the forest had to offer. Most of the town looks like anywhere in *Mitteleuropa* – sturdy concrete buildings with steeply pitched roofs – but turn off the main road down one of the shadowy arched passageways and suddenly you are confronted by a soaring church or maze of cobbled streets. The modern buildings occasionally give way to a house from another era, with shutters and timbered lattice-work. I was glad to discover that my hotel, the Romantik Hotel zur Oberen Linde, was one of these.

Like the English 'heritage' you find in B&Bs and tea shoppes, German heritage is both charming … and slightly twee. The hotel room's thick stone walls, low ceilings, extravagantly carved woodwork and swagged four-poster were snug and welcoming; it was the kind of place you'd gratefully retreat to as the cold took hold outside. The bar, on the other hand, plundered a rustic theme: table decorations of browning leaves, wrinkled berries and walnuts; wagon wheels propped against the walls and milk churns on the floor. The waitresses sported a Heidi look: red print dresses with bodice tops, lace collars and leg-of-mutton sleeves. There was a kitsch element to it that I realised I'd have to try to evoke in my gateau, especially since a vein of kitsch ran equally through the 1970s British version of the BFG.

However, I was principally here to visit Volker Gmeiner, owner of the Café König and also the Confiserie Gmeiner in Oberkirch, who was going to show me the building blocks of the delicious Black Forest Gateau he serves in his cafés. As with many of the artisans in this book, he turned out to be part of a long-standing family tradition: his grandfather was a baker, his father a baker and confectioner. His experience showed in the kitchen, where the cooking proceeded with the smoothness of a well-oiled machine.

I thought it best to confess up front to what we had done to his country's most popular dessert. 'In Britain, Black Forest Gateau tends to come out of a box. It's got dodgy sponge, overwhipped cream, cheap alcohol, and glacé cherries that have an unnaturally bright red colour, as though they've been subjected to a dose of radiation. You don't even want to put them in your mouth.'

'I get the impression they did everything wrong that they could,' Volker replied. His pink cheeks gave him a boyish look, and he seemed more amused than shocked. 'I'll show you the traditional good way to do it. I was taught that the dish has to have a bit of all tastes – sweetness and bitterness from the chocolate; salt from the sponge and the base; acid from the cherries. And a bit of many different textures, too. A crispy base balanced by smooth chocolate, and cherries for bite. For me, it's important that you can taste each ingredient separately, that you can get a sense of the components of the Black Forest Gateau.'

As he talked, Volker made a *pâte à bombe*, to stabilise the mousse. He put sugar and water in a pan on a gas ring and let it heat up to 120°C. In the meantime he beat whole eggs until thick, and then slowly and delicately added the sugar syrup, leaving the machine running until the mixture cooled.

'OK, we're ready to make the mousse.' Volker removed the *pâte à bombe* and set it aside while he melted chocolate in the microwave – a mixture of Valrhona's Araguani and their Manjari, which we use at the Fat Duck; it has citrus and cherry notes that would go well in the gateau. Once it was warm but soft, the chocolate was poured into the *pâte à bombe*. Volker mixed it with a spoon, spreading delicate stripes of pale brown around the surface in a rings-of-Saturn effect. 'Now I add cream, but as you know, the important thing for the perfect mousse is not to beat the cream too much as it's added or you'll lose the volume as the air is knocked out.'

'Yes. And it'll get too grainy and noticeably fattier as beating forces the fat out of the emulsion. You don't need to beat it a lot because the chocolate'll hold in air as it cools down.'

Volker got stuck in, plunging his hand into the mixture and turning it over. When it was ready he let me taste what was in the bowl, as though we were in a mother-and-child baking session. It had exactly the right sweetness – light but preserving the flavour and strength of the ingredients – and already there was a welcome cherry note from the dark chocolate.

The mixture was put into a piping bag and smoothed over a layer of dark sponge. On top of this, Volker piped three concentric circles, as though drawing an archery target. 'OK, now for the cherries,' he said. 'I use sour cherries from the Black Forest,' Volker told me. 'They have a short season – the end of July to the start of August – during which they're generally frozen for use all year round. You can't use sweet cherries: they would make the *Torte* too sweet, cloyingly so. We defrost the cherries a day in advance, then cook them with cinnamon and salt.'

The cherries were piped between each ring. The ridges of mousse prevented the cherries from falling out as you cut into the cake; that's why you had to resist the temptation to put one cherry dead centre as the bull's-eye. (It brought home to me, once again, the architectural aspect of the true Black Forest Gateau, and it triggered a memory. I had an honorary uncle called John, and my one good memory of the cake is going to his house in Brixton for Sunday lunch and eating a home-made version there. He was a retired architect, and maybe the BFG's elaborate superstructure was what fired up his culinary instincts. It was certainly his proudest culinary showpiece.)

Another 'floor' was then added to the construction, this time a disc of white sponge, which was squashed down so the chocolate mousse squidged out and up the sides. (This is a neat trick that chefs use all the time: make the sponge discs slightly smaller than the cake tin so that, as each layer is pressed down, mousse is forced out and up. It's far easier than taking the cake out of the tin later and trying to apply chocolate to the sides.) With a squeezy bottle Volker then drizzled the sponge with a mixture of half kirsch, half sugar syrup.

'You can't just use kirsch on its own. It's too strong and it flies away – "evaporates", I think you say. The quality of the spirit is very important: it mustn't be too sweet. I like to use one with 50 per cent alcohol – strong enough to stand up to the chocolate.'

Kirsch was also integral to the next stage. Volker added it to a pan containing hot water, sugar and gelatin and warmed it up. 'The gelatin holds the liquid in a kind of net,' he said. 'Another example of your architecture, Heston.'

I got the impression he might be teasing me just a little.

The intoxicating scent of kirsch suffused the room. Volker added a blob of cream to the pan and then poured the whole lot slowly back into a bowl containing more cream. 'The juggling of cream and kirsch here makes it an easier consistency to mix, and ensures not too much volume is lost,' he explained. 'As before, you've got to make sure the cream isn't overbeaten. You'll end up with too many air bubbles with thin walls that break and so reduce the volume.'

He scooped out the by-now sluggish white mass, plonked it on top of the sponge like a lick of shaving foam, and spread it out.

Another floor of dark sponge; another cream-splurge out the sides; another drizzle of the squeezy bottle in a spiralling motion towards the centre. The edifice was almost built. A final slop of kirsch cream and smoothing with a palette knife and it was done. A hat of greaseproof paper was placed on top and it was put in the fridge to cool for a couple of hours until the mousse set.

Once cooled, the gateau must be put on its foundation. Volker took a biscuit base and spread jam over it. 'It fixes the bottom of the cake to the base.'

'A kind of fruit glue,' I suggested.

'Architecture again,' he observed, as he placed the cake in position and smoothed more cream on top. 'You know, Black Forest Gateau is hugely popular here. I couldn't open my shops for the day without it. Any other cake, yes, but not the Black Forest Gateau. The elderly population in Baden-Baden keeps up the tradition of high tea. It's a good place for a *Konditorei*.'

'So the gateau is steeped in kirsch *and* tradition,' I offered, pleased with my wordplay.

In response, Volker fired up a blowtorch.

For a moment I wondered if I'd overstepped the mark, but he was just heating the cake tin a little to help the gateau slide out easily. On top of the cake he now placed a cutter that looked like a spoked wheel – 'I have to get it lined up with the centre, otherwise there will be pieces for rich people, and pieces for poor people' – and pressed down. Spot on. Equal shares for everybody this time.

A piped blob of whipped cream went on each portion, along with chocolate shavings and 'a little bit of snow' in the form of sifted sugar. The final touch was a few chocolate Christmas trees and some candied sour cherries.

'There you are,' Volker announced, 'the traditional Black Forest Gateau.' He didn't tinker with the sides but left them as they were. 'I don't care if there are a few holes and suchlike. I like the irregularities. The customer should be able to see that it's handmade.'

'So imperfection can be perfection?'

'Exactly.'

• The Tuscany of Germany •

It was ironic really. It had felt odd beginning an exploration of Black Forest Gateau by travelling to Pisa. And now here I was, in the Black Forest, being told that it was the Tuscany of Germany.

Hans-Peter Fies had a point, though. Olive trees grow in the region and, in season, you can get apricots, as well as pears, apples, wild plums and cherries. It's a fertile, farmers' landscape: Ringelbach still has a lot of rackety barns with firewood stored under the eaves. The bleat of sheep carry on the wind, and you can see people doubled over in cultivation on the steep hillsides that hem in the village.

By the main road, a waystone declares: WEIN – OBST & HONIG – SCHNAPPS. The area is famous for fruit and alcohol, and that's why I had come here. Volker Gmeiner had made it clear how easy it was for bad kirsch to swamp the virtues of the Black Forest Gateau, so I'd travelled to Ringelbach to visit the Franz Fies distillery and discover more about the process of turning fruit into a full-blooded spirit.

The distillery's presence is felt – or rather, smelt – before it's seen: the sweet sharp smell of high-proof alcohol catches in the nostrils as you walk through the village. I entered the reception room and noticed that, like Amedei, Franz Fies has its clutch of gold, silver and bronze. The walls were full of framed certificates attesting to the company's excellence. Hans-Peter's father set up the distillery after the war as a small farm concern, and it had clearly come a long way since then.

The basic principles and science of distilling are relatively straightforward. First, fermentation. Yeast fungi convert sugars to energy, producing alcohol as a by-product of that process. Add yeasts to a fruit (or grain or other carbohydrate source), therefore, and they will prey on its sugars, producing a mildly alcoholic liquid as they do so (between 5 and 12 per cent alcohol by volume, or ABV).

Second, evaporation. To create a spirit, the percentage of alcohol needs to be increased. Since alcohol is more volatile than water, and more easily brought to the boil and evaporated, if you heat up the fermented liquid, the alcohol turns to vapour first and so can be collected as it condenses.

The processes involved in producing a well-balanced spirit rather than toxic poteen or moonshine are, however, a lot more complicated than that, as I could see when I entered Hans-Peter's distillery. The dizzying aroma of liquor was even stronger in here, and the place looked like Frankenstein's laboratory: twenty-foot-high stainless steel drums towered over me, and a tangled network of pipes fed in and out of what looked like a giant deep-sea diver's helmet of burnished copper, with riveted portholes and pressure gauges.

'It's like something from *20,000 Leagues under the Sea*,' I exclaimed.

The diver's helmet turned out to be the still. 'First the fresh cherries are picked,' Hans-Peter said. 'This is in fact the most important part of the whole process. More important than all this machinery. The quality of the fruit is absolutely essential. The cherries must be very fine, no flaws. Bad fruit makes bad kirsch. It's as simple as that. After picking, the cherries are crushed and fermented in our upper factory. Then the mash comes down to the lower factory and is left for ten to twelve weeks. And then it comes into this copper still, where we heat it to about 78°C, at which point what we call the "ghost" flies away. It goes up that pipeline and into a closed room.'

'Yes. The alcohol vaporises.'

'Ja, ja. Genau.'

'The smell is really wonderful.'

'Yes? OK.' Hans-Peter sounded almost surprised. It was as though he'd got so used to it he didn't really notice any more. He took me over to the still's porthole. Peering through, I could see a briskly roiling liquid illuminated by a pinkish glow. 'The smell is from the cherries. And so is that colour. Later, as you'll see, it will be clear.'

'Is the temperature a crucial part of the process?' I wanted to know.

'I must heat very slowly, not too strong,' he explained. 'Between 75 and 80°C the pure alcohol comes off, along with some flavour and aroma compounds.'

'So by controlling the temperature you avoid collecting the water vapour?'

'Yes. But eventually the temperature does reach about 100°C, and then there is more water vapour, of course.'

'And this is the end of the first distillation?'

'Yes. Once all the alcohol is gone I can stop, and the rest of the mash is removed.'

The 'ghost' meanwhile has floated along pipes to the cooler. As its temperature reduces, it condenses and reverts to a liquid. It is now much purer and so no longer dark-coloured but clear.

'At the end of this cooking the alcohol is about 35–40 per cent ABV,' Hans-Peter told me. 'To increase the alcohol content and the flavour, we repeat the process: a second distillation that gives us about 70 per cent ABV.'

'And yet you then add spring water to dilute the spirit back to 40 per cent, so what's the point of this second distillation?'

'The quality of this distillate is very much better. The impurities and harshness of the first distillation are removed. It is purer and the taste is finer. You know, fermentation produces many volatile substances, not all of which you would want in the final product. Some – like methanol – are actually bad for our bodies! We class these substances into groups, according to how volatile they are, and during distillation we can use the variations in volatility to separate them from each other, leaving just the fraction that is richest in alcohol.'

It was hard to hear him over the insistent, almost melodic rattle of glass bottles, which shunted along a conveyor belt in the centre of the factory to be filled, sealed and boxed.

'The most volatile – and therefore the quickest to evaporate – include methanol and acetone. Because they're the first, you call them, I think, the "heads". These are removed as they cool and condense. Then comes alcohol, which is collected separately. Lastly there are the "tails", the things that are less volatile than alcohol. These are more difficult to deal with because you don't want to remove them completely: many of the substances give spirits character. For example, the tails include fusel oils. In small amounts these supply a desirable, slightly oily body to the product. Too much, however, can render it rough and unpalatable – *Fusel* is actually German for "rotgut". You'd know about it the next morning!'

'So after the first distillation the liquid is volatile and aggressive and not particularly complex. The second distillation brings out the intensity of the alcohol as well as an intensity of taste and flavour?'

'Yes, exact, exact.'

'Could I try the second distillation?' I asked.

'Of course. I would be happy for you to do so.' He took a spirit glass – a long-stemmed flute with a bulbous bowl – and dipped it in a metal barrel, then handed it over to me. 'It's a very intensive taste. Very pure. Very strong. Be careful. Have only a little bit.'

He wasn't kidding. Even a brief sniff of the contents made me want to lie down. My eyes started to water. It tasted very strong indeed. 'What percentage ABV is that?'

'About 75 per cent.'

'A few years ago I went to Armagnac to see a distiller. He told me that a good way to test the product is to pour some on your hands, rub them together, then cup them over your nose. Shall we try it?'

With his neat silvery hair and full moustache, Hans-Peter looked a bit like a movie actor from the 1920s, an impression reinforced by his tweed jacket and checked shirt. He had a sense of humour but he was also quite correct, so I wasn't entirely sure how this suggestion would be taken. It turned out he was entirely game, so we tipped our glasses on to our palms and then rubbed, as though about to apply aftershave. I put my hands up to my nostrils. As the alcohol vaporised I got a real hit of complex, intense cherry smell – including the cherry stone note that I liked so much and had found in Amedei's chocolate. It was something I definitely wanted to capture in my Black Forest Gateau, so I was very pleased to discover that kirsch could summon it up too. It was another example of how instructive this trip to the source had been: everybody I had met had passed on insights that magnified the gateau's potential. Even just wandering round Ringelbach and catching the faint wafts of alcohol in the air had prompted ideas: if I put kirsch in a spray bottle, and squirted it around before serving the gateau, would that provide an atmosphere of the Black Forest and heighten the eating experience, making it a little more authentic? I didn't know, but it would be fun trying it out back in the lab.

• Layer Cake •

'You've been a busy boy, Jocky.'

It sounded like a line from a British gangster flick – the sort of thing the boss says before punishing an underling who's been a bit too handy with an Uzi – but it was true: my pastry chef had been busy.

The work surface of the Fat Duck development kitchen was covered with slabs and strips ranging in colour from pale cream to darkest brown. They looked like planks and blocks from a child's building set – a reminder of the architectural aspect of the BFG. Jocky had consulted every cake and mousse recipe he could find, and baked them at a variety of temperatures and percentages in order to give us the widest possible choice from which to construct our gateau. There were jacondes and financiers, dacquoises and génoises, along with tubs of fresh cherries, compotes and purées, and even cherry and apricot pits. Nestling among them were ganaches and parfaits made with the chocolate we'd brought back from Amedei. Each item sat on greaseproof paper, labelled like an exhibit.

From this fantastic spread we had to choose the layers of our gateau, and their order and thickness, bearing in mind the chocolate and cherries that would cement it all together. I didn't even want to think about the maths of the maximum number of possible combinations.

'I've got the Black Forest Gateau that Volker made for me as a starting point,' I said to Jocky. 'Let's begin with his basic structure of seven layers and then play around with the rest. Three things really struck me while I was in Germany: Volker said that the gateau should contain four tastes – sweet, sour, salt and bitter – and emphasise the contrasts of dark and light. I'd like to capture both of those, if I can. And above all I want to somehow incorporate exactly the kirsch-memory I have from being there. If this is going to work, we've got to get the kirsch right. We'll start with the base and build upwards, trying to get the right balance of taste and texture.'

And so began an afternoon of spooning out mousses and compotes and putting them between sponges and biscuits. It took me back to a time when, as a kid, I'd try to construct an enormous sandwich containing only my favourite things: jam, jelly, Nutella, peanut butter, hundreds and thousands. Some of the results here were equally anarchic and inedible, but gradually we started to whittle down the choices.

Jocky had prepared a dried madeleine that had a really interesting texture, rather like a Langue de Chat biscuit. It was both light and crunchy and so could make a great base. And the chocolate sablés he'd cooked were promising too: they gave us the opportunity to incorporate milk chocolate as well as the dark, and had a thinness that meant we could increase the number of layers in the cake. I wanted in any case to cut down the height of the gateau, for it seemed to me that if it was too big to fit in the mouth then some of the flavour combinations would be lost.

So we had a tentative shortlist for the base. The sponge layers proved trickier. Many just didn't seem to fit in with my mental picture and taste-map of the Black Forest Gateau: they didn't match up to my memories of the German version, though we'd have to see how they responded to soaking in kirsch. A soft almond cake had the right kind of chewiness, and cherries and almonds certainly complemented one another, though I wondered if the almond took it too far in the wrong direction, too far from what people thought of as a Black Forest Gateau. I wanted to include as many contrasting textures as possible – stimulation for both head and palate – so anything a bit different had to be considered.

We built combinations into toppling towers. We tried out cherry and apricot preserves and found the apricot gave a better balance of acidity. On top of this went a chocolate sponge without flour that had a really pleasing delicacy to it. Jocky and I were unsure about which was the most suitable chocolate – Porcelana probably gave the best chocolate experience but Chuao accentuated the cherry character – and so decided to try to incorporate both. We found an unaggressive kirsch that instantly took me back to the Black Forest itself.

Things were coming together, but the maths of testing combinations wasn't the only factor we had to contend with. Normally, at the Fat Duck, experimentation is just like this – a mixture of instinct, blind alleys and continual testing – but there's no time limit involved. Recipes can take years to perfect, and often go through many metamorphoses to get there. Here we had a deadline: the eight dishes had to be finalised for filming in a week, and the Black Forest Gateau was proving to be the most difficult of the lot. I still had sponges to soak, vanilla stalks to dry out, and an idea about chocolate snow that I wanted to follow through … Were we going to be ready in time?

BLACK FOREST GATEAU

Each cake serves 4–6 (recipe makes enough for 3 cakes)

Here it is – a Black Forest Gateau composed of six delicious layers: a madeleine biscuit base topped with aerated chocolate, chocolate sponge, kirsch cream, ganache and chocolate mousse. More than any other dish, perhaps, this one can be let down by its ingredients. The salt plays a pivotal role, enhancing the flavours and tempering the cake's sweetness. And it's absolutely vital that you use the best chocolate, sour cherries and kirsch that you can get. The kirsch is especially important: I recommend Franz Fies (their address and website are included in the Directory), but if you can't obtain this, it's worth taste-testing a few – surely no hardship – to find one that works. It needs to be smooth, aromatic and full-flavoured.

One of the beauties of this recipe is its adaptability. The layers don't have to be assembled into a cake: many can be served up as desserts in their own right. Kids and grown-ups alike will love the chocolate mousse and aerated chocolate. Serving kirsch cream with a bowl of cherries would be an interesting echo of the cake's origins. This really is six recipes in one – and the possibilities are almost endless.

And the final touches, as always, make a difference. Spray a little kirsch round the dining room and serve the gateau on a wood-effect base and you have a context that, to my mind, makes it taste all the better.

Special equipment: 21.5 x 31.5cm brownie tin(s),* food mixer (optional), oven thermometer, 2.6 litre hard plastic container with lid (into which you have bored a small hole using a corkscrew), microwave (optional), whipping-cream canister and charges, vacuum-seal storage bag with one-way valve, vacuum cleaner, digital probe, wood-effect painting tool, non-stick silicone baking sheet (e.g. Silpat), 9 x 19cm loaf tin(s) with a depth of 5cm, piping bag, melon baller, large cardboard box, paint gun (optional), atomiser (optional)

Timing: Lots of layers mean lots of different cooking techniques. To assemble a whole cake in one day would undeniably be a fair amount of work. Better to think of this as architecture – a flatpack gateau – and spread out the building tasks. Prepare the chocolate sponge and kirsch cream up to a month in advance and keep them in the freezer, and make the biscuit base up to a week in advance, keeping it in an airtight container. The aerated chocolate can be prepared anytime: it will keep well in the fridge if sealed properly. That leaves only two layers to prepare on the day – the chocolate ganache and the chocolate mousse – neither of which is particularly laborious.

Ingredients list:
This is broken down into quantities for each component part below, but here's the entire shopping list for three cakes:

6 plump vanilla pods
50g sea salt
120g unsalted butter
18 large eggs
60g honey
120g plain flour
60g icing sugar
10g baking powder
380ml whole milk

500g top quality milk chocolate (such as Valrhona's Tanariva)
565g top quality dark chocolate (such as Amadei's Toscano Black 66%)
95g top quality dark chocolate (such as Amadei's Porcelana)
150g top quality dark chocolate (such as Amadei's Chuao)
215g groundnut oil
210g unrefined caster sugar
115g good quality cocoa powder
2 sheets of leaf gelatine
50ml top quality kirsch (e.g. Franz Fies)
515ml whipping cream
1 tsp glucose syrup
1 jar of apricot baking glaze
1 jar of top quality sour cherries in syrup (e.g. Amarena Fabbri)

For the madeleine biscuit base:
If making the wood-effect base at the same time, double these quantities and set aside half the mixture to use in that.

50g unsalted butter
1 large egg (60g)
30g honey
60g plain flour
30g icing sugar, sifted
5g baking powder ($^1/_2$ tsp)
pinch of table salt
15ml whole milk (1 tbsp)

For the aerated chocolate layer:
500g top quality milk chocolate (such as Valrhona's Tanariva)
65g groundnut oil

For the flourless chocolate sponge:
65g top quality dark chocolate (such as Amedei's Toscano Black 66%)
7 egg yolks (140g)
130g unrefined caster sugar

 A centimetre either side of these dimensions doesn't matter as the base will be trimmed after baking.

15g good quality cocoa powder (such as Green & Black's Organic), sifted
5 egg whites (150g)

For the kirsch cream:
2 sheets of leaf gelatin
5 egg yolks (100g)
90g unrefined caster sugar
250ml whole milk
220ml whipping cream
20ml top quality kirsch (e.g. Franz Fies)

For the chocolate ganache:
95ml whipping cream
1 tsp glucose syrup
pinch of table salt
95g top quality dark chocolate (such as Amedei's Porcelana)
20g unsalted butter, diced

For the chocolate mousse:
4 egg yolks (80g)
200g unrefined caster sugar
100ml whole milk
150g top quality dark chocolate (such as Amedei's Chuao)
generous pinch of table salt
200ml whipping cream

For the wood-effect base:
100g good quality cocoa powder (such as Green & Black's Organic)
200ml water
1 quantity madeleine biscuit base mix

For the dried vanilla pod stalks:
6 plump vanilla pods

For the finished Black Forest Gateau
The quantities below are enough for three cakes. You can either freeze the cakes you don't want to use at once, or make up one cake and save the rest of the prepared ingredients. For one cake, simply halve the chocolate ganache and chocolate cream recipes.

madeleine biscuit base rectangles
aerated chocolate
flourless chocolate sponge rectangles
kirsch cream
chocolate ganache
chocolate mousse
1 jar of apricot baking glaze
1 jar of top quality wild cherries in heavy syrup (Amarena Fabbri cherries are ideal but difficult to obtain. Griottines are more readily available, though they'll take the gateau's taste in a slightly different direction)
30ml top quality kirsch (e.g. Franz Fies)
500g top quality dark chocolate (such as Amedei's Toscano Black 66%)
150g groundnut oil
wood-effect base
dried vanilla pods, to decorate

MAKING THE MADELEINE BISCUIT BASE

1. Heat the oven to 200°C/400°F/Gas 6. Line a 21.5 x 31.5cm brownie tin with greaseproof paper or a little butter.

2. Melt the butter over a low heat, then leave to cool a little.

3. Beat the egg and honey together for 5 minutes, or until white and thick. (A food mixer with a paddle attachment is ideal for this job.)

4. Gradually add all the dry ingredients, then the cooled butter and finally the milk. Mix until they're all just combined. Do not overbeat.

5. Pour the mixture into the brownie tin. Bake for 10 minutes, or until a pale golden brown.

6. Turn the oven down to 100°C/212°F. (Use an oven thermometer to check this.) Cut the biscuit base into three 8 x 18cm rectangles. (It's not essential that they're exact at this point, as they will need to be trimmed again when assembling the gateau.) Lift these out of the tin and place on a baking tray.

7. Bake in the preheated oven for 20 minutes, or until a deep golden brown and crisp. Leave to cool and store in an airtight container until required.

MAKING THE AERATED CHOCOLATE

Here it is an especially good idea to get all the ingredients and equipment ready beforehand, so that the chocolate goes through the process quickly, stays liquid, and gets well aerated.

1. Line the 2.6 litre plastic container with greaseproof paper.

2. Break the chocolate into chunks and place in a medium-sized glass bowl. Place the bowl over a saucepan of simmering water and let the chocolate melt. (The bowl needs to be large enough that it can sit on top of the saucepan without its base touching the water: the aim is to soften up the chocolate on the gentlest of heats, so that it doesn't go grainy.) Alternatively, melt the chocolate at high power in a microwave for $1^1/_2$–2 minutes. (Again, be careful not to overheat it.)

3. Place a whipping cream canister in a bowl or pan of boiling water. (Warming the canister ensures that the chocolate stays molten when poured into it.)

4. Stir the oil into the bowl containing the melted chocolate then pour it all into the whipping cream canister. Attach the canister cap, and charge with three charges.

5. Shake the canister then squirt the chocolate on to the base of the 2.6 litre plastic container. Put on the container's lid, then place the container in the vacuum storage bag. Position the storage bag's valve over the hole in the container's lid. Switch on the vacuum cleaner and place the hose on the valve to suck the air out of the bag. The chocolate should rise and be riddled with small bubbles. As soon as it does so, remove the vacuum and close the valve as quickly as possible. To set the chocolate, place the box – still in the vacuum bag – in the fridge until required.

MAKING THE FLOURLESS CHOCOLATE SPONGE

1. Preheat the oven to 180°C/350°F/Gas 4. Line a 21.5 x 31.5cm brownie tin with greaseproof paper or a little butter.

2. Break the chocolate into chunks and place in a glass bowl. Place the bowl over a saucepan of simmering water and let the chocolate melt (or heat the chocolate at high power in a microwave for $1^1/_2$–2 minutes). Leave to cool.

3. Beat the egg yolks with 65g of the caster sugar for 5 minutes, or until white and thick. (A food mixer with a whisk attachment can perform this task.) Stir in the cocoa powder and melted, cooled chocolate.

4. Whisk the egg whites with the remaining sugar until soft peaks form. (The mixer can do this job too. If you have only one mixer bowl, a similarly sized stainless steel or glass mixing bowl will work. Make sure it is spotlessly clean: a dirty bowl is one of the commonest reasons for egg whites not stiffening.)

5. Gradually fold the egg whites into the egg yolk mixture, then pour this mixture into the brownie tin and bake for 20–25 minutes. The surface of the cake will look a little dry when removed from the oven, and it may sink slightly. Leave it to cool before cutting into three 8 x 18cm rectangles.

MAKING THE KIRSCH CREAM

1. Line a 21.5 x 31.5cm brownie tin with clingfilm.

2. Place the sheets of gelatin in a small bowl and pour over 100ml cold water. Leave for 15 minutes, or until soft.

3. Beat the egg yolks with the sugar for 5 minutes, or until white and thick. (The food mixer can do this job.)

4. Gently warm the milk in a small pan. Remove from the heat and stir in the beaten egg yolks. Return to a medium heat and cook for a further 2–3 minutes, stirring frequently. Use a digital probe to monitor when the temperature of the mixture reaches 80°C/175°F, at which point it should be taken off the heat. (It will have become thicker, with tiny bubbles appearing on the surface.)

5. Drain the gelatin and stir it into the warm mixture. (Make sure the mixture is not too hot or the gelatin will break. Make sure, too, that all the gelatin dissolves.) Leave until lukewarm.

6. Meanwhile, lightly whip the cream then add the kirsch. Fold this into the cooled gelatin mixture, then pour the mixture into the brownie tin and place it in the freezer to set for at least 1 hour.

MAKING THE WOOD-EFFECT BASE

1. Preheat the oven to 200°C/400°F/Gas 6. Melt the butter over a low heat, then leave to cool a little.

2. Beat the egg and honey together for 5 minutes, or until white and thick. (A food mixer with a paddle attachment is ideal for this job.)

3. Gradually add all the dry ingredients, then the cooled butter and finally the milk. Mix until they're all just combined. (Do not overbeat.) Set this madeleine mix aside.

4. Mix the cocoa powder and water and pour on to the far end of a non-stick silicone baking sheet set on top of a rigid baking sheet.

5. Drag the wood-effect painting tool over the batter and towards you, pivoting it back and forth as you go. (It's a process similar to pouring paint into a tray and dragging a roller through it to spread it out.) Place in the fridge and leave to chill for 1 hour.

6. Take the butter out of the fridge and, using a spatula, spread the madeleine mix over it. Place in the oven for 10 minutes, or until a light golden brown.

7. Remove from the rigid baking sheet and allow to cool. Once cooled, invert the wood-effect base on to the plate that will be displaying the gateau, and peel away the silicone baking sheet.

MAKING THE DRIED VANILLA POD STALKS

1. Cut the vanilla pods lengthways into four.

2. Tie a knot at the end of each strip, then twist it to give a gnarled effect.

3. Place on a plate and leave to dry overnight at room temperature.

MAKING THE CHOCOLATE GANACHE AND CHOCOLATE MOUSSE AND ASSEMBLING A BLACK FOREST GATEAU

1. Line a 5cm deep, 9 x 19cm loaf tin with clingfilm.

2. For the chocolate ganache: gently heat the cream, glucose syrup and salt. Break the chocolate into a bowl then stir in the warm cream. When the chocolate has melted entirely, add the butter and stir until that too has melted. Spoon the mixture into a piping bag and place it in the fridge for at least an hour to stiffen up.

3. Meanwhile, if need be, trim the madeleine base so that it fits the bottom of the loaf tin, leaving a $1/2$cm gap between it and the sides of the tin. Trim the flourless chocolate sponge to the same dimensions as the madeleine base. Cut the aerated chocolate to these dimensions, and trim it so that it is no more than 1cm thick.

4. Before putting the madeleine base in the tin, spread it with a generous layer of apricot baking glaze. Put the aerated chocolate on top and place these in the bottom of the tin. (If you're making the cake without the aerated chocolate layer, replace it with a piece of flourless chocolate sponge.)

5. Remove the piping bag containing the ganache from the fridge. Along the length of the top of the aerated chocolate, about 2–3mm from the edge, pipe a thick line of ganache. Repeat on the other side. (Looked at from above, the rectangle of aerated chocolate should now have two stripes of ganache, each of which runs parallel to the longer edges.)

6. Drain the cherries and reserve the syrup. Fill the gap between the two lines of ganache with a double row of cherries. (The idea is that every person is served a slice containing a pair of cherries, so calculate the number you'll need accordingly and be sure to space them well. Keep in mind roughly where you've placed them, which will make step 14 easier.)

7. Mix 60ml of the reserved cherry syrup with the kirsch.* Dip the chocolate sponge in this soaking syrup then position it on top of the ganache and cherries.

8. Remove the kirsch cream from the freezer and trim it to the same dimensions as the other layers. Manoeuvre it on top of the chocolate sponge using a palette knife or fish slice. Put the gateau in the freezer while you prepare the chocolate mousse.

9. Beat the egg yolks with the sugar for 5 minutes, or until white and thick. (A food mixer with a paddle attachment can be used for this.)

10. Gently warm the milk in a small pan. Remove it from the heat and stir in the beaten egg yolks. Return to a medium heat and cook for a further 2–3 minutes, stirring frequently. Use a digital probe to monitor when the temperature of the mixture reaches 80°C/175°F, and remove from the heat.

11. Finely chop the chocolate and place it in a medium-sized bowl. Pour the warm milk and eggs over the chocolate and stir until the chocolate has melted. Add the salt and leave to cool.

12. Whip the cream until soft peaks form. Fold the cream into the cooled chocolate mixture.

* Taste the cherry syrup before mixing it with the kirsch. If it is rather flavourless, tip it into a small pan, add a tablespoon of unrefined caster sugar and bring to the boil. When it has reduced by half, take it off the heat and leave to cool slightly before stirring in the kirsch.

13. Remove the gateau from the freezer. Make sure the clingfilm is taut against the sides of the tin. Pour the chocolate mousse down the sides of the tin until it reaches a level 1cm above the kirsch cream layer. Return the gateau to the freezer and leave it for at least an hour, to firm up the layer of mousse.

14. Using a melon baller, scoop out a double row of indentations along the gateau. (Ideally, they should be above the cherries that were added in step 6.) Return the gateau to the freezer for a least an hour: it needs to be properly frozen in order to get the right effect with the chocolate coating.

15. For the coating, break the chocolate into chunks and place in a small glass bowl. Melt the chocolate by placing the bowl over a pan of simmering water, or by heating it at high power in a microwave for $1^1/_2$–2 minutes. Leave to cool slightly before stirring in the groundnut oil. (If you don't plan to coat the cake with the paint gun, take 100g of this chocolate, cut it into shavings and scatter over the cake just before serving.)

16. Fill the base of the paint gun with the melted chocolate mixture and attach the nozzle. To avoid redecorating the kitchen in chocolate brown, set the large cardboard box on its side (which effectively provides a protective roof and walls to work in). Remove the gateau from the freezer. Carefully lift it out of the loaf tin and on to a plate. Remove the clingfilm and place the gateau in the cardboard box. Spray the gateau with the chocolate, turning carefully as you go. Return it to the freezer until 20 minutes before serving.

17. To serve, place the gateau on the wood-effect base. Use a skewer to bore a small hole 2–3 inches into the centre of the bottom of each indentation, down towards the cherry below. Agitate the skewer a little to increase

the hole's diameter. Pour in cherry syrup until it reaches the top of the bore-hole (but doesn't spill out into the indentation itself). Place a sour cherry, stalk end up, in each indentation, and sit a dried vanilla pod in each cherry, to make a decorative stalk. For the full effect, fill an atomiser with kirsch and squirt it round the room just before serving the gateau — it will magically bring a little of the Black Forest to the dinner table.

TREACLE TART & ICE CREAM

… he felt it was a better use of his time to eat his way steadily through his steak and kidney pie, then a large plateful of his favourite treacle tart.

J. K. Rowling, *Harry Potter and the Order of the Phoenix*

INTRODUCTION

Although I remember the classic green and gold tin of Tate & Lyle's Golden Syrup on the kitchen shelves at home, I don't know what it was used for because we didn't have treacle tart. Ice cream is a different matter. It's an indelible part of my memories of childhood. There was the excitement when I heard the fairground jollity of the ice-cream van's jingle, followed by the rush to tell Mum, sort out the change and get out in the street in time to buy a 99, preferably with an extra Flake. (For me the chug of the ice-cream van's engine idling still summons up summer more powerfully than anything else, except perhaps the buzz of wasps or the whirr of lawnmowers.) There was the intermission at Saturday Morning Film Club, when screenings of *Flash Gordon* or *The Lone Ranger* would be stopped abruptly and a stampede of kids would make for the woman selling tubs of ice cream, each with its little pink plastic spoon under the lid.

Most of all, though, ice cream brings to mind weekly trips with my sister and grandmother to Church Street Market off the Edgware Road. Visiting the junk shops was a drag but the last part of the trip more than made up for it. We'd stop off at the Regent Snack Bar – an ice-cream parlour decorated in pistachio green with a model of a cone hanging above the door – where Gran would treat both of us to a tub of vanilla ice cream. We weren't allowed to eat it until we got home, which made the two-minute walk seem like the longest of my life.

Somewhere during that eternal walk, an ice-cream fanatic was born. You could say that that perfect taste haunted me, shaping my expectations and enjoyment of ice cream. More than any other food in this book, ice cream reflects my feelings about the role of memory, nostalgia, history and ritual in cooking: the way in which the past – formative, fondly remembered experience – sets a kind of template for what we want from what we eat, a benchmark of perfection.

And the trappings also play a part in this, often without us even realising it. If I served up ice cream at the Fat Duck in, say, a pistachio-coloured bowl with a pink plastic spoon and broadcast the sounds of wasps, mowers and a quietly chugging engine, would its taste be enhanced – at least for me? I've yet to try it, but I will, and I bet it does (especially if I set the stopwatch going and make myself wait two minutes). Perfection is about tapping into those kinds of memories: that's why it's personal to each of us. For these recipes I've drawn on my own memories, and those of others, with the aim of establishing a consensus of sorts – some memories have an almost universal pull, and good cooking often manages to summon these up. But in the end, if you want perfection, it's your own history that you have to delve into and put on the plate.

My passion for ice cream is a case in point. Driven by childhood memories of the perfect vanilla ice cream, I explored every aspect of its manufacture. My first forays into science concerned how it was made: the formation of ice crystals; the introduction of air cells to weaken the matrix. Eventually I arrived at the texture I wanted, but the right flavour eluded me. I tried adding chocolate, a coffee bean – nothing worked. In desperation, I visited Foubert's in Chiswick, run by a Sicilian who had worked in the Regent Snack Bar. Even here the vanilla didn't taste as I remembered …

Then I saw Luciano trowel vanilla and coffee ice cream into a tub. That's what I used to have, I suddenly remembered. My memory had been playing tricks on me. My ideal vanilla was, in fact, half-and-half.

Was it perfection?

You'd better believe it.

HISTORY

• Treacle •

'They lived on treacle,' said the Dormouse, after thinking a minute or two.
Lewis Carroll, *Alice's Adventures in Wonderland*

Although treacle was slow to catch on as a sweetener, its name originates from ancient times. It comes from the Greek *theriake*, meaning an antidote to the bite of wild beasts, and was employed as a cure for all kinds of poisons, right up to the Middle Ages.

Perhaps the slow spread of the product is a result of its medicinal history. At first, apothecaries made treacle from their own secret recipes. But as demand from chemists and distillers grew, it became a valuable article of trade. For a time, Venice had a virtual monopoly on production, but by the fifteenth century, Genoa and Flanders were supplying most of England's treacle. Eventually, sugar refineries were set up in London, and the home-manufactured product supplanted the imports. London treacle was born.

Refining raw sugar cane involves crushing then boiling the cane until it has thickened sufficiently to allow the growth of the sugar crystals that will eventually become sugar. Treacle was made at this stage with what was drained off from the sugar cane during successive boilings. It was almost black in colour and had a faint burned-caramel flavour, like molasses. (This is now called 'black treacle'. 'Light treacle', better known as golden syrup, is made from the syrup obtained during the first boiling of sugar cane, a refining method that was only introduced around 1880.)

Mass production led to supply outstripping demand from distillers and apothecaries, and by the seventeenth century the excess was marketed in its natural state as a sweetener. For the poor, especially in the north, a spoonful of treacle helped their meagre diet go down: it was added to parkin and oatmeal biscuits, and puddled on top of porridge.

As the number of British colonies grew (and access to cheap labour along with them), the gathering and processing of sugar cane became more economical. Once refined sugar was affordable, it soon replaced treacle as the masses' sweetener of choice. This and the development of golden syrup heralded treacle's transition from sweetener to dessert ingredient, adding colour, moisture and taste to a variety of dishes.

It is not known when and where treacle tart was thought up – when treacle went from walk-on part to star performer in a dessert – but one of treacle's early roles provides a possible clue. By the reign of Charles II, treacle rather than licorice was being used to make gingerbread. The royal recipe called for large amounts of candied peel and coriander seed, but the domestic version couldn't possibly afford that level of spicing and so relied far more heavily on treacle for flavour. Somewhere a chef with an inventive imagination may well have tasted festive gingerbread and decided that putting it in a pastry case would add something special.

• Ice Cream •

I doubt the world holds for anyone a more soul-stirring surprise than the
first adventure with ice-cream.

Heywood Broun

The story of ice cream satisfyingly encapsulates two themes of this book: the way in which much of food history soon becomes a frothy confection of myth, exaggeration and romanticism; and the importance of science in the kitchen.

Authoritative books will tell you that Arabs in Sicily began by icing their sweetened aromatic drinks known as *sharbats* with snow from Mount Etna, and ended up inventing granitas and water ices. They will say that Marco Polo saw ice cream being made in China and brought the idea back to Italy, and that Catherine de' Medici hired an Italian chef, Buontalenti, who introduced the French court to ice cream in 1533. Legend also has it that two more Italians, de Mirra and Marco, brought ices to the court of Charles I, who later gave his official ice-cream maker a lifetime pension with the proviso that he reveal the recipe to no one.

Historical evidence contradicts all these stories. It's now commonly believed that Marco Polo never actually reached China in his travels, and there's no record of Charles I's supposed ice-cream supremo. If he did actually exist, then it's a very well-kept secret indeed. Most of these tall tales appear only in the nineteenth century, and seem to be generated by marketing men and ice-cream makers and vendors, as though they felt the need not only to churn their product, but to give it some spin as well.

The final disproof is not historic but scientific: before the middle of the seventeenth century, almost no one in Europe could make ice cream because they didn't know the chemical process that makes it happen.

The most basic technique for manufacturing ice cream depends on the 'endothermic effect': if you add some form of salt to ice, it significantly lowers the freezing point of the mixture. Add another liquid to the mix, and this too will freeze and solidify via conduction.

It is true that Arabs and Italians played a significant part in the dissemination of this crucial culinary know-how. In the thirteenth century, the Arab historian of medicine Ibn Abu Usaybi'a talks of making artificial ice from cold water and saltpetre, and indeed historians largely agree that the Arabs acquired their knowledge from China and passed it on during their occupation of Spain. The first reference to this process in Europe is in the Italian physician Zimara's *Problemata* in 1530, but it remained the province of doctors and scholars for another century or so. Water ices began to appear in Italy, France and Spain in the 1660s, and the earliest French recipe was published in 1674. The earliest English version came some forty years later, in *Mrs Mary*

Eales Receipts, a cookbook by Queen Anne's confectioner.

As the frequent mention above of courts, kings and queens suggests, ice cream was at first a pleasure only for the wealthy. Making ice on a commercial basis was enormously costly, and so enthusiasts tended to harvest and store natural ice in specially constructed ice houses. By 1800 these were a feature of many European stately homes, but ice cream was still largely denied to those without the money and space to indulge themselves. Once again it was science that introduced ice cream to a new audience: in 1843 machines were invented in both England and America that froze and churned the mixture – the first step towards mass production. And the market for this increased output was in part the result of the upheavals and unification of Italy in the mid-nineteenth century: many Italian emigrants ended up in England and brought their ice-cream expertise with them. The British masses soon acquired a taste for their wares, made possible by the importation of farmed ice, initially from the United States and later from Norway.

More scientific revolution followed. By the beginning of the twentieth century mechanical refrigeration had largely superseded the ice-and-salt approach, meaning manufacturers were no longer at the mercy of warm winters or fluctuations in salt production.[*] This, allied to the development of refrigerated railway trucks, massively expanded the opportunities for manufacture and delivery. Once domestic freezers were invented, liberating the consumer from the need to eat immediately, ice cream's popularity became unstoppable.

THE QUEST FOR THE BEST

• Milking It •

The fat in milk and cream is part of the magic that makes ice cream. It keeps the ice crystals from becoming too large, and it accounts for the richness and smoothness of the end product. To make really delicious ice cream, it was vital that I got hold of the best milk I could, so I went to the village of White Waltham in Berkshire.

Over the last decade, Waltham Place Farm has worked hard to become biodynamic – an agricultural approach that is far removed from the intensive farming that has shrivelled the environment and the food it produces. Biodynamics developed from a series of lectures given by the philosopher Rudolf Steiner in Koberwitz (now Kobierzyce in Poland) in 1924. At its heart is the belief that there should be an integrated relationship between farmers and the plants, animals and soil they work with. The aim is to have a self-sufficient farm, maintaining a mix of habitats.

[*] In many parts of the world, however, salt and ice are still used: making ices using salt, ice and a hand machine is a very satisfying way of doing it, and a rewarding piece of practical science.

The fields should be managed in a way that supports animal life, and the soil nourished with therapeutic preparations. Biodynamic farmers are aware that their farms are part of the wider natural environment and act accordingly. Even the planetary rhythms and their influence on the growth of animals and plants are considered. Quality not quantity is a fundamental part of the biodynamic vision, and I had enjoyed the benefits of this at the Fat Duck: Waltham Place supplies us with fruit and vegetables, and I was hoping that it would start planting for us in the near future.

The farm has another thing to recommend it: it's only a ten-minute drive from my home, which is fortunate because milking means an early start.

Although it was barely light when I arrived, Chris Stevenson was already waiting impatiently for me. Chris is about as far from the traditional image of the milkmaid as you are likely to get. With his long moustache and sideburns, he looked more like Lemmy from Motörhead. His eyes glittered with nervousness or amusement, I wasn't sure which. 'Right, let's go and see the cows,' he said, and plodded off.

The mist of early morning was clearing to reveal a classic English scene. We walked past solid outbuildings of weathered red brick and purple clapboard. A cluster of turkeys stalked us, expecting food. Although it was late autumn, the vegetable gardens spread out lush and colourful: squashes and beets were neatly flanked by dahlias and marigolds, grown to attract insects and ward off bugs with their heady scent and bright blooms. Rare breeds of sheep – Jacob and Castlemilk Moorit – foraged happily in fenced enclosures. The Jersey cows looked magnificent. They were a glossy caramel or clotted-cream colour and still had their horns, which somehow made them look nobler. (Intensive dairy farms saw off the horns. Though it's claimed this is for safety, there's also – as always – an economic consideration: without horns you can cram more cows into a shed. To me it seems a sorry desecration of the animal's dignity.)

I had chosen Jersey cows because their milk has 25 per cent more butterfat than milk from most other breeds, allowing me to have the 'clean' taste that milk gives to ice cream as well as a real creaminess. As we walked along the muddy track towards the milking shed, however, Chris told me to expect other differences in the milk from their biodynamic cows. 'Intensive farms have an increased risk of contamination so they pasteurise the milk – heating it to kill off any bugs. The problem is heat kills off lots of good things along with the bad. The milk lacks vitality and flavour. Here at Waltham Place we're small enough to keep proper control over hygiene, so we don't have to pasteurise.'

As any mother who has breastfed will know, what you eat affects the taste of milk. Most commercial dairy operations give their cows only one type of grass. 'This is at odds with nature, and so it's not good for the cows or their milk,' said Chris. 'If you think back to a time before intensive cultivation, fields for grazing had a huge variety. There'd be herbs, rye, wild flowers and other stuff in there, and the cow would instinctively select what it needed for a healthy balanced diet. Here the Jerseys graze on grass leys that are as near as possible to what they would feed on naturally. And you can taste that in the milk. No question.'

As we arrived at the milking shed and Peggy, Becky and Cathy trotted inside, Chris explained that we'd be milking by hand. He claimed the machine had broken down, though I wondered whether he was tricking me into a very literal 'hands-on' experience. He still had that amused glint in his eye. Anyway, it seemed appropriate, in such a timeless setting, to be doing things the old-fashioned way. I rolled up my sleeves, while Chris showed me how to do it.

First, he 'stripped out' the cows: squeezing their teats to get rid of the milk that had collected in them overnight and then washing and drying them. Then, squatting on a large red

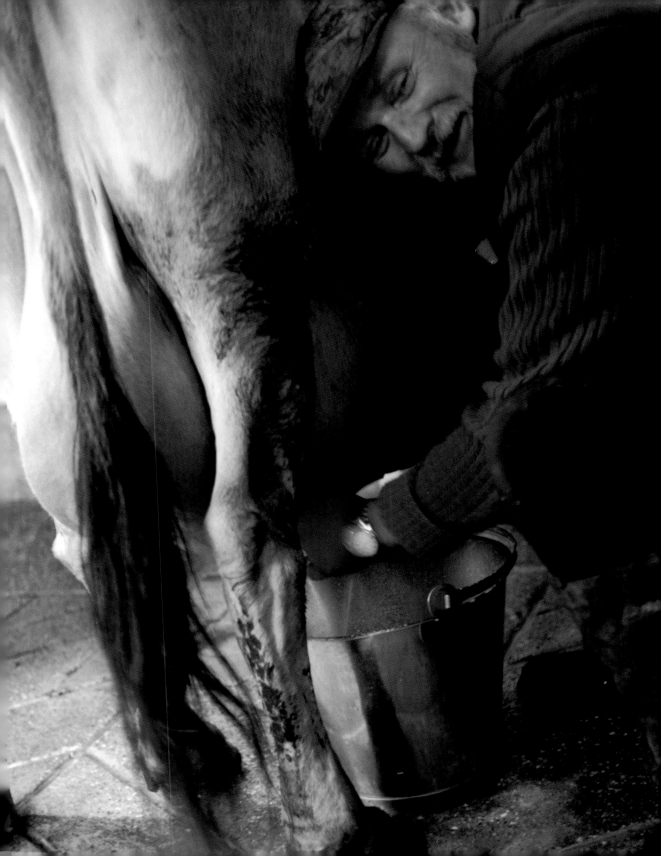

plastic jerrycan and resting his head affectionately against Peggy's flank, he began pulling, gently but firmly, on two of her teats. He settled into a piston-like rhythm, and the shed was gradually suffused with a rich, milky aroma. All too soon he had filled half a bucket and it was my turn. I knew already this would be one of those things that looks simple until you try it.

Most difficult was knowing how much force and pressure you could exert without hurting the cow. Peggy sensed she was in unfamiliar hands and Chris had to call out 'Good girl' a few times to steady and reassure her. Under his guidance I became more skilful and the trickle of milk became if not a stream then at least a runnel.

'How much do you want?' I asked. Already my fingers were beginning to ache.

'Well, there's enough there for a cup of tea. But we won't be getting any milk on our cornflakes at this rate,' Chris replied.

I let him take over. Even at his speed, hand-milking took about twenty minutes per cow (a machine can do the same job in two), and by the end, even his fingers were aching. But we had eleven litres of fresh milk to play around with. The next stage was to turn some of it into cream.

Chris had already put a bucketful of fresh milk into a sink of hot water. 'While milk and cream are inside the cow,' he explained, 'they're at a warm enough temperature that the two mix properly. As soon as milk leaves the cow and cools down in the bucket, the cream begins to separate out. You can't just stir it back in because it'll become too lumpy. Instead you have to warm it again until the cream and milk recombine.' As he talked he assembled the parts of the creamer, attaching a series of silver metal attachments to a small motor, on top of which he placed a metal basin. The contraption looked no bigger or more complicated than a food processor, and by the time he'd finished, the milk was ready to be poured in the top.

Different attachments determine whether you get double cream and skimmed milk, or single cream and semi-skimmed. Eventually I wanted to try out each of them as the basis for my ice cream, but we began with double and skimmed. The rotor whirred into life and, minutes later, a thick yellow paste was oozing out of one nozzle while a white stream flowed out of the other.

The double cream was delicious but the skimmed milk was a revelation. Normally skimmed milk is thin, watery and characterless – useful if you're looking for milk that has no danger of overpowering other tastes but hardly a satisfying drinking experience. This, on the other hand, was smooth, rich and full-flavoured, almost chewy and with subtleties of taste. Using Jersey milk or cream in an ice cream was going to be really interesting: I could hardly wait to get back to the Fat Duck and start trying it out.

As it happens, I didn't have to wait, thanks to liquid nitrogen. One of liquid nitrogen's properties is that it boils at -196°C. (We use it at the Fat Duck to make Nitro-poached Green Tea and Lime Mousse, a fantastic palate-cleanser at the start of a meal.) For ice cream you simply add liquid nitrogen to the mix and it boils, bubbles and chills almost immediately.[*]

Along with some of the usual chef's paraphernalia – hand whisk, mixing bowl – I'd also brought a canister of the stuff. As soon as Chris had separated the milk and cream, I put some of the latter in a bowl, added sugar and whisked while pouring in the liquid nitrogen. Gusts of white condensed vapour ballooned out over the table like low-lying mist in a spooky graveyard, then disappeared almost as swiftly to leave a bowlful of smooth, creamy ice cream. From cow to

 With a substance this cold, care needs to be taken while handling it to avoid a nasty freezer burn. Make sure you understand what is involved and take the necessary precautions if you're intending to try this at home.

cornet in four minutes! Even Chris seemed impressed. 'Mmm, that's rich, that is,' he said as his face broke into a satisfied smile.

As I drove away from the farm I reflected on what I'd seen and learned – not just in terms of what would be useful for the perfect ice cream but also in terms of wider considerations on the future of farming. Waltham Place does show us a kind of perfection. Certainly, if the taste was anything to go by, the farm yields far better milk than its high-production rivals. But it goes deeper than that. The quality of the produce goes hand in hand with the quality of life of the animals – they appear to be happy. If you think this is simply dewy-eyed romanticism on my part (and there's no doubt that Waltham Place Farm can have that kind of effect), then consider this: on intensive dairy farms most cows are spent by the age of seven or eight, after which it's the cull market for them, to be turned into steak and kidney pies. Holsteins, which form about 80 per cent of British stock, often manage a mere two and a half years. Yet Peggy, the cow I'd milked this morning, is fourteen and still going strong. Waltham Place demonstrated that there are other – and better – ways to farm. Better for Peggy, certainly, but also better for us – for our morals, our health and the taste of the food we put on the table.

• 'Out of the Strong Came Forth Sweetness' •

My ice cream was taking shape, but I also had a tart to start. A trip to Tate & Lyle was in order.

It was only when I visited the company's factory in London's Docklands that I realised that, although the green and gold tin had an iconic status for me and was a vivid part of my youthful memories of Mum's kitchen shelves, I had never really looked at it properly.

At the entrance to the factory, however, there's a large stone bas-relief that makes you see the label anew. There's the motto, etched in large letters, and there's the lion. Only I now saw, for the first time, that he's a dead lion, and what look like flies are buzzing around his head.

The staff at Tate & Lyle are extremely loyal, enthusiastic and knowledgeable about their product and its hundred-year history (the syrup is often referred to there as 'Goldie', as though it were a character in its own right). They know by heart all the seminal facts and dates, and have a touching appreciation for the memorabilia – they showed me marvellous old cookbooks that ingeniously weaved treacle into every recipe, and a (full) tin from the First World War that had a metal base and lid but cardboard sides, so as to save resources. They of course knew that the flies are in fact bees, and that the motto and scene come from the Bible. They told me that, in Judges 14, Samson kills a lion on his way to the Philistines, and on the way back notices that bees have made a honeycomb in the carcass. This inspires him to set the Philistines a riddle: 'Out of the eater came forth meat, and out of the strong came forth sweetness.' It was hard to see how this related to treacle, except for the fact that it has an undeniable sweetness, but apparently Abram Lyle was a very religious man and the image was his idea. Despite – or perhaps because of – its idiosyncrasies, the trademark has remained virtually unchanged ever since, a true branding classic. Indeed, the lion is almost too powerful: many people believe it's called Lion's Golden Syrup.

Mr Tate and Mr Lyle never met. They began as rival sugar refiners in the 1860s and the companies only merged in 1921. Lyle spotted the potential of golden syrup early on, feeding it first to his employees and, as demand grew, supplying it to shopkeepers in barrels. The company is still practically the only manufacturer of treacle in the country.

The manager, Ian Clark, took me on a tour of the factory. It was, as you might expect, a strange mix of old and new. We first visited the can-making room, which had none of the

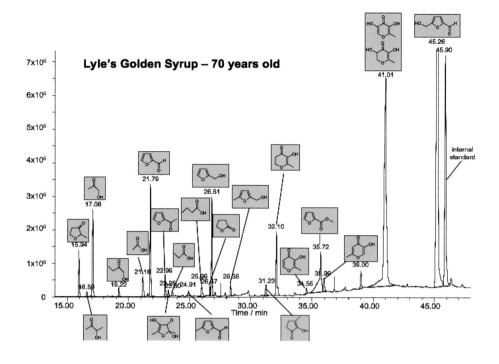

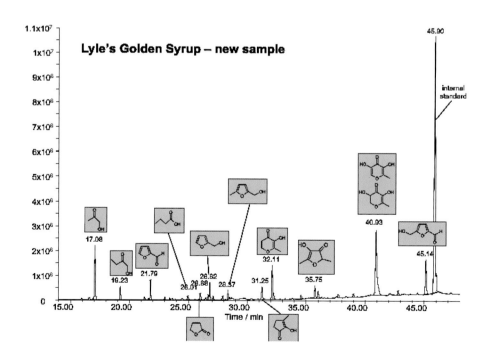

prefab functionality of modern industry: here there were high ceilings, solid brickwork and bolted iron girders, a feeling of space. As at Amedei, the machines had a satisfyingly retro look to them – bulky, weighty and painted a dour green or black. The room was dominated by three ten-foot-high Ferris wheels that gave each can a ride while testing to see if it was airtight. The rejects fell to the bottom.

The can-making room might have seemed like a museum piece (it reminded me of the East Hall of Kensington's Science Museum: the oversized Georgian and Victorian engines with their elaborate networks of pistons and pulleys), but the filtering and inversion room looked positively space-age. Steel silos soared upwards and a web of silver pipes spread and intertwined in all directions. Once again I was reminded of *Charlie and the Chocolate Factory*.

'All these tubes and vessels and dials. This is the Wonka room, isn't it?' I said.

'You could say that,' Ian giggled enigmatically, rather like Willy Wonka himself (an impression reinforced by the fact that regulations meant he was wearing a cobalt-blue hairnet under a moss-green baseball cap).

'There's a wonderful smell of molasses and toasted cereal. What's happening here?'

'This is the nerve centre of the Goldie process,' he told me. 'It's where the inversion takes place, the most important part of the procedure. I'll explain it to you later, in the lab: I've got some coloured balls that make it simpler.' (I told you the staff were keen.)

The heat was near tropical: through a small bolted porthole in one of the pipes I could see a fierce red glow. 'That's the evaporator,' Ian said. 'We trickle the syrup through a carbon bed to make it a more attractive colour, then the evaporators feed it up to the next floor.'

Squeezed in below the roof are three huge steel drums lying on their side: the storage tanks containing some twenty-three tons of treacle. From here, gravity propels the treacle downwards to the syrup filling room, where the tins are rattled along racks and conveyor belts to be filled and sealed. The place is slightly sticky underfoot and the characteristic rich, sweet smell wafts through the room. Ian and I walked upstairs to the lab so he could show me the science behind that thick, sticky sweetness.

With its veneered cupboards and work surfaces, the Tate & Lyle laboratory would look like a large domestic kitchen, except that every available surface is filled with bottles of liquid marked with dates and percentages and intriguing combinations such as 'brandy & nutmeg' or 'rum & cinnamon'. The room is at the top of the factory, and through the windows I could see across large swathes of Docklands. One hundred years ago, the area must have been an industrial powerhouse, with the fug of different factories clouding the air with aromas. It has since become something of a wasteland – dominated by pylons and moribund pubs – but already there are signs of renewal. A futuristic-looking DLR station is taking shape opposite, and optimistic estate agents advertise riverside apartments. Tate & Lyle seems to carry on regardless, secure in the integrity of its product and selling a whopping thirteen million tins a year.

Ian explained to me the process of inversion that is so central to the creation of golden syrup. 'Sugars come in many forms: sucrose, glucose, fructose, maltose and lactose, among others. The starting point for golden syrup is sucrose, which is the most common and one of the sweetest. That's what you've got in your sugar pot. It has the distinction of keeping its

pleasant taste even in high concentrations. But for golden syrup we need to change the sugar's crystalline structure into something with a runny smoothness, and we do this by splitting it into other sugars. Here, take these.'

He handed me two balls, one red, one yellow.

'Sucrose is made up of two simpler sugars: glucose and fructose. Imagine the red ball is a fructose molecule, the yellow a glucose molecule. Hold one ball in each hand and bring the two together and you've got sucrose.' I stood there obligingly, like a magician setting up his next trick. 'Now, if you heat sucrose in the presence of acid, the sucrose splits into its constituent parts.' Ian pushed my hands apart; the trick was under way. 'This messes up the orderly crystalline structure, resulting in a thick liquid. And the disorder prevents the sucrose from re-forming – rogue molecules of glucose or fructose keep getting in the way.' He handed me a third ball and brought my hands back together. Hey presto! The presence of another ball meant the neat bonding of one glucose molecule with one fructose molecule was no longer possible. (Much as playing goose-berry tends to kill off romance: two's company, three's a crowd.)

This was the theory. Now Ian showed it in action. He mixed together 350 grams of demerara sugar, 150 millilitres of water and 750 milligrams of citric acid powder until he had a grainy brown soup. Then he heated up the concoction to about 80°C and let it simmer for fifteen minutes. Gradually the sweetness lessened and the mixture thickened.

'So, once the sugar's inverted you've got a syrup with an acidic note to it. What's the next stage, Ian?'

'Add sodium bicarbonate to bring the pH back up to neutral and stop the inversion process.'

I tasted the results. It was syrup all right, but not quite what I was after. 'Lyle's Golden Syrup has got a particular flavour, a particular characteristic that's not what you get when you do this. So something else must be going on as well as inversion. How do you get that flavour?'

'Golden Syrup is a lot more concentrated than this. At our refinery, brown sugar is boiled under a vacuum, driving off a lot of the water and intensifying the flavour. But then, as it cools down and the white sugar begins to recrystallise, we remove that too, which concentrates the flavour further. The product of this process is known as a "Jet" and we can repeat the process as many times as we need to get the flavour, colour and consistency we want. To give you some idea: Golden Syrup is a mixture of Jets 2 and 3; Jet 5 is black treacle.'

'Have you got some here? I'd love to taste it.'

Ian fetched samples of Jets 2 and 3. There was a marked colour difference between the two: the dark caramel of the second Jet had transformed to a much darker reddy brown in the third. The change in colour was mirrored by a noticeable difference in taste.

'Jet 3 has much more of the treacle flavour that you'll recognise,' suggested Ian.

'Yes, it's got a slight licorice aspect, some butterscotch and a real nutty note that reminds me above all of monkey nuts, especially the shell.'

For me this was a pivotal moment: I'd not really registered the nutty flavour in treacle before, and I suddenly saw how I could use a technique from classic French cuisine to accentuate this in my treacle tart, adding to its complexity and depth of taste. It was one of those lovely epiphanies that you hope for during each research visit or experiment, and rarely get. With this recipe, I was at last beginning to see the way forwards. Paradoxically, however, my next trip was pointed in the opposite direction – back into the past.

• Court on Camera •

There are always mysteries in old cookbooks, because even the most unpoetical depend on the existence of a living tradition for the cook to know when the result is correct.

Charles Perry, from *In Taste: Proceedings of the Oxford Symposium on Food & Cookery*

With its spacious courtyards, pleasing proportions and soaring octagonal red-brick towers, Hampton Court is one of the glories of Tudor architecture. It's thrilling to look at – but not half as thrilling for me as what's inside: the Hampton Court kitchens.

There are no Pyrex beakers or stainless steel work surfaces, no distillator or centrifuge, but in many ways these are the ultimate research kitchens. (There's even a black witch's cauldron in one of the vast stone fireplaces, suggesting that a kind of alchemy really does take place here.) They can be rigged up as they would have been in the Tudor, Elizabethan or Jacobean periods. The aim is to 'learn from doing' – using recipes and utensils from the past, in the original setting, to see what light it sheds on a specific area of social history. You've heard of method acting? This is method cooking: historians investigate exactly what kitchen equipment was used and have copies made; they travel to the Canary Islands to obtain the right cochineal beetle for sixteenth-century food colouring; and they've been known to don waistcoats and breeches dyed with onion skins because that's what would have been worn at the time. For the last few years I've been working with them to develop historical British food for the Hind's Head.

My guides for the day, Marc Meltonville and Richard Fitch, were wearing black T-shirts rather than hand-woven hemp, but their immersion in culinary history was none the less impressive. If anyone could fill me in on the historical background of treacle tart, these guys could. They were a formidable double act, plucking dates out of the air for any ingredient you cared to mention and finishing off each other's sentences.

'We serve a treacle tart at the Hind's Head,' I began, 'and we've done a lot of work developing it. I originally wanted to recreate one of the earliest recipes, which had dark treacle, apple, dried fruit and ginger, but it turned out to be too far removed from what people now think of as treacle tart. So this time I wanted to see how far we can raid history but still keep within the boundaries of people's expectations.'

'The earliest thing we've found that looks like treacle tart is called "Tart of Bread",' Marc told me. 'It doesn't use treacle, but it's in the right style, and so that's what we're making here.' He picked up an incredibly sculptural, solid, rounded cone of sugar and hammered at it with a wooden mallet. It sheared in large chunks that then had to be worked over using a pestle and mortar.

'That sugar's unusual. Where did you get it?' I wanted to know.

'It's from Iran,' said Richard. 'They boil down the cane juice then pour it into cone-shaped moulds, where it's left to cool and crystallise. Before Henry Tate patented a sugar-cube cutter, sugar was always sold in the form of these "loaves" – that's how Sugar Loaf Mountain in Brazil got its name: it's the same cone shape.'

'You can really smell the molasses.'

'Yes. It's single-refined, so although some of the molasses would drain away while the cone was inverted, there'd still be a lot in there.'

Marc ground the sugar until it was a fine powder – a hard bout of manual work – then made equally fine breadcrumbs and mixed them together in a glazed earthenware bowl. Next, rose water was added.

'The recipe just says "some",' said Richard, 'so there's a lot of guesswork involved. That's part of the reason for experimenting here at Hampton Court.'

'When is this recipe from? What year?'

'It's from *The Good Housewife's Handmaid for the Kitchen*, published in 1594,' he said, without hesitation.

Marc poured molten butter on to the sugar, breadcrumbs and rose water, and stirred until it was all thoroughly incorporated. By now it looked like a stodgy breadcrumb mix. Richard brought over a heavy pan into which he'd placed pastry. He scraped in the mix, pressed it down with his fingers, then trimmed the edges off the pastry.

'Would anything be added on top?' I wondered.

'You might sprinkle over sugar.' He placed the pan on a copper tray, and laid this on top of a tray containing hot coals. Above the two trays went a third, containing more hot coals. 'This oven's even more of an experiment than the rest,' he said. 'It should be 180–200°C. I reckon the tart'll take twenty minutes or so.'

'So, while that's cooking, tell me about the next link in the treacle chain after Tart of Bread.'

'Well, there is no direct link. We've looked through the extensive collection of books here and there's no recipe for treacle tart until the 1920s.'

'The 1920s?! OK, what about the earliest use of the word "treacle" in a dish?'

'Well, as you know, Heston, the product golden syrup, sold and marketed as such, only appears in the 1880s,' explained Richard. 'But people have been getting that extraction through-out history whenever they've refined sugar. Traditionally, in England, "treacle" meant any of the syrups you got from refining. So when it says "treacle" in a recipe, we haven't really got a clue what goes in it—'

'—in our collection,' Marc continued, 'the earliest use is in an eighteenth-century book called *A Collection of Above 300 Receipts* by Mary Kettilby. It's a recipe for thick gingerbread, and it continues in much the same form into the late nineteenth century, containing ginger, flour, treacle and eggs.'

By now, Tart of Bread was done. Richard lifted off the coals. 'The top's browned off nicely. Let's give it a try.'

'At least it looks like treacle tart,' observed Marc.

'Yes, it's the right texture,' I said. 'Like a slightly moist madeleine, with a cakey note. And the taste of rose water really comes through. It's very nice indeed. I don't think it's that far removed from the modern palate at all.'

'I agree,' Richard affirmed. 'It's definitely in the right area. It might not be the grand-father of treacle tart but it's certainly a distant relative.'

'Could do with some custard, though,' Marc said ruefully.

Already, using historically accurate ingredients was reaping rewards: the low water-content of the single-refined sugar meant the tart had a really good crispy crust on top – some-thing you'd never have got using normal sugar. It was a small but valuable insight into past prac-tices and kitchen lore.

Richard and Marc were not finished, though. They had other experiments for me to try.

'Before golden syrup was invented, references to treacle often had black treacle in mind, so we've tried a recipe using that. It calls for breadcrumbs again, plus treacle, currants and ginger—'

'—the amounts are all guesswork. Old recipes tend to give vague measurements such as "a small bigness". It's very much trial and error.' Richard mixed together the breadcrumbs, ginger and currants, then poured black treacle – glossy and viscous, like engine oil – into the bowl. It bonded thickly to the other ingredients. 'Now we add melted butter to loosen it up.'

'It's actually not so far from the Tart of Bread recipe, is it?'

'No,' Marc agreed.

'What about salt? I feel it has to have that to cut the sweetness and give a richer, more rounded flavour.'

'None of the old recipes mentions it—'

'—but none of the old recipes mentions what to them is blindingly obvious,' finished Richard. 'They'll just say "season" and leave it at that. And when they say "spice it", they mean the entire range of your spice box. It could mean sugar, as that's among the spices, or something else—'

'—these books were written long before the era of coffee-table cookbooks that are used for inspiration. They're more of a reminder. That's why there are no precise measurements.'

Richard had been mixing the ingredients for some time. The result looked a lot like mincemeat. He put the concoction in a metal pan. 'No pastry case: at this time "tart" meant it was left open.' Sugar was sprinkled over and it went in the copper tray and into the oven.

'What's the date of this recipe?' I asked.

'The first half of the nineteenth century – early Queen Victoria,' Marc replied.

The smell told us when the tart was done. 'It's still soft,' said Richard. 'That's good. But it's not as crisp as the other was. That's the black treacle at work. I'm sad to say there's virtually no taste.'

'Yes,' I had to admit. 'It's bready, a bit toast-like. It's strange, but the Tart of Bread is in some ways closer to the modern treacle tart than this is, even though it's some 250 years older. It's as though we've come full circle.'

'But even in this recipe you can see the continuity,' Marc pointed out. 'Apart from the black treacle, this has a lot of things you might find in a modern treacle tart.'

Marc and Richard had also prepared Mary Kettilby's thick gingerbread recipe. It took some cutting with a sharp knife and proved to be not so much hard as dense, somewhere between a biscuit and a cake, and very different from what the modern palate would expect. 'Think parkin not Victoria sponge,' advised Marc. 'They're not into that kind of cake yet.'

It was a reminder of how important context is: this kind of gingerbread might seem strange and uninviting to us now, but it was a staple of the eighteenth and nineteenth centuries, when it would have been eaten sliced, with a cup of tea or a glass of sherry. Cooking is intertwined with custom and habit, the style of the times, and the Hampton Court kitchens are a great way of reminding yourself of this, and of seeing the change and continuity that surround cooking.

As always with a visit to Hampton Court, I had been given far more than I could possibly make sense of in one go. But already I'd got a sense of the backbone of the recipe, of the ingredients that had gradually coalesced into what we think of as treacle tart today. Playing around with those ingredients would be intriguing, especially if I could somehow give a nod to the dish's origins.

• Getting a Reading at Reading •

In Patrick Süskind's novel *Perfume*, Jean-Baptiste Grenouille has a nose so sensitive it can distinguish different types of wood or smoke or stone by smell alone.

> He had gathered tens of thousands, hundreds of thousands of specific smells and kept them so clearly, so randomly, at his disposal, that he could not only recall them when he smelled them again, but could also actually smell them simply upon recollection.

My sense of smell is pretty good, but many is the time I've wished I had Grenouille in my employ – and now that wish was all the keener because I wanted to differentiate between the many subtle aromas that make up golden syrup so that I could experiment with the composition of my tart. I could have done with Jean-Baptiste's nose. Fortunately, I knew a man with the next best things.

For several years I've been visiting Reading University to work with Professor Don Mottram, who has access to a gas chromatograph and mass spectrometer. These machines can separate out the various flavour components contained in a substance. The mass spectrometer provides a computer read-out that shows, by means of graphed peaks, what compounds are present, and in what quantities. The gas chromatograph also gives you the opportunity to stick your nose in a tube and try to detect each successive aroma. For me it has been a great way of searching out surprising but effective food combinations – white chocolate and caviar, for example, and foie gras, almonds and sour cherries. By isolating particular flavour compounds in one food, and then cross-referencing these against a database, I can discover which foods have a compound in common. Of course, this doesn't mean they're bound to suit each other, but the hidden connections revealed by the computer provide a great spur to creativity and culinary investigation.

It's serious science, but there is an undeniable Willy Wonka aspect to the technology, so it seemed appropriate that I'd be testing golden syrup with it. I'd brought with me a normal green tin's worth, along with a glass jar of seventy-year-old Tate & Lyle's Golden Syrup that Ian Clark had lent me so that I could explore the effects on flavour of ageing. Don set up the machines and I, effectively, set my nose to the grindstone …

The high-tech scratch 'n' sniff approach eventually resulted in an intriguing list of foods that might go well with treacle: popcorn, butterscotch, cooked banana, candyfloss, dried fruit, coffee. Back at the development kitchen we stocked up on ingredients until the place looked like a farmers' market – fresh figs tumbled across the work surface in a riot of deep purple streaked with vibrant green, interspersed with clusters of black, green and yellow bananas and tubs of purée and compote – and then we tried out ideas, looking for a combination of texture and flavour that would bring something extra to a treacle tart.

Mary-Ellen made strips of fig and banana purée and baked them in the oven, while I smoked a banana in ginger essential oil and even froze a banana with liquid nitrogen so that I could grate it into fine flakes. We prepared each potential ingredient in every way we could think of, then added them to a batch of tarts and cooked and tasted. All of them were good – and the addition of coffee seemed to me outstanding – but all of them took the dish in a direction that was just too far from what we think of as treacle tart.

It wasn't exactly back to the drawing board, though. At Reading the seventy-year-old syrup had produced a really interesting result. The peaks of the computer read-out zigzagged across the page like a mountain range. The older treacle contained the same flavour compounds as the normal stuff, but each was intensified. Age had had a beneficial effect. I decided there and then to have a go at replicating that effect because it would definitely add something to the recipe.

So I put a tin of golden syrup in a water bath on a low heat for a couple of weeks, crossed my fingers, fought the temptation to tinker with it, and then tasted the results. The treacle definitely had more depth and individuality – perhaps not as much as three-quarters of a century might achieve, but certainly enough to enhance my tart. I'd found the ingredient that would make it special.

TREACLE TART & ICE CREAM

Serves 8–10

Here, the key is to keep the pastry as cold and relaxed as possible at all times. If it's too warm, the fat begins to melt. If it's overworked, the gluten develops too much and the pastry loses its lightness. So don't overdo the mixing and rolling: work quickly and briefly. Cool all the equipment – greaseproof paper, rolling pin, marble pastry board if you have one – in the fridge before you start. And return the pastry to the fridge whenever you feel it's getting too warm. The fridge's coldness will harden up the butter and the resting time will relax the gluten, after which it will be easy to work with once more.

Coldness is, of course, also the key to the ice cream. I'd had problems with domestic ice-cream makers because they didn't get the mixture cold enough. The stuff I used at Waltham Place Farm – liquid nitrogen – was one solution, but it's difficult to obtain and difficult to work with. I seemed to be stuck between a rock and a hard place – either too cold or not cold enough – and then I remembered dry ice. At -80ºC it would freeze the mixture properly without causing havoc in the kitchen. And, as the main source of eerie mist effects on stage and screen, it would be easier to obtain than a canister of liquid nitrogen.

The Fat Duck's Nitro-poached Green Tea and Lime Mousse is served up surrounded by a swirl of vapour. With a bit of practice, this ice cream could be made at the table, providing a fantastic piece of theatre as the billowing mists of dry ice clear to reveal a cook, in goggles, bearing a bowl of ice cream that's out of this world.

Special equipment: digital probe, oven thermometer, loose-bottomed tart tin (28cm diameter and 3cm deep), baking beans or several handfuls of small change, protective goggles, safety gloves, dry ice, food mixer

Timing: Making the pastry requires care and patience: it will take a few hours, though for much of this time the pastry is simply chilling in the fridge. Once this is done, the tart should be relatively uncomplicated – the filling involves only a little heating and mixing. And, once you've got the hang of dry ice, the ice cream takes no time at all. (You can even do it in advance, though I'd say it's at its best when first made.)

For the vanilla salt:
2 plump vanilla pods
50g sea salt

For the pastry:
400g plain flour
1 heaped tsp table salt
400g unsalted butter, chilled and diced
100g icing sugar
zest of 1 lemon, finely grated
seeds from 1 vanilla pod
2 large egg yolks (about 40g)
2 large eggs (about 120g)

For the treacle tart filling:
200g unsalted butter
3 large eggs (about 180g)
75ml double cream
2 tsps table salt
2 x 454g tins of golden syrup *
half an 800g loaf of brown bread
zest of 3 lemons
juice of 2 lemons (or enough to make 60ml)

For the Jersey milk ice cream:
500ml Jersey whole milk
300ml double cream
80g unrefined caster sugar
100g glucose syrup
1kg dry ice

MAKING THE VANILLA SALT

1. Split the vanilla pods with a knife and scrape out the seeds.

2. Work the seeds into the salt with your fingers and leave to infuse until needed.

PREPARING THE PASTRY

1. Tip the flour and salt into a large bowl. Using your fingertips, rub in the butter until the mixture resembles breadcrumbs. (Given the amount of butter, you may need to add and rub it in batches.)

2. Quickly stir in the icing sugar, lemon zest and vanilla seeds. Add the egg yolks and the whole eggs and mix until combined. Tip on to a sheet of clingfilm, wrap it up and leave to rest in the fridge for at least 3 hours.

3. Meanwhile, preheat the oven to 150°C/300°F/Gas 2. Lightly butter and flour the tart tin and place it on a baking sheet.

4. Dust a piece of greaseproof paper with flour. Take the pastry out of the fridge and remove the clingfilm. Place the pastry on the grease-proof paper. Cut off approximately one third of the dough and reserve in case needed to patch holes in the pastry base. (If unused it can be frozen or baked off as biscuits.) Shake over more flour, then top with a second piece

 Ideally, this should be aged. Preheat the oven to 70–80°C/160–175°F (the latter temperature is the absolute maximum). Make sure the tin is well sealed, then place in the oven for at least 24 hours. (It can be left for up to 100 hours, during which it will continue to improve in depth and complexity. And it will keep for a long time, so it's worth doing several tins at once.)

of greaseproof paper. Begin to roll the pastry flat, moving the pin from the centre outwards. Keep turning the pastry through 90° every few rolls. Aim for a thickness of 3–5mm and a diameter of 45–50cm. Once the pastry is rolled out to the correct thickness, peel back the top layer of greaseproof paper, trim off any excess, then wind the pastry on to the rolling pin, removing the other layer of paper as you go. Unwind the pastry over the flan tin and gently push it into the base and edges. Place in the fridge for 30 minutes.

5. Once the pastry has firmed up, remove it from the fridge. Prick the base with a fork to stop it puffing up. Take a new piece of grease-proof paper, scrunch it up and smooth it out several times (this makes it easier to put in position), then place it over the pastry base. Put baking beans or – even better – coins on top. Return the lined pastry case to the fridge for at least 30 minutes.

6. Remove the case from the fridge and put in the oven to bake for 25–30 minutes, until the pastry is a light golden brown. You may need to return the case to the oven for 10–15 minutes if, after removing the beans or coins, the base is slightly tacky.

PREPARING THE FILLING AND COOKING THE TART

1. Preheat the oven to 150°C/300°F/Gas 2. Remove the crusts from the brown bread and discard. Tear the bread into pieces and blitz in the food processor to make breadcrumbs. Weigh out 170g and set aside.

2. Make a beurre noisette by putting the butter in a pan over a medium heat. When the butter stops sizzling (a sign that the water has all evaporated, after which it will soon burn) and develops a nutty aroma, remove it from the

heat immediately. Strain it into a jug and leave to cool until needed. Discard the blackened solids in the sieve.

3. Put the eggs, cream and salt in a bowl and whisk until combined. Pour the golden syrup into a pan and heat gently until liquid.

4. Pour 115g of beurre noisette into the warmed golden syrup, and stir. (Try to avoid tipping in any sediment that may have collected at the bottom of the jug.)

5. Pour the buttery syrup into the egg and cream mixture. Stir in the breadcrumbs and the lemon zest and juice.

6. Transfer the mixture to a large jug. Pour two-thirds of it into the pastry case. Slide the tart into the oven and pour in the remainder of the filling. Bake for 50–60 minutes or until the tart is a deep brown colour. Remove from the oven and leave to cool before taking out of the tin.

7. Slice and serve with a few grains of vanilla salt and a dollop of Jersey milk ice cream.

MAKING THE ICE CREAM

1. Put the milk, cream, sugar and glucose syrup in a pan and heat gently until the sugar has dissolved and the glucose is liquid. Set aside.

2. Put on safety gloves and protective goggles and open the packet of dry ice. Wrap it in a tea towel and then a hand towel and smash it into a powder with a rolling pin. (Make sure that there are no large lumps of dry ice as these will remain as lumps in the ice cream.) Unfold the towels and shake the powdered dry ice into a glass bowl.

3. Pour the milk and glucose mix into the bowl of a food mixer. (From now on you need to work reasonably rapidly to avoid freezing up the equipment.) Shake a little of the dry ice into the mixing bowl and, using the mixer's paddle, mix on the first (lowest) speed until the dry ice dissolves and its vapour clears. Continue to add dry ice a little at a time until the ice cream has absorbed all of it. (It may be easier to do this in two batches. It's important to add the dry ice in small quantities to prevent the ice cream going grainy.) Once the dry ice is absorbed, beat the ice cream on the second speed until smooth.

4. Quickly scrape the ice cream out of the mixer* and into a container. Store in the freezer until required. It is best eaten within 24 hours.

* If undissolved chunks of dry ice remain at the bottom of the mixer bowl, leave them to dissolve entirely, then run the bowl under hot water.

FOOD SAFETY

Salmonella, E. coli, botulism … It often seems as though there's a new food scare every week. The scare stories show that it's absolutely vital to establish a proper and effective hygiene routine in your kitchen. One of the major causes of food poisoning is cross-contamination: the transferral of bacteria from one foodstuff to another. Below I will outline the best practices for preventing this.

But the scare stories can also encourage a culture of fear. Remember the listeria hysteria of the late 1980s, which prompted many people to avoid soft cheese altogether? The ultra-cautious approach would see us reduced to a diet of overcooked meat and hard-boiled eggs, with no access to mayonnaise or chocolate mousse. Half the world's greatest culinary pleasures would be denied us. Fortunately though, freedom of choice means we are still able to eat meat on the bone and cheese made from unpasteurised milk.

We should celebrate that freedom by exploring the marvellous ingredients the world has to offer, but we also need to live up to the responsibility of our choices: find out where your food comes from and how it is made and handled; search out suppliers and artisans who care about what they are doing and take the trouble to get it right. These are simple actions that go a long way towards minimising any risks involved. And reinforce this by ensuring the food stays safe when it is being prepared in your kitchen.

- **Wash your hands regularly using a bactericidal hand cleaner.**
  Busy as they are, your hands are one of the most effective ways of carrying bacteria from one food to another. Wash them not only when you first enter the kitchen (and, of course, after touching the waste bin or pets) but also after touching raw meat, fruit or vegetables. Extra care needs to be taken with foods that won't be cooked – salad, fruit, bread, etc. – because there'll be no opportunity for transferred bacteria to be destroyed by heat.

- **Clean work surfaces, cutting boards and knives after each task with a spray sanitiser that both cleans and disinfects.**
  After your hands, these are probably bacteria's best means of spreading across the kitchen. (Professional kitchens have separate colour-coded chopping boards for meat, fish and vegetables. It's a good practice to get into at home as well.) Your sense of smell is a good ally in making sure this has been done properly. If a knife or a sieve smells of the last thing you used it for, it needs further cleaning.

- **Regularly wash, disinfect or dispose of wiping cloths and dishcloths.**

  These too can be breeding grounds for bacteria. The best approach is probably to use paper towels where possible. Cross-contamination is lessened if you use different cloths for different jobs: one for wiping worktops, one for drying hands, one for drying dishes, etc.

- **Store raw meat so that it can't touch or drip on other foodstuffs.**

  Keep it separately in sealed containers on the bottom shelf of the fridge. Don't store it alongside other foodstuffs, and keep raw meat separate from cooked meat. Take care when defrosting meat in the fridge: the liquid produced can spread bacteria if it drips.

- **The outside of a chicken's egg can carry a lot of bacteria.**

  So treat it with the same vigilance as you would raw meat.

- **Try to complete each stage of a task before going on to the next.**

  If you're peeling and chopping onions, peel the lot and discard the peelings, then clean the work surface before you begin to chop. You'll not only lessen the potential for cross-contamination but also enjoy a more methodical and orderly kitchen.

EQUIPMENT

Eating is one of the few things we do that draws on all of our senses at the same time. Cooking, similarly, is above all about touch, taste, smell, sight and sound – sniffing out the aromas that tell you a herb has released its essential oils; watching the colour-change penetrate the surface of a seared steak or slice of tuna; hearing the noisy bubbling of butter in the frying pan cease as the last of its water content departs. The eyes, ears, nose, mouth and fingers are the really essential tools of the cook's trade, and no amount of fancy equipment can replace them. None the less, there are a few, largely inexpensive, pieces of hardware that should be part of any cook's arsenal.

Thermometers

Temperature is of vital importance in cooking, and two pieces of equipment will help make you master of it. First, I'd recommend an oven thermometer: it's amazing how inaccurate oven dials can be, and how much heat can be lost through an open oven door or the introduction of a cold roasting tin. Cooking at the wrong temperature, even by a few degrees, is probably the easiest way to mess up a meal. An oven thermometer will ensure that, if a recipe calls for 200°C, you're able to reach and maintain that temperature.

Second, a battery-operated digital probe is the best way of achieving perfectly cooked meat, fish and pastries, an ideal that in itself should be justification for having one. As the recipes in this book show, cooking meat, for example, is a complicated juggling act of trying to reconcile the different temperatures at which meat browns, tenderises and totally dehydrates. A digital probe takes the heartbreak out of this.

Scales

Accurately measuring ingredients is as vital to successful cooking as regulating temperature, yet scales are often no more accurate than oven thermostats, especially where small amounts are called for. Make sure you have a good set of scales that is accurate even below 100g. (To test them, take a pat of butter, cut off 50g – often the wrapper is marked at 25g intervals – and weigh it.)

Equipment Online

Most of these items are available in any good kitchen shop. However, should you have difficulty obtaining them, the following three online stores stock good versions of each.

Hansens Kitchen Equipment Ltd
306 Fulham Road
London SW10 9ER
tel: 020-7351-6933
fax: 020-7351-5319
www.hansens.co.uk

Nisbets
Fourth Way
Avonmouth BS11 8TB
tel: 0845-1110285
fax: 0845-1435555
www.nisbets.co.uk

Pages
121 Shaftesbury Avenue
London WC2H 8AD
tel: 020-7565-5959
fax: 020-7565-5960
www.pagescatering.co.uk

To find a reliable set of scales, it is worth consulting www.scalemagazine.com. The Jennings CJ300 is a good, relatively inexpensive model.

Soda siphons are available from:
www.johnlewis.com

Sausage equipment and supplies are available from:
www.naturalcasingco.co.uk

For pizza, ice cream and Black Forest Gateau, a Kenwood Major mixer was used. A list of stockists is available at:
www.kenwoodworld.com

Vacuum-seal storage bags are available at many department stores, and can also be found at:
www.spacebag.com

Atomisers can be found in branches of Boots, and paint guns, blowtorches, protective gloves and goggles are obtainable from almost any hardware store, DIY shop or builder's merchant. The wood-effect painting tool (basically a small paddle with a wood-effect rubber stamp round the leading edge) is available at art shops and some DIY stores. A short-handled pizza peel can be bought in many professional cookware stores (see also the 'Pizza' section of the Directory).

DIRECTORY
RESTAURANTS, SUPPLIERS AND OTHER USEFUL ADDRESSES

General Information

Organic Farming
www.soilassociation.org

Slow Food Movement
www.slowfood.com

Food Standards Agency
www.food.gov.uk

Farmers' Markets
www.farmersmarkets.net

Spices
www.seasonedpioneers.co.uk
www.steenbergs.co.uk

Suppliers by area
www.foodloversbritain.com

Roast Chicken and Roast Potatoes

L'Arche Cafeteria
Autoroute 39
L'aire du Poulet de Bresse
tel: 00-33-(0)3-85-76-30-97
fax: 00-33-(0)3-85-76-32-37

Boucherie Trolliet
102 Cours Lafayette
69003 Lyon
France
tel: 00-33-(0)4-78-62-36-60
fax: 00-33-(0)4-78-95-34-12
www.boucherie-trolliet.com

Les Adresses de Georges Blanc
01540 Vonnas
France
tel: 00-33-(0)4-74-50-90-90
fax: 00-33-(0)4-74-50-08-80
www.georgesblanc.com

You can get hold of Bresse chickens at:
C. Lidgate
110 Holland Park Avenue
London W11 4AU
tel: 020-7727-8243
fax: 020-7729-7160

A reliable alternative is:
Label Anglais
S. J. Frederick and Sons
Temple Farm
Roydon
Harlow
Essex CM19 5LW
tel: 01279-792460
fax: 01729-793558
www.labelanglais.co.uk

MBM (potatoes) has offices in many parts of Britain. The main contact details are:
tel: 01354-652341
fax: 01354-654145
www.mbm.uk.com

See also:
www.pouletbresse.com

Pizza

Pizzeria Brandi
Salita S. Anna di Palazzo 1–2
(Via Chiaia)
Napoli
Italy
tel: 00-39-081-416928
fax: 00-39-081-400294
www.brandi.it

Il Pizzaiolo del Presidente
Via dei Tribunali 120
80138 Napoli
Italy
tel: 00-39-081-210-903

L'Antica Pizzeria da Michele
Via Cesare Sersale 1–3
80100 Napoli
Italy
tel: 00-39-081-553-9204
www.damichele.net

Pizzeria La Notizia
Via Caravaggio 53–55
80112 Napoli
Italy
tel: 00-39-081-714-2155
www.pizzaconsulting.it

For '00' flour:
Antimo Caputo Srl
Corso San Giovanni a Teduccio 55
80146 Napoli
Italy
tel: 00-39-081-752-0566
fax: 00-39-081-559-0781
www.molinocaputo.it

It is also available online at:
www.nifeislife.com

Malt syrup: You can obtain
Clearspring Japanese brown rice
malt syrup from:
www.goodnessdirect.co.uk

Mozzarella: Garofalo Mozzarella di
Bufala is available at Waitrose and
online.

Smoked sea salt: Available from
the Anglesey Sea Salt Company
(www.seasalt.co.uk) and Waitrose

See also:
www.fornobravo.com
www.woodstone-corp.com
www.pizzamaking.com
www.fabflour.co.uk

Bangers & Mash

Piperfield Pork (Graham Head)
The Dovecote
Lowick
Berwick-upon-Tweed
Northumberland TD15 2QE
tel: 01289-388543

Crombie's of Edinburgh
97 Broughton Street
Edinburgh EH1 3RZ
tel: 0131-556-7643
fax: 0131-556-3920
www.sausages.co.uk

MBM (potatoes) – see entry under
'Roast Chicken and Roast
Potatoes' above.

**Ludlow Marches Food and
Drink Festival**
The Buttercross
Ludlow
Shropshire SY8 1AW
tel/fax: 01584-873957
www.foodfestival.co.uk

For smoked olive oil:
www.organicsmokehouse.com

See also:
www.sausagelinks.co.uk
www.sausagefans.com
www.sausagemaking.org

Steak

Peter Luger, Inc.
178 Broadway
Brooklyn
NY 11211
USA
tel: 001-(718)-387-7400

Empire Diner
210 Tenth Avenue
New York
NY 10011
USA
tel: 001-(212)-243-2736
fax: 001-(212)-924-0011

Katz's Delicatessen
205 East Houston Street
New York
NY 10002
USA
tel: 001-(212)-254-2246
fax: 001-(212)-674-3270
www.katzdeli.com

Gray's Papaya
2090 Broadway
New York
NY 10023
USA
tel: 001-(212)-799-0243

WD-50
50 Clinton Street
New York
NY 10002
USA
tel: 001-(212)-477-2900
www.wd-50.com

Robert's Steakhouse
Penthouse Executive Club
603 West 50th Street
New York
NY 10036
USA
tel: 001-(212)-245-0002
www.penthouseexecutiveclub.com

For Longhorn steaks:
Pedigree Meats
Huntsham Farm
Goodrich
Ross-on-Wye
Herefordshire HR9 6JN
tel: 01600-890296
fax: 01600-890390
www.huntsham.com

Smoked sea salt: Available from
the Anglesey Sea Salt Company
(www.seasalt.co.uk) and Waitrose

See also:
www.eblex.org.uk
www.beefyandlamby.co.uk

Spaghetti Bolognese

Antica Trattoria della Gigina
Via Stendhal 1
40128 Bologna
Italy
tel: 00-39-051-322-300
fax: 00-39-051-418-9865

Osteria Francescana
Via Stella 22
41100 Modena
Italy
tel: 00-39-059-210-118
fax: 00-39-059-220-286

La Pasta di Aldo
Via Castelletta 41
62015 Monte San Giusto
Macerata
Italy
tel: 00-39-0733-53105
fax: 00-39-0733-530480
www.lapastadialdo.it

Fish & Chips

La Pasta di Aldo has no representative in the UK, making it difficult to obtain, and there's no spaghetti in the range. The best alternative is:

Rustichella d'Abruzzo SpA
Piazza Vestini 20
65019 Pianella
Pescara
Italy
tel: 00-39-085-971-308
fax: 00-39-085-972-521
www.rustichella.it

It is available in some delicatessens and online at www.guidetti.co.uk

As far as fish suppliers go, there's no substitute for cultivating a good local fishmonger. If you have trouble finding one in your area, try www.foodloversbritain.com

A Salt and Battery
112 Greenwich Avenue
NY 10011
New York
USA
tel: 001-(212)-254-6610
fax: 001-(212)-254-6693
www.asaltandbattery.com

James Knight of Mayfair & Cecil & Co. (fish)
tel: 020-7587-3070

MBM (potatoes) – see entry under 'Roast Chicken and Roast Potatoes' above.

White rice flour: Doves Farm rice flour is available supermarkets and at www.goodnessdirect.co.uk Otherwise, try www.thai4uk.com

See also:
www.seafish.org

Marine Stewardship Council
www.msc.org

Marine Conservation Society
Unit 3
Wolf Business Park
Alton Road
Ross-on-Wye
Herefordshire HR9 5NB
tel: 01989-566017
fax: 01989-567815
www.mcsuk.org
www.fishonline.org

Black Forest Gateau

Café König
Lichtentaler Strasse 12
76530 Baden-Baden
Germany
tel: 00-49-(0)7221-23573
www.chocolatier.de

Confiserie Kaffeehaus Gmeiner
Hauptstrasse 38
77704 Oberkirch
Germany
tel: 00-49-(0)7802-2629
www.chocolatier.de

Amedei Srl (chocolate)
Via San Gervasio 29
56020 La Rotta (Pontedera)
Pisa
Italy
tel: 00-39-0587-484849
fax: 00-39-0587-483208
www.amedei.it

Franz Fies GmbH (kirsch)
Schwarzwalder Edelobstbrennerei
Kastelbergstrasse 2
77704 Oberkirch-Ringelbach
Germany
tel: 00-49-(0)7802-4445
fax: 00-49-(0)7802-4478
www.fiesbrennerei.de

For Amarena Fabbri cherries, consult:
Call Caterlink Ltd
Callywith Gate Industrial Estate
Launceston Road
Bodmin
Cornwall PL31 2RQ
tel: 01208-78844
fax: 01208-73030
www.caterlink.co.uk

See also:
www.seventypercent.com

Treacle Tart and Ice Cream

Waltham Place Farm (milk for ice cream)
Church Hill
White Waltham
Berkshire SL6 3JH
tel: 01628-825517
fax: 01628-825045
www.walthamplace.com
The gardens, shop and tearoom are open on specific days from May until September. They are well worth a visit.

Tate & Lyle Plc
Sugar Quay
Lower Thames Street
London EC3R 6DQ
tel: 020-7626-6525
fax: 020-7623-5213
www.tateandlyle.com

Hampton Court Palace
East Molesey
Surrey KT8 9AU
tel: 0870-752-7777
0870-751-5175
fax: 020-8781-5362
www.hrp.org.uk
The 'Events and Exhibitions'
section of the website gives
details of when you can visit the
kitchens to see Tudor cookery at
first hand.

Glucose syrup:
This can be obtained from:
some supermarkets, or online
from www.jane-asher.co.uk or
www.squires-shop.com

Dry ice:
The best site I have found for
getting (gloved) hold of dry ice is:
http://ind.yara.co.uk/en/
products_services/dry_ice/.
They will supply a minimum of
10kg of dry ice in 1kg slabs (it's
the slabs you want, not the
pellets). It's got no real shelf life
and you can't store it in your
freezer, so you need to have it
delivered as near as possible to
the day you want to use it. Keep it
in its original container and, as it
evaporates, pack with newspaper
the gaps that develop between
slabs.

Heston's Restaurants

The Fat Duck
High Street
Bray
Berkshire SL6 2AQ
tel: 01628-580333
fax: 01628-776188
www.fatduck.co.uk

The Hind's Head Hotel
High Street
Bray
Berkshire SL6 2AB
tel: 01628-626151

BIBLIOGRAPHY

This is not an exhaustive list by any means. I've tried to include books that seem to me to be definitive in their field, along with others that provide a great starting point for further exploring particular areas covered in this book. They are all informative, incisive and entertaining, and would be an excellent addition to any kitchen bookshelf.

General

Simon Hopkinson and Lindsey Bareham, *The Prawn Cocktail Years*, Macmillan 1997.
Laura Mason and Catherine Brown, *Traditional Foods of Britain: An Inventory*, Prospect Books 2004.
Jeffrey Steingarten, *The Man Who Ate Everything* and *It Must've Been Something I Ate*, Review 1999, 2002.

History

Andrew Dalby, *Food in the Ancient World*, Routledge 2003.
Alan Davidson, *The Oxford Companion to Food*, OUP 1999.
Theodora Fitzgibbon, *The Food of the Western World*, Hutchinson 1970.
Jean-Louis Flandrin and Massimo Montanari, *Food: A Culinary History*, Columbia University Press 1999.
Jane Renfrew, Maggie Black, Jennifer Stead and Peter Brears, *Food & Cooking in Britain*, series published by English Heritage 1985.
Reay Tannahill, *Food in History*, Three Rivers Press 1988.
C. Anne Wilson, *Food & Drink in Britain*, Academy Chicago 2003.

Science

Peter Barham, *The Science of Cooking*, Springer 2001.
Harold McGee, *On Food & Cooking*, Hodder & Stoughton 2004.

Advanced Science

S. Beckett, *The Science of Chocolate*, The Royal Society of Chemistry 2000.
H. D. Belitz, W. Grosch and Peter Schieberle, *Food Chemistry (3rd Revised Edition)*, Springer-Verlag 2004.
Stanley P. Cauvain and Linda S. Young (eds.), *Baking Problems Solved*, Woodhead Publishing 2001.
T. P. Coultate, *Food: The Chemistry of its Components*, The Royal Society of Chemistry 2002.
W. P. Edwards, *The Science of Sugar Confectionery*, The Royal Society of Chemistry 2000.
P. J. Fellows, *Food Processing Technology: Principles and Practice*, Woodhead Publishing 2000.

R. A. Lawrie, *Meat Science*, Woodhead Publishing 1998.

Robert T. Marshall, Richard W. Hartel and H. Douglas Goff, *Ice Cream*, Kluwer Academic/Plenum Publishers 2003.

J. B. Rossell (ed.), *Frying: Improving Quality*, Woodhead Publishing 2001.

Yoko Takechi (ed.), *The Fifth Taste of Human Being: Umami the World*, Cross Media 2005.

Bresse Chickens

Quentin Crewe, *Foods from France*, Ebury Press 1993.

Potatoes

Alex Barker and Sally Mansfield, *Potato*, Lorenz Books 1999.

Lindsay and Patrick Mikanowski, *Potato*, Grub Street 2005.

Alan Romans, *The Potato Book*, Frances Lincoln Publishers 2005.

Pizza and Pasta

Nikko Amandonico, *La Pizza*, Mitchell Beazley 2001.

Marcella Hazan, *The Essentials of Classic Italian Cooking*, Macmillan 1992.

Claudia Roden, *The Food of Italy*, Chatto & Windus 1989.

Dough

Raymond Calvel, Ronald L. Wirtz and James J. MacGuire, *The Taste of Bread*, Kluwer Academic/Plenum Publishers 2001.

Jeffrey Hamelman, *Bread: A Baker's Book of Techniques and Recipes*, John Wiley & Sons Inc. 2004.

Meat

Bruce Aidells and Denis Kelly, *Bruce Aidells' Complete Sausage Book*, Ten Speed Press 2000.

Hugh Fearnley-Whittingstall, *The River Cottage Meat Book*, Hodder & Stoughton 2004.

Donald MacPherson, *Tender, Tasty Beef – Every Time*, report sponsored by the Royal Highland and Agricultural Society of Scotland and the Royal Smithfield Club, 2003.

Fish

Bernadette Clarke, *Good Fish Guide*, Marine Conservation Society 2002.

Chocolate

Sara Jayne-Stanes, *Chocolate: The Definitive Guide*, Grub Street 2005.

Ice Cream

Caroline Liddell and Robin Weir, *Ices: The Definitive Guide*, Grub Street 1995.

ACKNOWLEDGEMENTS

First I'd like to thank all the chefs who devoted their time, energy and imagination to showing me some amazing food, especially Georges Blanc, Massimo Bottura, Ernesto Cacialli, Enzo Coccia, Carlo Cortesi, Wylie Dufresne, Volker Gmeiner, Adam Perry Lang and Hiroshi Sudo.

Second I'd like to thank all the artisans, gastronomes, restaurateurs, managers, PR representatives, farmers and suppliers who indulged my fascination for how things work and patiently answered all my questions: Alison Ashman, Fred Austin, Laurent Berthelin, David Blagden, Enzo Caldarelli, Eugenio, Carmine and Antimo Caputo, Chris Carter, Christian Chotard, Dino Ciccarelli, Ian Clark, Sandy Crombie, Tom Dixon, Luigi and Maria Donnari, Dewey Dufresne, Hans-Peter Fies, Andrew Francis, Michael Gianmarino at Lombardi's, Alan Griffiths, Claire Harrison, Graham Head, Ferne Hudson, the Lewis family at Orleton Farm Shop, Peter Pattrick, Gianluigi Peduzzi, Nicky Perry, Jody Storch, Cecilia and Alessio Tessieri, Maurice Trolliet and Mike Wall, along with Matt and Nicky at A Salt and Battery, the team at Waltham Place Farm – Chris Stevenson, Vinnie McCann, Val Turner, Beatrice Krehl, Steve Castle, Suki Mann and Nicky and Strilli Oppenheimer – and everyone at Peter Luger, Brandi, Da Michele and Solania.

Neither the book nor the series could have happened without enormous behind-the-scenes work by a number of drivers, fixers, co-ordinators and translators. I'm especially grateful to Irene Agrillo, Paolo Benzi, Damon Bundschuh, Dario Canciello, Frank Dunne, Isabelle Faure, Jodie Penfold, Venetia Phillips, Faye Rogafki, Deirdre Traynor Jones and Gabriel Walsh. I'd also like to thank all the farmhands, factory workers, sous-chefs, waiters and waitresses to whom I wasn't introduced but whose hard work, professionalism and enthusiasm underpin everything described in this book.

Filming was often gruelling, but the team at the BBC made sure it was fun as well. A massive thanks to Gary Hunter for making all this happen and allowing me to gain a good friend in the process. I owe a lot to Michael Massey, whose energy, determination, encouragement and imagination were the linchpin of the TV series. He was skilfully backed up by Andrew Fettis, whose expertise and inventiveness contributed much to the programmes, and by Dawn Lake and especially Peter Strachan, who did some great filmwork under difficult circumstances. They were a great crew to work with. I'm grateful to Juliet Hadden for taking the legwork out of some of the paperwork; and special mention must go to the Emma Robertson, without whom neither the TV series nor this book could have happened. Her research skills, recipe testing, food knowledge and devotion to the cause are second to none.

The studio sessions were extremely complicated, and I'm grateful to everybody who helped make them run smoothly: Lou Abercrombie, Kate Adam, Eleanor Bailey, Robin Brigham, Luis Carreola, Maree Cochrane, Abi Fawcett, Tim Green, Lisa Harrison, Tara Kane, Paul Keyworth, Fiona Llewellyn, Chris Meed, Steve Moss, Andy Muggleton, Lucie Parker, Jo Pratt, Micky Reeves, Tanya Severn, Rudi Thackray, Maria Ttofian, Frank Webster, Joe Wildman and Andy Young. I'd also like to acknowledge the generosity of Divertimenti, Fujitora, I. Grunwerg Ltd, All-Clad cookware and above all Poggenpohl in helping to fit out the kitchen.

Several experts have been generous with their time and ideas. Above all I'm indebted to Ivan Day, Harold McGee, Doctor Bernard Mackey, Professor Don Mottram and Dr Ann Marie Friend, Jeffrey Steingarten, Professor Andy Taylor and Rachel Edwards-Stuart, Robin Weir, and doctors Terry Sharp and Sam Millar at Campden & Chorleywood Food Research Association. Their limitless curiosity helped to form many of the ideas in this book.

I've had a fantastic publishing team whose passion was a vital part of this book's creation and development. My agent, Zoë Waldie, had the vision and determination to bring the book to life in the first place. My publisher, Mike Jones, provided the enthusiasm and encouragement necessary for its completion. Emily Sweet edited with great intelligence and sensitivity, bringing order to the chaos of the final stages of the book's progress. Thanks must also go to Rachel Calder at Tessa Sayle and Monica Brown at Lotus PR; and to Caz Hildebrand for brilliantly masterminding the book's design and Simon Wheeler for taking the photos. During our travels he was valued as much for his acerbic wit as for his uncanny ability to capture the spirit of the action.

Many of my staff at the Fat Duck and Hind's Head went way beyond their duties in providing assistance. Thanks must go to my head chef, Ashley Watts, and my pastry chef, James 'Jocky' Petrie: without them to help steer the mother ship, this book would not have been possible. Mary-Ellen McTague and Dominic Chapman energetically tested, tasted and discussed – their input was essential to the project. And my development chef, Chris Young, gave me the best possible support in turning culinary ideas, no matter how outlandish, into reality. Finally, the organisational skills of my very patient and longsuffering assistant, Roisin Wesley, were the only thing that allowed me to juggle a hectic film schedule and still find time to cook.

Photographic Acknowledgements:

AKG-Images: 233
Alinari: 66, 172
Americana images/Scott Mitchell: 134
Corbis: 204, 205, 209, 231, 232, 234
Mary Evans Picture Library: 20, 99, 162, 270
Rapho/Marc Tulane: 27
Topfoto: 100, 195

INDEX